New Creation Eschatology
and the Land

New Creation Eschatology and the Land

A Survey of Contemporary Perspectives

STEVEN L. JAMES

WIPF & STOCK · Eugene, Oregon

NEW CREATION ESCHATOLOGY AND THE LAND
A Survey of Contemporary Perspectives

Wipf & Stock
An Imprint of Wipf and Stock Publishers
199 W. 8th Ave., Suite 3
Eugene, OR 97401

www.wipfandstock.com

PAPERBACK ISBN: 978-1-5326-1913-7
HARDCOVER ISBN: 978-1-4982-4525-8
EBOOK ISBN: 978-1-4982-4524-1

Manufactured in the U.S.A.   09/27/17

He said to me, "Son of man, this is the place of My throne and the place of the soles of My feet, where I will dwell among the sons of Israel forever."

—Ezekiel 43:7 [NASB]

Contents

Preface

With this work two of my fascinations in the discipline of theological and biblical studies converge. The first is the topic of the final state of the redeemed, specifically the nature of the everlasting life that believers are to experience in the new heavens and new earth. The second is the question of Israel, particularly the fulfillment of Old Testament promises regarding the possession of land. Over the last decade as I have meditated upon what God has revealed about these topics in Scripture, I have become increasingly aware of two things. The first is that the Scripture reveals more about these topics than most Christians realize or care to admit. The second is that these topics, far from being peripheral or tangential interests, have relevance for the individual Christian's walk and for the church. Though in the current work I charge some individuals as being inconsistent in their approaches to the topics above, I am grateful to God for their respective contributions to the discussion. It is my hope that the current work is a contribution to the dialogue already taking place and that the discussion of the new creation in biblical and theological studies continues to increase. My ultimate prayer is that the present work would be true to God's word and pleasing in his sight as I strive toward a better understanding of his promises for the new creation and look forward to the realization of those promises.

Acknowledgments

Because this book is essentially the product of the doctoral dissertation that I completed at Southwestern Seminary, my gratitude appropriately goes to those who have supported me during that entire educational pilgrimage. Without the continued support and encouragement of colleagues, friends, and family, I am convinced that I would not have seen the completion of this work. No other individual has been a greater influence upon my entire theological education than Craig Blaising. I am grateful for his patient guidance, encouragement, and affirmation. Gerardo Alfaro and Michael Vlach provided helpful comments throughout the process of completing the work. I am also thankful for the many conversations with professors at Southwestern, especially those in the Theological Studies division.

Robert Boss lent his ear to the main argument and provided much encouragement. Kevin Crouch and Vern Charette were sounding boards at various points throughout the project. Other sources of encouragement were Jonathan Watson, Travis Trawick, Kyle Walker, Benjamin Hawkins, and Matt Harrison. Throughout the process of writing, I also received moral support from Jennifer Charette and Emily Jones, both of whom I worked alongside in the Office of the Provost at Southwestern. I also thank Charissa Wilson, my assistant, who has provided encouragement throughout and light proofing of the final draft. Gregory Smith, also a colleague in the Provost's Office, has listened to my thoughts on new creation eschatology perhaps more than any other individual. I am grateful to him for his thoughtful interaction and encouragement every step of the way.

Throughout the journey, I have felt the prayers of my church and family members. Having godly parents has been one of the greatest assets that I have had in life. Undoubtedly, they have spent many hours interceding on my behalf before the Lord from beginning to completion of the project.

They are a testimony to the Lord's faithfulness in my life and time and again offered much-needed encouragement when discouragement was setting in. My wife's parents have also provided help in a number of ways.

The greatest help and support has come from my wife, Heather. I admire her for the work that she does in our home, in the education of our children, and in her efforts to complete a biblical studies graduate degree. There is no other individual who has sacrificed more during the completion of this work, and to her I am forever grateful. My children, Annalee, Abigail, Samuel, and LilaRae have provided much laughter, love, and encouragement. I will never forget being asked day after day, "Daddy, what page are you on?" Finally, I thank the Lord who has showered me with blessings without number and has sovereignly overseen the support and encouragement from others. His word has nourished me in times of famine and continues to do so.

Abbreviations

ABD	*The Anchor Bible Dictionary*
AB	The Anchor Bible
AJ	*Asbury Journal*
BibSac	*Bibliotheca Sacra*
BBR	*Bulletin for Biblical Research*
BECNT	Baker Exegetical Commentary on the New Testament
BZNW	Beihefte zur Zeitschrift für die neutestamentliche Wissenschaft und die Kunde der älteren Kirche
CC	Continental Commentaries
ChrCent	*Christian Century*
CJ	*Concordia Journal*
ConBNT	Coniectanea biblica, New Testament
ConC	Concordia Commentary
CTR	*Criswell Theological Review*
EJ	*Evangelical Journal*
FOTL	Forms of Old Testament Literature
ICC	The International Critical Commentary
JCTR	*Journal for Christian Theological Research*
JETS	*Journal of the Evangelical Theological Society*
JRT	*Journal of Religious Thought*
JSJSup	Supplements to the Journal for the Study of Judaism

JSNT	*Journal for the Study of the New Testament*
JSNTSup	*Journal for the Study of the New Testament, Supplement Series*
JTSA	*Journal of Theology for Southern Africa*
LNTS	*Library of New Testament Studies*
MSJ	*Master's Seminary Journal*
NAC	The New American Commentary
NCBC	New Cambridge Bible Commentary
NIDB	*New Interpreter's Dictionary of the Bible*
NICNT	The New International Commentary on the New Testament
NIGTC	New International Greek Testament Commentary
NIVAC	The New International Version Application Commentary
NSBT	New Studies in Biblical Theology
NT	New Testament
NTS	*New Testament Studies*
OED	*The Oxford English Dictionary, 2nd ed.*
OT	Old Testament
PNTC	The Pillar New Testament Commentary
PSCF	*Perspectives on Science and Christian Faith*
ThTo	*Theology Today*
TRE	*Religion Past and Present: Encyclopedia of Theology and Religion*
TynB	*Tyndale Bulletin*
WBC	Word Biblical Commentary
WTJ	*Westminster Theological Journal*
ZNW	*Zeitschrift für die neutestamentliche Wissenschaft und die Kunde der älteren Kirche*

Introduction

The eschatological portrait painted by the Old Testament [OT] is one in which creation has a propitious future. Donald Gowan argues that in the OT there is promised a threefold transformation of creation—that of the human person, human society, and nature.[1] While described in terms of radical discontinuities from the present, the future includes the restoration or renewal of the present creation. This restored "new" creation is described in texts such as Isaiah 25, 35, 65, and 66.

In the OT, the restored creation is characterized as one of unprecedented peace, justice, and righteousness for the whole earth. It also is intimately connected to the fulfillment of promises concerning the restoration of the particular people Israel within a particular land. In recent years, there has been a recovery of what may be called "new creation eschatology" which utilizes texts that include language concerning this territorial restoration. While drawing upon certain features of the texts—e.g., God's presence upon a renewed earth, the redemption of the natural world, and peace among all nations—to inform their conception of the final state, many recent new creationists deny that the particular territory of Israel has a role in God's promised future. Their neglect or rejection is especially interesting in light of the intimate relationship in the texts between the restoration of creation and the restoration of Israel territorially. Rather than a disposable element, the territorial restoration of Israel informs the framework of peace, justice, and righteousness that is to come upon the earth.

This book is a biblical/theological investigation of the territorial restoration of Israel within recent new creationism. I examine a number of well-known recent new creationists, including N. T. Wright, J. Richard

---

1. Gowan, *Eschatology in the Old Testament*. The basis for Gowan's threefold conception, which in turn gives structure to his book, is Ezekiel 36:22–38.

Middleton, Russell Moore, Douglas Moo, and Howard Snyder. For the purposes of this work, the labels *new creationism* and *new creationists* will refer to the writings of this select group. I show that there is a logical inconsistency between new creationists' use of OT texts for new creation hope and their exclusion of the territorial restoration of Israel in the new creation. I argue that this exclusion fails to appreciate territorial particularity as a necessary feature of those OT texts. Finally, I suggest that affirming the territorial restoration of Israel 1) represents a consistent utilization of OT new creation texts, 2) is harmonious with New Testament [NT] texts commonly used to deny territorial restoration, and 3) leads to a consistent new creation eschatology that emphasizes the materiality of the final state, a materiality that often has been rejected in the form of type or shadow.

The Way Ahead

In chapter 1 I introduce new creationism. In contrast to the historical dominance of spiritual, heavenly, non-temporal conceptions of the final state, the last two decades have witnessed a rise of conceptions that include the redemption of material, earthly, and temporal reality. In introducing recent new creationism, I focus on the primary emphases of selected new creationists.

In chapter 2 I observe that new creationism posits an essential continuity between the old and new creation: the new earth is the old earth renewed. I show that, in light of 2 Peter 3 and Romans 8, the selected new creationists envision a renewal of the present earth. This vision necessitates a level of continuity between the present creation and the future creation and can be seen in a variety of themes within these perspectives. In some cases new creationists conceive a relationship that entails a correspondence of identity between particular features of present materiality and particular features of future materiality.

In chapter 3 I offer a synthesis of the views of the territorial promise of land in recent theology. The synthesis includes theologians who have devoted whole works to the theme of land as well as those who have contributed works not solely focused on the theme but nonetheless are contributions to the scholarly study of the theme. The purpose of the chapter is to show that understanding the fulfillment of the land promise as a metaphor is common. I provide evidence that new creationists agree with that common interpretation. In concluding the chapter, I suggest that the diverse metaphorical interpretations surveyed can be categorized as follows: spiritualized (or Christified) and universalized (or expanded), respectively.

In chapter 4 I argue that a metaphorical understanding of the territorial land promise of Israel is inconsistent with new creation conceptions that envision a restored earth. I note that one area in which this inconsistency is evident is in new creationists' utilization of OT prophetical texts. I provide a brief examination of the utilization of these texts by new creationists to argue for continuity between the present creation and the renewed creation. These passages include those which speak directly to God creating new heavens and a new earth (e.g., Isa 65–66). Also important are those texts which speak to restoration and cosmic peace in the context of Zion and Jerusalem and the effect that this has upon other nations (e.g., Isa 2:2–4 [cf. Mic 4:2–3]; 11; 32; Ezek 36–37; Zech 2, 9). In the examination, I focus on the emphasis of a restored creation within recent new creationism and upon the question of correspondence introduced in chapter 2. The point is to challenge the conclusion that the territory of Israel should be spiritualized or universalized.

In chapter 5 I argue that territorial particularity is a distinguishing and necessary feature of the biblical texts utilized in recent new creationism. I offer an alternative to the positions introduced in chapter 3, arguing that affirming the territorial restoration of Israel 1) represents a consistent utilization of OT new creation texts, 2) is harmonious with NT texts commonly used to deny territorial restoration, and 3) leads to a consistent new creation eschatology that emphasizes the materiality of the final state, a materiality that often has been rejected in the form of type or shadow. I note a small group of theologians who have argued that upholding the territorial restoration of Israel actually bolsters a new creation conception.

In the conclusion, chapter 6, I offer several implications. I explain that the current study helps to show that a consistent new creation view should affirm the territorial restoration of Israel. I also point out areas for further research which logically issue from the current work such as a further examination of the overall hermeneutic of new creationists, studies on the nature of the territorial particularity of Israel in the new creation, the question of the role of nations in the final state, and further work on the framework of OT prophetical texts that include the territorial restoration of Israel. I note recent treatments of "place" within theology and the implications of the territorial particularity of Israel in light of the modern return of Jews to the Holy Land.

1

New Creation Eschatology
and Its Recent Forms

Craig Blaising argues that throughout the history of Christian thought there have been two basic models for conceptualizing the final state of the redeemed.[1] First, the spiritual vision model tends to view the final state as a heavenly and timeless existence. The second, the new creation model, emphasizes an earthly, material, time-sequenced, and embodied existence in a new heavens and new earth. The models that Blaising proposes are helpful in distinguishing tendencies throughout the history of the church.[2] Though the two conceptions have their respective emphases, one should

1. Blaising, "Premillennialism," 157–227. Blaising explains an interpretive model as "a heuristic device for comprehending complex views." Ibid., 160. His description of the "two models of eternal life" as he calls them (160–64), along with his examination of the respective models throughout church history (164–81), serve as a foundation for his argument for premillennial return of Christ. Also see Blaising, "New Creation Eschatology," 7–24. While the emphasis in the discussion of the two models is upon the final state, contemporary discussions of personal eschatology often revolve around passages of Scripture that inform a proper understanding of what occurs at the death of the believer when he is comforted in the presence of Christ, though without a body (e.g., Luke 23:43 and Phil 1:23). The term normally used to describe this state is heaven, a term that has a wide range of meaning in Scripture (see Reddish, "Heaven," 90–91).

2. I use the word tendencies because there exists neither a strict definition of a spiritual vision view nor a new creation view. The various views, because of slight nuances, could be thought of as being positioned on a linear spectrum where movement to either the left or the right would indicate a conception of the final state that emphasizes the spiritual and heavenly elements or, alternatively, one that emphasizes material and earthly elements.

1

not think of the two conceptions as necessarily exclusive. Still, there is widespread consensus that the history of the church has been dominated by conceptions that could be categorized within Blaising's first model, the spiritual vision, and that the emphases of the new creation model generally have been ignored or rejected.[3]

However, over the past few decades there has been a rising theological interest in biblical descriptions of a new creation. In 1979, Anthony A. Hoekema published *The Bible and the Future*.[4] In this work, Hoekema argues that the world will be renewed and that the final state will have relative continuity with the present creation.[5] Although there seems to be dependence upon Hoekema among contemporary evangelical theologians arguing for a new creation conception, widespread discussion of the issue was not manifested in the literature in the two decades that followed the publication of Hoekema's work. Within the last fifteen years, though, a number of theologians from various faith traditions within evangelicalism have expressed a notable interest in the issues that Hoekema addressed over thirty years ago. The result has been a growing discontent with conceptions that emphasize the nature of the final state as primarily spiritual in nature. While not eschewing all elements of a spiritual vision model, the recent new creationism emphasizes characteristics that have been absent—or at least minimized—in the spiritual conceptions of the final state which have dominated church history.

The issues involved in recent dialogue include not only distinctions between the intermediate state and the final state of believers (and, hence, the relationship between heaven and the final state[6]), but also the relationship between this world and the next (including whether the present universe will be annihilated or renewed and purified), ethical concerns

---

3. In addition to Blaising's essay, other works in which this dominance can be seen include McDannell and Lang, *Heaven*; McGinn's series *The Presence of God*, 5 vols. (1 additional volume forthcoming); Russell, *History of Heaven*; Santmire, *Travail of Nature*; Snyder, *Models of the Kingdom*; and Viviano, *Kingdom of God in History*.

4. Hoekema, *Bible and the Future*. See especially chapter 20, "The New Earth," 274–87.

5. Hoekema highlighted a traditional feature of Dutch Reformed thought that was new creationist in that it affirmed continuity between the present heavens and earth and the new heavens and new earth. Examples from the tradition include Bavinck, *Reformed Dogmatics* (especially vol. 4); Berkhof, *Christ the Meaning of History*; Berkouwer, *Return of Christ*; and Kuyper, *De Gemeene Gratie*. Additionally, in his explanation of new creationism, Hoekema quotes the language of the Belgic Confession (Art. 37) which states that Christ will come to cleanse the old world in fire and flame.

6. See fn 1 in the current chapter.

regarding the impact of human activity in this world to life in the new earth (including creation care, responsible stewardship of the earth, societal and cultural concerns, worldview, the built environment, and even an emphasis on urban renewal), the relationship of the new heavens and new earth to history, and the idea that the work of Christ includes not only the salvation of the individual, but also the redemption of the entire creation from the effects of sin.[7]

For the purposes of this work, I will focus on recent biblical/theological contributions to new creationism within evangelical theology.[8] Each of the theologians in view affirm a restored creation and exhibit a heavy reliance upon OT texts to describe a promised time of unprecedented peace, justice, and righteousness. The rationale behind the current selection of theologians will become evident as the topic of territorial particularity and its relation to these recent forms is developed in subsequent chapters. For the purpose of simplicity, from this point on I will use the phrase "new creationists" or "new creationism" to refer to the selected theologians and their conceptions, respectively.

7. The growing discontent regarding the tendency toward a spiritual vision eschatology throughout history spans across various denominations and ecclesial traditions. A wide range of essays and articles from a Christian perspective have appeared within the last decade, each one emphasizing one or more of the issues mentioned above. Examples of brief non-technical articles and essays that embody a new creation emphasis include Arand and Herrman, "Attending to the Beauty of the Creation," 313–31; Clapp, "Animals in the Kingdom," 45; Jacobsen, "We Can't Go Back to the Garden"; Hamner and Johnson, "Holy Mission," 1–8; McCartney, "*ECCE HOMO*," 1–21; Mcacham, "Heaven Can't Wait," 30–36; Surburg, "Good Stuff!," 245–62; Truesdale, "Last Things First," 116–22; Williams, "On Eschatological Discontinuity," 13–20; Williams, "Rapture or Resurrection," 9–37; and Williams, "Regeneration in Cosmic Context," 68–80. Recent books that have emphasized the issues above include Alcorn, *Heaven*; Bauckham, *Bible and Ecology*; Bauckham, *Living With Other Creatures*; Bouma-Prediger, *Beauty of the Earth*; Hegeman, *Plowing in Hope*; Jacobsen, *Sidewalks in the Kingdom*; Jacobsen, *Space Between*; Lawrence, *Heaven*; Marshall and Gilbert, *Heaven is Not My Home*; Plantinga, *Engaging God's World*; Williams, *Far as the Curse if Found*; Wittmer, *Heaven is a Place on Earth*; and Wolters, *Creation Regained*. While an investigation into what might be the cause or causes behind the growing discontent is needed, along with a thorough analysis of the literature included in the growing discontent, such an investigation is neither possible nor necessary for the purposes of the current work.

8. This work does not cover the themes and trajectories of arguments for a new creation concept that are outside of mainstream Christian thought, whether among social, scientific, and cultural studies or concepts from non-Christian religions.

N. T. Wright—Life After Life After Death

N. T. Wright, professor at the University of St. Andrews, is well-known in evangelical Christian circles for his robust apologetic for the reality of Christ's bodily resurrection and also for his controversial views on justification.[9] Regarding eschatology, Wright argues for what he believes is a more biblical understanding of the final state of believers than that which has predominated in the past. Wright's new creationism is most explicitly presented in his 2008 work *Surprised by Hope: Rethinking Heaven, the Resurrection, and the Mission of the Church.*[10] Responding to what he conceives as ignorance within today's church, Wright confronts the idea that the Christian hope is going to heaven when one dies and the idea that heaven is the ultimate destination or final home for the Christian.[11] He makes the charge that this limited conception of hope actually demeans the bodily resurrection of Christ and the promises that describe God's kingdom rule coming to the earth with the new Jerusalem coming down from heaven "uniting the two [heaven and earth] in a lasting embrace."[12]

---

9. For Wright's reconstruction of the life of Jesus and the history of early Christianity, see his *Christian Origins and the Question of God Series*. At the time of this writing, four volumes of the proposed six-volume series had been released: *New Testament and the People of God; Jesus and the Victory of God; Resurrection of the Son of God;* and *Paul and the Faithfulness of God.* For other works that deal with Wright's arguments for the reality of Jesus' resurrection, see especially Wright, *Challenge of Jesus;* Borg and Wright, *Meaning of Jesus;* and Stewart, *Resurrection of Jesus.* For his controversial views on justification see, in addition to the above works, Wright, *What Saint Paul Really Said;* Wright, "Redemption from the New Perspective," 69–100; Wright, *Paul: Fresh Perspectives;* Wright, "4QMMT and Paul," 104–32; Wright, "New Perspectives on Paul," 243–64; and Wright, *Justification.* A recent work in which Wright has compiled many of his previous essays on Pauline theology is Wright, *Pauline Perspectives.*

10. Wright, *Surprised by Hope.* The work synthesizes the more detailed arguments found in the *Christian Origins and the Question of God Series.* A helpful and brief precursor to Wright's argument in *Surprised by Hope* can be found in his *New Heavens, New Earth.*

11. In the preface, Wright speaks to this ignorance and states what he feels the church needs to recapture: "the classic Christian answer to the question of death and beyond, which these days is not so much disbelieved (in the world and church alike) as simply not known . . . . most people simply don't know what orthodox Christian belief is." Wright, *Surprised by Hope,* xii, 12. He offers the following works as evidence of the misunderstanding of the term heaven as the ultimate destination: Stanford, *Heaven;* McGrath, *History of Heaven;* and the more thorough aforementioned historical surveys by McDannell and Lang and Burton Russell, respectively.

12. Wright, *Surprised by Hope,* 19.

Alternatively, Wright argues, the literal bodily resurrection of Christ (and of all believers in the future) implies a hope that embraces aspects of material and earthly life after death.[13] For Wright, this material and earthly hope raises doubts as to whether individual salvation should be the center and driving feature of the hope for the future: "Instead of looking first at the promise to the individual and working up from that to the renewal of creation, we begin with the Biblical vision of the future world—a vision of the present cosmos renewed from top to bottom by the God who is both creator and redeemer. That is the context within which we will then be able to speak of the second coming of Jesus and then of the bodily resurrection."[14]

Wright's view of redemption, the plan of which is to liberate what has come to be enslaved, includes the entire cosmos.[15] In his opinion, the NT is concerned more with life after life after death (i.e., life after heaven) than it is with life after death, that is heaven in the sense of a temporary bodiless state of death.[16] Salvation is not simply going to heaven when a person dies. Instead, it encompasses God's promised new heavens and new earth and the believer's participation in "that new and gloriously embodied reality."[17]

---

13. For Wright, Jesus' resurrection was the beginning of an entirely new world in which Christians could presently play a part. It signified "a very this-worldly, present-age meaning: Jesus is raised, so he is the Messiah, and therefore he is the world's true Lord; Jesus is raised, so God's new creation has begun—and we, his followers, have a job to do!" Ibid., 56.

14. Ibid., 80. In a footnote, Wright makes the reader aware that he is in dialogue with Moltmann, *Theology of Hope*; Moltmann, *Coming of God*; Pannenberg, *Systematic Theology*, esp. vol. 3; Polkinghorne and Welker, *End of the World and the Ends of God*; Colwell, *Called to One Hope*; Bauckham, *God Will Be All in All*; and Bauckham and Hart, *Hope Against Hope*. Wright also references his *Millennium Myth*.

15. At the conclusion of one chapter, he states, "What I am proposing is that the New Testament image of the future hope of the whole cosmos, grounded in the resurrection of Jesus, gives as coherent a picture as we need or could have of the future that is promised to the whole world, a future in which, under the sovereign and wise rule of the creator God, decay and death will be done away with and a new creation born, to which the present one will stand as mother to child." Wright, *Surprised by Hope*, 107.

16. Wright introduces the concept of life after life after death in *Surprised by Hope*, 148–52. It is this *surprising* future hope that leads directly "to a vision of the *present* hope that is the basis of all Christian mission." Ibid., 191.

17. Ibid., 197. For Wright, this salvation should lead to a rethinking of the main work of the church. He writes, "It's no good falling back into the tired old split-level world where some people believe in evangelism in terms of saving souls for a timeless eternity and other people believe in mission in terms of working for justice, peace, and hope in the present world. That great divide has nothing to do with Jesus and the New Testament and everything to do with the silent enslavement of many Christians (both conservative

The Christian hope becomes "a full, recreated life in the presence and love of God, a totally renewed creation, an integrated new heavens and new earth, and a complete humanness—complete not in and for itself as an isolated entity, but complete in worship and love for God, complete in love for one another as humans, complete in stewardship over God's world, and so, and only in that complete context, a full humanness in itself."[18] For Wright, salvation is a transformation that began to take place at the resurrection of Christ within space, time, and matter. The result of the transformation is not an abandonment of space, time, and matter, but their renewal. When the final resurrection occurs, "we will discover that everything done in the present world in the power of Jesus' own resurrection will be celebrated and included, appropriately transformed."[19]

J. Richard Middleton—Holistic Redemption

Professor of Biblical Studies at Roberts Wesleyan College and professor of Bible and Culture at Northeastern Seminary, J. Richard Middleton proposes that the biblical story of redemption is holistic, encompassing all creation.[20] For Middleton, it is important to distinguish between Scripture's use of the terms creation and redemption and how these terms are understood in the

and radical) to the Platonic ideology of the Enlightenment." Ibid., 193.

18. Wright, *New Heavens, New Earth*, 23.

19. Wright, *Surprised by Hope*, 294. While Wright does not fully explain what "everything" means in his conception, what is clear is that there are social, political, and cultural similarities between the temporal present state and the everlasting transformed state (See, for example, chapter 13, "Building for the Kingdom," and the Appendix in *Surprised by Hope*).

20. For his extensive proposal of holistic redemption, see Middleton, *A New Heaven and a New Earth*. Middleton states that the primary purpose of the book "is to sketch the coherent biblical theology (beginning in the Old Testament) that culminates in the New Testament's explicit eschatological vision of the redemption of creation." Then he notes the following subsidiary purposes: 1) to "explore some of the ethical implications of a biblically grounded holistic eschatology for our present life in God's world"; and 2) to investigate "what happened to the biblical vision of the redemption of the earth in the history of Christian eschatology." Ibid., 15–16. The appendix of the book is a helpful addition to the works noted in fn 3 of the present chapter regarding the question of how a heavenly destiny came to dominate Christian thought. A brief introduction to Middleton's argument of holistic redemption can be found in Middleton, "A New Heaven and a New Earth," 73–97. Elements of Middleton's proposal can be found in Walsh and Middleton, *Transforming Vision*, especially chapter 5, "Transformed by Redemption" (74–90) and in Middleton and Gorman, "Salvation," 5:45–64.

modern western worldview. According to Scripture, he contends, *creation* "includes the entire human socio-cultural order," not simply nature.[21] Likewise, *redemption* includes the reversal of the Fall and restoration to God's good intention, not a dualistic Platonic redemption "conceived as transferal from a lower, inferior realm (variously understood as body, earth, matter, nature, or the secular) to a higher, more valued or esteemed realm (understood as soul, heaven, spirit, the realm of grace or the sacred)."[22] Middleton describes his vision of salvation as follows:

> [T]he redeemed human race will once again utilize their God-given power and agency to rule the earth as God intended—a renewal of the human cultural task, but this time without sin. . . . Far from being the end or cessation of history, this is history's true beginning, free from the constraints of human violation vis-à-vis God, or other humans, or the earth itself. The climax of the biblical story, which many have called the "eternal state," is fundamentally this-worldly. When God brings his original purposes to fruition, we find not escape from creation, but rather new (or renewed) creation.[23]

Middleton calls the traditional idea of heaven "a hybrid idea" because it conceives that the believer will experience everlasting fellowship with God in a non-physical realm, but with a resurrected, i.e., physical, body.[24] Consequently, he is comfortable to do away with "the notion of 'heaven' as an eternal hope, since this notion is thought to be fundamentally incompatible with authentic biblical faith."[25] The believer's everlasting hope

---

21. Middleton, "A New Heaven and a New Earth," 74. Middleton points to the parallels between the biblical idea of creation and beliefs in ancient Mesopotamia, referencing his own work *The Liberating Image*, chapters 3–5. Middleton notes that even many who promote creation care make the reductionist mistake in that they "tend to reduce 'creation' to nature or the environment, with little reflection on the fact that human beings, and all the cultural and social formations that they have developed over history, are also part of the created order." Middleton, *A New Heaven and a New Earth*, 22.

22. Middleton, "A New Heaven and a New Earth," 75.

23. Middleton, *A New Heaven and a New Earth*, 70.

24. Middleton, "A New Heaven and a New Earth," 73.

25. Middleton notes several works which, in varying degrees, have accepted this view. "A New Heaven and a New Earth," 73 fn 2. Middleton's plot of the biblical story as outlined in "A New Heaven and a New Earth" and developed more fully in *A New Heaven and a New Earth* (ch. 3) "serves to reinforce the holistic and this-worldly character of God's purposes." He concludes that "eschatological redemption consists in the renewal of human cultural life on earth rather than our removal from earth to heaven. Close

of redemption should be cosmic in its scope, comprising all aspects of life as a part of God's redemptive plan and his righteous rule.[26] Middleton concludes, "The inner logic . . . of holistic salvation is that the creator has not given up on creation and is working to salvage and restore the world (human and nonhuman) to the fullness of shalom and flourishing intended from the beginning. And redeemed human beings, renewed in God's image, are to work toward and embody this vision in their daily lives."[27]

Russell Moore—Life and Life More Abundantly

Russell Moore's cosmic eschatological approach entails a new creation understanding of the final state of the redeemed. Moore, president of the Ethics and Religious Liberty Commission of the Southern Baptist Convention, describes God's restoration of all creation in vivid terms.[28] He writes

---

attention to the unfolding biblical story reveals that there is simply no role for heaven as the final destiny of the righteous." Middleton, *A New Heaven and a New Earth,* 58. He also writes "that there is not one single reference in the entire biblical canon (Old and New Testaments) to heaven as the eternal destiny of the believer. Although this idea has a vastly important role in popular Christian imagination (and even in some theologies), not once does Scripture itself actually say that the righteous will live forever in heaven." Middleton, *A New Heaven and a New Earth,* 72.

26. Cf. Walsh and Middleton, *Transforming Vision,* 80. The holistic redemption, Middleton argues, is set forth in both testaments. He writes that "the entire Old Testament reveals an interest in mundane matters such as the development of languages and cultures, the fertility of land and crops, the birth of children and stable family life, justice among neighbors, and peace in international relations. The Old Testament does not spiritualize salvation, but rather understands it as God's deliverance of people and land from all that destroys life and the consequent restoration of people and land to flourishing." Middleton, *A New Heaven and a New Earth,* 25. These OT descriptions culminate "in the New Testament's eschatological vision of the redemption of creation." Middleton, "A New Heaven and a New Earth," 15.

27. Middleton, *A New Heaven and a New Earth,* 27. In regard to the relationship between the way that creation and humans worship, Middleton states the following: "If mountains worship God by being mountains and stars worship God by being stars, how do humans worship God? By being human, in the full glory of what that means. Humans, the Bible tells us, are cultural beings, defined not by our worship, for worship is what defines creation (all creatures are called to worship). But the human creature is made to worship God in a distinctive way: by interacting with the earth, using our God-given power to transform our earthly environment into a complex world (a sociocultural world) that glorifies our creator." Ibid., 41.

28. Formerly Moore was Dean of the School of Theology and Senior Vice President for Academic Administration at The Southern Baptist Theological Seminary, where he also served as Professor of Christian Theology and Ethics.

that the picture "is not of an eschatological flight from creation but the restoration and redemption of creation with all that entails: table fellowship, community, culture, economics, agriculture and animal husbandry, art, architecture, worship—in short, *life* and that abundantly."[29] After God's ultimate triumph of all evil and death itself, believers will experience an everlasting state in which they exist bodily upon the earth which has been transformed and regenerated.[30] Similar to Wright, Moore states that the "point of the gospel is not that we would go to heaven when we die."[31] Rather, the gospel points to God winning back his good creation by restoring and recreating "a world that vindicates his original creation purposes."[32]

Douglas Moo—Nature in the Plan of God

While he seems to be more cautious than Wright in keeping the redemption of human beings at the heart of God's plan and evangelism as the church's primary goal, Douglas Moo proposes "that the attitude of an 'either/or' when it comes to evangelism and environmental concern is a false alternative."[33] Moo, professor of NT at Wheaton College, expresses concern

29. Russell D. Moore, "Personal and Cosmic Eschatology," 859. Moore's analysis of what the church has believed (873–92) manifests the dominance of what Blaising calls the spiritual vision understanding of eternal life and thereby parallels the histories cited earlier in the chapter in fn 3. It is also in general agreement with Middleton's description of the hybrid idea that consists of a belief in bodily resurrection and a final state that is essentially spiritual and heavenly, implying non-materiality.

30. He writes, "This new earth includes all of the covenant promises of God fulfilled. God dwells with his people, in Christ. He welcomes them to the tree of life. The city of Jerusalem is rebuilt and glorious, with the wealth of the nations streaming into it (Rev. 21:22–26)." Ibid., 873.

31. Ibid., 912. He writes further, "Eternity means civilization, architecture, banquet feasting, ruling, work—in short, it is eternal *life*. The new earth is not the white, antiseptic, hyperspiritual heaven some Christians expect as their eternal home. Nor is it simply the everlasting family reunion with calorie-free food and super powers, as some hope." Ibid.

32. Ibid., 913. For Moore, this idea should impel the Christian to action in the present life. For his understanding of the effects of a new creation eschatology upon the Christian's present life (hope, ethics, social and political action, and corporate witness), see especially Moore, *Kingdom of Christ* and the section on how the doctrine of eschatology impacts the church today in "Personal and Cosmic Eschatology," (917–25). One may also consult the various articles at http://www.russellmoore.com/papers/ which speak to these issues.

33. Moo, "Nature in the New Creation," 454. He likens this dichotomy to that of

at the lack of attention given to the cosmos within the discussion of escha-tological fulfillment.[34] For him, the restoration of the cosmos, including both humanity and nature, should not be spiritualized.[35] A significant con-tribution of Moo to recent discussion is an article in which he argues that Paul's use of the phrase "new creation" in Galatians 6:15 and 2 Corinthians 5:17 should be understood primarily as the description of a new age that has come through Christ's first coming and will be consummated upon his return.[36] Moo attempts to provide justification for using the phrase "new creation" to refer to something wider than individual human transforma-tion—the renovation of the cosmos and the fulfillment of new heavens and new earth prophecies such as Isaiah 65 and 66.[37] Moo concludes that there are implications regarding Christian stewardship of nature: " 'New Cre-ation' is manifested in the present through transformed Christians who live in transformed relationships with God, with one another, with all people, and with the world of nature. 'New Creation' will be consummated when these relationships are perfected by God himself and when he brings his created world to its final state of glory."[38]

While Moo admits the difficulty of knowing with certainty the con-tinuity between the present heavens and earth and the new heavens and earth, he concludes: "But this much can at least be said: the new world is a place of material substance. The phrase 'heaven and earth' is a merism that

---

evangelism versus social concern during the 1960s and 1970s and understands both to be "profoundly out of keeping with the witness of Scripture" (454). Cautioning against subordinating Scripture to environmental concerns, Moo points out that evangelicals have responded at times "by retreating to a kind of rigid historical exegesis that deliber-ately brackets out the concerns of our own world." He calls this "a mistake in the opposite direction, in its extreme form creating an unbridgeable ditch between the Bible and the issues that press upon us so insistently." Moo, "Creation and New Creation," 40.

34. Moo, "Nature in the New Creation," 458.

35. Moo uses the term nature to denote "the sub-human world of creation." Ibid., 459.

36. Moo, "Creation and New Creation," 39–60.

37. Regarding the Isaianic prophecies and their relation to the Pauline passages in which he is interested, Moo writes that "in his familiar prophecies about a 'new heavens and new earth,' Isaiah envisages an ultimate salvation that extends beyond the people of Israel or even the land of Israel to include the entire comos [sic]: a 'new heavens and new earth' (Isa 65:17–22; cf. 66:22–24). It is quite unlikely, given the usual meaning of 'creation' in Paul, that he would use 'new creation' to allude to this Isaianic expectation without some reference to the cosmos." Ibid., 45–46.

38. Ibid., 59.

refers to the entire universe."[39] Moo envisions an earthly, material existence for believers, one in which they are rightly related to the rest of nature as God intended from the beginning.[40]

Howard A. Snyder—The Healing of Creation

Like the previous theologians surveyed in this chapter, Howard A. Snyder, Professor of Wesley Studies at Tyndale Seminary in Toronto, affirms the future of the redeemed as embodied existence upon the earth. At the heart of Snyder's view is his understanding of the scope of sin. He describes the post-Fall situation as follows:

> Something has gone horribly wrong on earth, and it affects—infects, really—everything. Scripture is very clear that this problem is at once spiritual, moral, theological, social, economic, political—and yes, physical. We can't simply isolate one strand of the problem and separate it from the rest of the diseased reality that is our fallen world.
>
> The human and earthly problem is, in other words, *ecological*—our entire human existence in all its dimensions is diseased. The spiritual, the physical, the social, and political are all intertwined.[41]

According to Snyder, the tendency to focus solely on individual sin and salvation and the tendency toward dualism have led to a devaluing of the non-human creation.[42] These tendencies have dominated the history of the church and made predominant the view that has made the salvation of

39. Moo, "Nature in the New Creation," 464.

40. Moo is in the process of writing a book with his son Jonathan on creation care which is to be in Zondervan's Biblical Theology for Life series.

41. Snyder and Scandrett, *Salvation Means Creation Healed*, xvi. A preliminary argument to Snyder's treatment in this work can be found in Snyder, "Salvation Means Creation Healed," 9–47. The emphasis on individual salvation has been questioned even among the Reformed. See, for example, Granberg-Michaelson, "Covenant and Creation," 27–36.

42. Snyder challenges the dualistic understanding of matter, writing that in the Bible "Spirit and matter are not two different worlds. They are interlaced dimensions of the one world God created in its entirety and intends to redeem, save, liberate, and heal in its entirety." Snyder, *Salvation Means Creation Healed*, x. Part of Snyder's emphasis, like that of Moo, is creation care. He offers four views which distort the biblical view of creation. Ibid., 42–45.

souls not merely the center of God's redemption plan, but the circumference of that plan.

Snyder argues that as a result of the wide scope of sin, redemption has a wide scope as well. Because sin is comprehensive, the cure has to be comprehensive as well.[43] So, while affirming the centrality of Christ's work of the reconciliation of individual souls to himself, Snyder argues for a wider understanding of Christ's work of reconciliation:

> The reconciliation won by Christ reaches to all the alienations that result from our sin—alienation from God, from ourselves, between persons, and between us and our physical environment. The biblical picture therefore is at once personal, ecological, and cosmic. As mind-boggling as the thought is, Scripture teaches that this reconciliation even includes the redemption of the physical universe from the effects of sin, as everything is brought under its proper headship in Jesus (Rom 8:19–21).[44]

Redemption as a biblical theme certainly includes the spiritual realm but it also includes the physical realm, specifically the promise of a new heaven and a new earth.[45] One sees this cosmic reconciliation especially in Paul's writings and the book of Revelation, but, for Snyder, the picture reaches its climax in OT restoration texts such as Isaiah 11.[46] The reconciliation in view is not one in which humanity is taken out of the creation, but one in which redeemed humanity lives upon a renewed earth.[47] Snyder concludes that this is the gospel. Ultimately, for Snyder, for one to affirm the redemption of the individual from sin and the reconciliation of individuals to Christ through faith while ignoring or denying the reconciliation

43. Thus, "If salvation means creation healed, then salvation must be as deep and wide, as high and broad, as creation itself." Ibid., 146.

44. Ibid., 99.

45. Snyder writes, "The redemption God is bringing promises a new heaven and a new earth. What does this really mean? Biblically, it *does not* mean two common but extreme views: it does not mean only saving the earth from oppression or ecological collapse, nor does it mean disembodied eternal life in heaven and the annihilation of the material universe. Rather, it means reconciliation between earth and heaven, the heavenly city descending to earth (Revelation 22), the reign of God that in some way reconstitutes the whole creation through God's work in Jesus." Ibid., 98.

46. Ibid., 98–102.

47. Snyder writes, "In place of sub-biblical or Neo-Platonic views that place spirit above matter and radically split present from future, the global church needs a biblical earth-and-heaven ecological worldview that is in fact the biblical worldstory of the kingdom of God." Ibid., 138.

and redemption of creation incorrectly limits this gospel. The goal, Snyder concludes, "is not to reach heaven, but to have full fellowship with God and one another now and in the final new creation. Creation healed! This is salvation, true healing salve. It is the good news."[48]

Biblical Foundations: Texts and Themes

In arguing for their understanding of the final state, new creationists draw attention to certain biblical texts. They claim that they simply are attempting to recover what has been at best neglected and at worst denied throughout the history of the church. As new creationists, specifically the ways in which they utilize biblical texts, are analyzed, certain emphases become apparent. An overview of these themes serves as further introduction to the conceptions of new creationists and as a foundation for subsequent chapters, especially regarding the way in which they utilize OT prophetical texts to argue for a restoration of the earth while excluding the territorial restoration of Israel within those texts.

The Coming of God's Kingdom

In the Sermon on the Mount, Jesus teaches his disciples the manner in which to pray. Part of this prayer is that God's kingdom would come and that his will would be done on earth as it is in heaven.[49] Wright and other new creationists argue that Jesus' prayer is pointing to a perfect rule that will take place on the earth, something that can only be accomplished when sin and death have been completely eradicated.[50] Wright calls this perfect

48. Ibid., 227.

49. It may be concluded that Jesus' model prayer conveys a desire that the rule of God on the earth prior to Christ coming again would parallel his rule in heaven, where God currently dwells (c.f. Heb 8:1–2; 4:14; 8:1; 9:24; 1 Pet 3:22). Understood in this way, Christians are to possess a desire that the rule of God would look as close to God's perfect rule in heaven as is possible in a state where sin and death exist.

50. New creationists generally affirm some sense of an already-not yet tension of kingdom fulfillment in the NT, including, for instance, the affirmation that Christians are already citizens of heaven according to Phil 3:20 and Col 1:13 (see Wright, *The Resurrection of the Son of God*, 229–36). However, as will be seen, they generally understand that the prayer that the kingdom of God come and that God's will be done on earth is describing a future event to be fulfilled on the earth following the return of Christ. For new creationists such as Howard Snyder, this future orientation has implications for the

rule the marriage of heaven and earth which "is the ultimate rejection of all types of Gnosticism, of every worldview that sees the final goal as the separation of the world from God, of the physical from the spiritual, of earth from heaven. It is the final answer to the Lord's Prayer, that God's kingdom will come and his will be done on earth as in heaven."[51] It is for this, Wright maintains, that Jesus taught us to pray.[52] In his discussion of the intermediate state, Moore concludes the following: "For believers, the intermediate state is blessedness, to be sure. But in heaven there is yet eschatology. The ultimate purpose of God is not just the ongoing life of believers but that his kingdom would come, his will would be done 'on earth as it is in heaven' (Matt. 6:10). That awaits the end of all ends, the return of Jesus and the final overthrow of death."[53] Jesus' model prayer envisions a future earthly condition. Middleton, after quoting Matthew 6:10, concludes, "It is the biblical eschatological hope that one day God's salvation (which is being prepared in heaven) will be manifest fully on earth. Then earth will be fully conformed to heaven."[54]

For new creationists, the time of the earth being conformed to heaven is intimately related to the manifestation of God's kingdom on the earth and can be seen in passages like Isaiah 52:7–12 which envision a time when Israel's God will return to be king, "*that all the ends of the earth may see the salvation of our God.*" This text, Wright notes, "means the end of exile, the defeat of evil, and the return of Israel's God to Zion."[55] Moore writes, "Throughout the prophets, the Spirit points to a final order in which the curse on creation is reversed: animal predation is no more (Isa. 11:6–9), nature itself will be in harmony with humanity (Isa. 60:19–22), the demonic

---

Christian's desire that there would be manifestations of that perfect rule during this age. Snyder writes that "if we believe God really intends to answer Jesus' prayer that God's 'will be done, on earth as it is in heaven' (Matt 6:10), we will work now to show the truth of God's reign in all areas on earth." Snyder, *Salvation Means Creation Healed*, 158. However, the point of Jesus' statement seems to rest in the desire that a future rule of God is going to have a comprehensive effect upon the entire earth.

51. Wright, *Surprised by Hope*, 104. The first answer, according to Wright, is the first Easter "when Hope in person surprised the whole world by coming forward from the future into the present." Ibid., 29. In a discussion of Rom 8, Wright states that "we Christians are caught in between creation and new creation, and this shows in how we pray and what we pray for." Ibid., 279.

52. Ibid., 201, 15, 93.

53. Moore, "Personal and Cosmic Eschatology," 902.

54. Middleton, "A New Heaven and a New Earth," 96.

55. Wright, *Surprised by Hope*, 202.

order is crushed (Isa. 27:1; Hab. 3:13), and all the nations stream to Israel bringing their wealth into her gates (Isa. 60:1–14; Micah 4:1–5)."[56] The prophesies of these OT texts, which are crucial for new creationists, are realized through God's kingship. Because many OT texts envision earthly fulfillment, new creationists such as Moore do not limit the kingdom to the general rule of God over his creation. He writes, "The Kingdom is not seen in the Old Testament as simply the general sovereignty of God . . . . The kingdom of God is instead the reign of God through his human mediator-king over a world in submission to his righteous rule. This envisions the restoration of the Edenic order when God ruled through a human vice-regent, Adam, and put 'all things under his feet' (Ps. 8:5–8)."[57]

Wright connects Daniel's prophecy of the son of man having authority and dominion over the nations (Dan 7) to Isaiah's messianic prophecy concerning judgment which "creates a world where the wolf and the lamb lie down side by side" (Isa 11).[58] Relating prophecies of judgment and defeat of God's enemies (Isa 11:1–5; 42:1–2; 61:1–11) with prophecies of the pouring forth of the Spirit (Joel 2:28–32) and with the messianic language of Isaiah 11, Moore concludes, "This messianic kingdom will rout the defiant spirits and nations, will serve as a model for God's creation purposes, will vindicate Israel's covenant claims, and will restore shalom to the universe in both its human and nonhuman aspects."[59]

Snyder's concept of *shalom* resulting from the healing of creation is also connected with texts that envision the kingdom which is to come. Referring to Micah 4:4 and Zechariah 3:10, he writes, "Here is true *shalom*, peaceful and fruitful harmony between God, people, and the land."[60] He writes further,

> Christians firmly believe that, viewed eschatologically, "the kingdom of the world has become the kingdom of our Lord and of his Messiah, and he will reign forever and ever" (Rev 11:15). Both the Old and New Testaments prophesy a renewed earth community, "new heavens and a new earth, where righteousness is at home" (2 Pet 3:13; cf. Isa 65:17; 66:22; Rev 21:1). Here is universal *shalom*

56. Moore, "Personal and Cosmic Eschatology," 859.

57. Ibid.," 862.

58. Wright, *Surprised by Hope*, 138.

59. Moore, "Personal and Cosmic Eschatology," 863–64. Moore also cites Zech 9:9–10; Isa 9:1–10; and Dan 7:14 as envisioning a reign that will extend to the ends of the earth and last forever.

60. Snyder, *Salvation Means Creation Healed*, 126.

with all peoples and the whole earth: "they shall all sit under their own vines and under their own fig trees, and no one shall make them afraid" (Mic 4:4; cf. 2 Kgs 18:31; Isa 36:16). Eschatologically speaking, Christian community is restored earth community, refined and purified by God's judgment and renewal.[61]

Discussing nature in the new creation, Moo emphasizes kingdom texts while connecting the restoration of nature to the restoration of the whole cosmos.[62] He concludes, "Kingdom and creation cannot be set against each other."[63]

The center of the future kingdom is the new Jerusalem that John sees in Revelation 21:10—22:5, another text which new creationists utilize. The city is seen "coming down out of heaven from God" (Rev 21:2, 10; cf. 3:12).[64] Wright notes that "when we come to the picture of the actual end in Revelation 21–22, we find not ransomed souls making their way to a disembodied heaven but rather the new Jerusalem coming down from heaven to earth, uniting the two in a lasting embrace."[65] He calls Revelation 21–22 "the last and perhaps the greatest image of new creation, of cosmic renewal, in the whole Bible."[66] The new Jerusalem is a city with physical characteristics, containing matter and form. It consists of nations and kings (Rev 21:24). It is a place in which "there will no longer be any curse; and the throne of God and of the Lamb will be in it, and his bond servants will serve him; they will see his face, and his name will be on their foreheads"

61. Ibid., 215.

62. In his extended discussion of Rom 8:19–22, Moo argues that Paul's dependence upon texts such as Isa 11:10–14; 24:21–23; 27:6; 42:1, 6; 49:6; 54:3; Jer 4:2; and Ps 72:8–11 suggests a connection between Paul's conviction about physical restoration to prophecies of the kingdom. Moo, "Nature in the New Creation," 463 including fn 51.

63. Ibid., 486.

64. The concept of the city coming from heaven seems to fit with Jesus' words of comfort to his disciples as recorded in John 14:1–3. Perhaps Jesus is referring to the city when he tells them that he is going to prepare a place for them. The idea that this eschatological city is currently in heaven may be implied also by Gal 4:26 and Heb 11:16; 12:22–24; 13:14. In a similar fashion, believers are assured that their salvation or inheritance is prepared and kept in heaven (Matt 25:34; 1 Pet 1:4) and that their hope and reward is in heaven (Col 1:5 and Matt 5:12; cf. Luke 6:23). These verses, while seeming to imply the idea that the reception of the inheritance entails believers going to heaven, actually correspond to a new creation conception in which the inheritance, the reward, and the content of the hope is brought to believers on the earth and heaven is simply where they are stored prior to that point in time when they are realized on the earth.

65. Wright, *Surprised by Hope*, 19.

66. Ibid., 104.

(Rev 22:3–4).[67] Wright concludes, "We notice right away how drastically different this is from all those would-be Christian scenarios in which the end of the story is the Christian going off to heaven as soul, naked and unadorned, to meet its maker in fear and trembling."[68] Snyder utilizes the description of the new Jerusalem in Revelation 21:24–27 to argue that the "biblical vision of *creation—incarnation—new creation*" involves human culture. For him, John's vision provides impetus for Christians "to engage today's global society effectively and redemptively at every level" because every dimension of human society will be redeemed.[69] Moore notes that John's description of the eternal city is "consistent with the rest of biblical eschatology" and that the description "is surprisingly 'earthy.' Eternity means civilization, architecture, banquet feasting, ruling, work—in short, it is eternal *life*."[70] Middleton also reflects on the materiality of the new Jerusalem: "The very description of the New Jerusalem as a bride 'prepared' for her husband should remind us of Jesus going to 'prepare' a place for the disciples. Indeed, both preparations take place in heaven. In Revelation 21, however, the New Jerusalem (which is both a holy city and the people of God—that is, redeemed humanity in their concrete socio-cultural, even urban, character), comes down out of heaven. Here it is very clear that the final, permanent dwelling place of God with humanity is on earth. . . . God will be enthroned there (on earth) . . . ."[71]

That this is an everlasting (as opposed to timeless) existence corresponds to what John writes in the very next verse: "they [the bond-servants of God] will reign forever and ever" (Rev 22:5).[72] For new creationists, the

---

67. Unless otherwise noted, the NASB translation will be used throughout this work.

68. Wright, *Surprised by Hope*, 104.

69. Snyder, *Salvation Means Creation Healed*, 141.

70. Moore, "Personal and Cosmic Eschatology," 912.

71. Middleton, "A New Heaven and New Earth," 92.

72. Middleton makes this point, writing, "The word 'forever' is crucial, for it disabuses us of the idea of some temporary earthly 'Millennium,' to be followed by an eternal 'heavenly' state." Middleton, "A New Heaven and New Earth," 92 fn 33. Elsewhere, he states that "when a dominant Platonic background of otherworldly aspirations is combined with belief in a temporary earthly millennium, all the biblical promises and descriptions of the redemption of the cosmos (and there are many) tend to be squeezed into this thousand-year rule of Christ, which leaves the final state to be reinterpreted as 'heaven.'" Middleton, *A New Heaven and a New Earth*, 286. Along with the fact that there is no wickedness or curse in the city and that, if read chronologically, John's vision is after the final judgment, the statement concerning the saints' everlasting reign seems to exclude the possibility that there is a time in which Christ will reign on the earth (whether or not

appearance of the new Jerusalem is the signal that the Kingdom of God has been consummated.

Bodily Resurrection

The bodily resurrection of the dead is a traditional point of Christian doctrine.[73] New creationists emphasize the importance of bodily resurrection for understanding the eschatological kingdom. According to Wright, resurrection should not be viewed as simply a description of life after death, nor should it be limited to a spiritual concept. Instead, it has specific reference to the physical reality of *bodily* life that follows the *bodiless* state in heaven.[74] In his argument for bodily resurrection, Wright discusses the parable of the tares of the field.[75] In this parable, Jesus explains to his disciples that after the Son of Man throws the tares into the "furnace of fire" (i.e., after the resurrection and the casting of the unrighteous into γέεννα, cf. Matt 5:22 and 18:8–9), the "righteous will shine forth as the sun in the kingdom of their Father" (Matt 13:42–43). Wright notes that an echo of Daniel 12:3 in the parable is evidence that Jesus was referring to bodily resurrection.[76] Further, Wright states, "When Jesus speaks of the reward awaiting God's people, he can simply refer to 'to resurrection of the righteous' in the normal Jewish way (Luke 14:14). . . . he is exactly on the map of first-century Jewish belief."[77] Moore writes that the reality of bodily resurrection is taught in the OT: "Job hoped for the day when, in his flesh, he would see the Creator in whom he trusted (Job 19:25–27). The Prophet Daniel foresaw a day of cosmic tumult, followed by the judgment of humanity. On that day,

---

it is a literal thousand years) which will be followed by an eternal state that resembles more of a spiritual vision conception.

73. Examples of texts that promise future resurrection and immortality include Isa 25:6–9; 26:19–21; Ezek 37:1–26; Dan 12:2; John 5:25–29; 6:40, 54; 11:21–26; Rom 8:11, 23–25; 2 Cor 4:14; 5:1–5; 2 Thess 4:14–17; 2 Tim 1:10.

74. Wright argues that in the ancient world the term resurrection "was never used to mean life after death." Instead, "*Resurrection* was used to denote new bodily life *after* whatever sort of life after death there might be. When the ancients spoke of resurrection, whether to deny it (as all pagans did) or to affirm it (as some Jews did), they were referring to a two-step narrative in which resurrection, meaning new bodily life, would be preceded by an interim period of bodily death." Wright, *Surprised by Hope*, 36.

75. Ibid., 38.

76. Wright, *Surprised by Hope*, 38.

77. Ibid.

he revealed, the graves will be opened, and God's people will be resurrected in honor and glory and God's enemies will be resurrected in defeat and judgment (Dan. 12:1–3)."[78]

When describing the bodily resurrection of believers, new creationists build upon the reality of Christ's resurrection.[79] For example, Moore writes "Our future resurrection life will mean being conformed fully to the resurrection life Jesus now experiences (1 Cor. 15:49). Those who deny bodily resurrection, Paul argues, deny the central truth of the Christian claim: the resurrection of Jesus."[80] Paul writes that Jesus' resurrection is the "first fruits of those who are asleep" (1 Cor 15:20).[81] There will be similarities between Jesus' post-resurrection body and the post-resurrection bodies of believers. Interestingly, following his resurrection, Jesus' body is similar in many ways to the body that he had prior to his death.[82] Wright and Middleton argue that 1 Corinthians 15 teaches that believers will be resurrected in a body similar to the present one in its materiality. Wright concludes, "The contrast [Paul] is making is not between what we would mean by a present

---

78. Moore, "Personal and Cosmic Eschatology," 860.

79. As stated above, one of the areas in which N. T. Wright has been lauded in conservative evangelical circles is regarding the historicity of Jesus' resurrection. Receiving heavy criticism from liberal proponents who deny Jesus' resurrection, Wright has argued that the resurrection of Jesus is foundational for Christian doctrine (see works listed in fn 9 of the current chapter). Wright's interest in the historicity of Jesus' resurrection seems to be in line with his research on new creation eschatology, especially regarding the implications of Jesus' resurrection upon the resurrection state of believers. The connection between the two is manifested clearly in Wright, *Surprised by Hope*.

80. Moore, "Personal and Cosmic Eschatology," 871.

81. For a discussion of ἀπαρχή, especially regarding the nuances of the concept of first fruits, see Thiselton, *First Epistle to the Corinthians*, 1223–24. Thiselton concludes that the implication of the language is an "ordered sequence of temporality, representation, and promise or pledge of what is to come" (1224).

82. See Matt 28; Luke 24; John 20–21; and Acts 1. We must be careful to affirm both continuity and discontinuity between the mortal body and the immortal body. Wright concludes, "[I]n the renewal of our bodies, we may assume that there will be continuity without the suggestion of absolute physical identity. God does not need to search for the same atoms and molecules that once constituted us; if he did, there would not be nearly enough to go round, since we all wear second-hand clothes in that respect. We are all of us, as C S Lewis [sic] says, like a curve in a waterfall; our bodies are in a state of physical flux." Wright, *New Heavens, New Earth*, 20. The emphasis among new creation proponents does seem to be on the continuity, probably since they are reacting against more of a dualistic approach to the spiritual and the material caused, at least in part, by a misunderstanding of the dichotomy in Scripture between the natural or fleshly body and the spiritual body, as, for example, in 1 Cor 15:44.

physical body and what we would mean by a future spiritual one, but between a present body animated by the normal human soul and a future body animated by God's spirit."[83] The difference is not one of spiritual vs. material but one of mortal vs. immortal.[84] Middleton writes that "a careful reading of 1 Corinthians 15 reveals that the discontinuity Paul emphasizes is between the body *as corrupted by the fall* and the body *finally freed from the bondage of sin.* That is, the primary reason why eschatological redemption differs from our present life in the world is that it entails the removal of sin and death."[85]

In 1 Corinthians 15 Paul connects Christ's resurrection to the hope of the gospel. He writes that, without the resurrection of Christ, Christian faith and preaching would be vain, death and sin would still prevail, and there would be no hope of resurrection (1 Cor 15:12–19). But Christ was resurrected and believers will be as well. In new creationism, the reality of bodily resurrection excludes spiritual conceptions of the final state. Resurrection is about life, and life abundantly lived (John 10:10). As Wright states, "Resurrection doesn't mean *escaping from* the world; it means *mission to* the world based on Jesus's *lordship over* the world."[86] In this way, bodily resurrection is at the heart of the Christian hope, pointing to the reality of Christ's victory over sin and death. This, Wright states, is what underlies the concluding verse of 1 Corinthians 15:

> For Paul, the bodily resurrection does not leave us saying, "So that's all right; we shall go, at the last, to join Jesus in a nonbodily, Platonic heaven," but, "So, then, since the person you are and the world God has made will be gloriously reaffirmed in God's eventual future, you must be steadfast, immovable, always abounding in the Lord's work, because you know that in the Lord your labour is not in vain." Belief in the bodily resurrection includes the belief

83. Wright, *Surprised by Hope,* 44 (cf. 155–56). Wright's extended interpretation can be found in his *Resurrection of the Son of God,* 312–61.

84. For a treatment of Paul's concept of spiritual body, see Lampe, "Paul's Concept of a Spiritual Body, 103–14; Also, for a technical treatment of the σῶμα πνευματικόν, see the excursus in Thiselton, *First Epistle to the Corinthians,* 1276–81.

85. Middleton, "A New Heaven and New Earth," 76. Elsewhere, Middleton asks, "Could Paul in 1 Corinthians 15 be thinking of a parallel between our putting off the mortality of our present bodies in order to get dressed up (if we might put it so) for the resurrection, on the one hand, and God putting off the perishable cosmos and replacing it with more permanent clothing (a new heaven and a new earth), on the other?" Middleton, *A New Heaven and a New Earth,* 203.

86. Wright, *Surprised by Hope,* 235.

that what is done in the present in the body, by the power of the Spirit, will be reaffirmed in the eventual future, in ways at which we can presently only guess.[87]

Another text regarding bodily resurrection that is emphasized among new creationists is Romans 8. Howard Snyder sees verse 11 as "the promise of physical resurrection after the pattern and by the power of Jesus' rising."[88] Later in the chapter, Paul presents believers as looking eagerly for their adoption as sons (Rom 8:23). To that end they have received the pledge ("first fruits") of the Spirit. The adoption is described as "the redemption of our bodies."[89] Middleton states that "human liberation, as Paul understands it, cannot be limited to the inner person (affecting only the 'soul'); instead, 'redemption' (a term characteristically used in connection with the exodus [see Exod. 6:6; 15:13]) is applied in verse 23 to our very bodies—an unusual (though entirely appropriate) reference to the resurrection from the dead."[90] The important point is that redemption is both physical and spiritual. The resurrection of the body underscores the goodness of the materiality of human existence.

Traditionally, an important text concerning the resurrection of the body has been 2 Corinthians 5:1–10. Contrasting the *earthly tent* with the *dwelling from heaven*, some have denied that in this text Paul is teaching bodily resurrection at the return of Jesus.[91] While acknowledging that "it certainly sounds as though he [Paul] is contrasting embodied life on earth with the hope of the living in heaven forever," Middleton and other new creationists conclude that, even in this passage, Paul's ultimate hope is for the resurrection of the body.[92] As Middleton states, "[Paul] hammers home

---

87. Ibid., 156.

88. Snyder, *Salvation Means Creation Healed*, 94.

89. I am in agreement with Moo's treatment of τὴν ἀπολύτρωσιν τοῦ σώματος ἡμῶν: "The genitive, in light of the biblical stress on the permanence of 'bodily' life through resurrection and transformation, must be objective—it is the body that is redeemed—rather than ablatival—'redemption *from* the body.'" Moo, *Epistle to the Romans*, 521 fn 67.

90. Middleton, *A New Heaven and a New Earth*, 159.

91. See, for example, Charles, *Eschatology*, 458–59; Davies, *Paul and Rabbinic Judaism*, 310–11; Dodd, *New Testament Studies*, 110; Guy, *Doctrine of the 'Last Things'*, 117; Knox, *St. Paul and the Church of the Gentiles*, 136–137; and Pilcher, *The Hereafter in Jewish and Christian Thought*, 165–68. A part of these interpretations is the view that Paul's theology had developed between 1 and 2 Corinthians, showing a growing influence of Hellenistic themes upon his former traditional Jewish eschatology.

92. Middleton, "A New Heaven and a New Earth," 93.

the point that he fully expects 'not to be naked' (5:3), that he does 'not wish to be unclothed' (5:4); instead he longs to be clothed with his heavenly dwelling (5:2). In other words, Paul's explicit hope is not for existence as a 'naked' soul or spirit (presumably in heaven), but for eternal embodied life (on earth)."[93] The view that these verses should be seen in light of the ultimate hope of the resurrection of the body typifies the new creation response to those who understand these verses as denying the reality of the materiality of the resurrected body.[94]

Reconciliation of All Things

Moore writes, "The point of the gospel is not that we would go to heaven when we die. Instead it is that heaven will come down, transforming and

93. Ibid. For an extensive treatment of Middleton's understanding of the relationship between the resurrection and earthly rule see his *A New Heaven and a New Earth*, 131–54. Wright notes the appearance of this idea in 2 Cor 4: "If all we had were the final verses of chapter 4, it might be possible to say—and some do try to argue this—that Paul was referring to a future hope in which the body would be left behind and a pure spirit would remain . . . . Is this not three-quarters of the way down the road to Plato, eager to be done with the perishable mortal body and to be left with the glorious, immortal, and disembodied soul?" Wright, *Surprised by Hope*, 153. For a technical treatment of the relationship between the terms γυμνοὶ ("naked") and ἐκδύσασθαι ("to be unclothed") and their negative sense in 2 Cor 4:3–4, see Harris, *Second Epistle to the Corinthians*, 384–91. Harris's conclusion is that the two terms "together form an allusion to some aberrant view of which Paul disapproves," namely, "the view of the hereafter held by the precursors of Gnosticism at Corinth (1 Cor 15:12), who appear to have taught, as a corollary of baptismal resurrection, that the Christian hope consisted primarily of emancipation from corporeal defilement. Similarly, v. 3 may be Paul's rebuttal of the fallacious deduction made by these Corinthian 'protognostics' that the expression ἐνδύσασθαι ἀθανασίαν ('to put on immortality') used in 1 Cor 15:53–54 implied that the believer's final destiny was disembodied immortality—'assuming, that is, that when we have put in [*sic*] on, we shall find ourselves to be not disembodied [but permanently embodied]." Harris, *Second Epistle to the Corinthians*, 389. For Harris's detailed treatment of the influence of this 'protognosticism,' see "Paul's Opponents in 2 Corinthians" in the introduction, esp. 77–87.

94. Regarding 2 Cor 5:8, Moore writes, "This heavenly state is always in view of the ultimate day of history, however, when bodies are raised and death is overturned forever (1 Cor 15:50–57)." Moore, "Personal and Cosmic Eschatology," 871. Wright argues more extensively against the Platonic influence of dualism (Wright, *Surprised by Hope*, 153–56), concluding that Paul is referring to "a new house, a new dwelling, a new body, waiting within God's sphere (again, 'heaven'), ready for us to put it on over the present one so that what is mortal may be swallowed up with life." Ibid., 153. Wright treats 2 Cor 4:16—5:10 extensively in his *Resurrection of the Son of God*, 364–71.

renewing the earth and the entire universe."[95] The transformation in view renews and heals rather than replaces the existing creation.[96] In Colossians 1:19–20, Paul writes that all things, whether things on earth or things in heaven, will be reconciled in Christ. Middleton states,

> Salvation is here conceived as reconciliation or making peace between those who are at enmity, presumably by removing the source of that enmity, namely, sin. Indeed, verse 20 contains the idea of atonement through the blood of Christ; this is how reconciliation is achieved. But in contrast to much Christian preaching, which emphasizes that the blood of Christ was shed for "me" (and we are told to put our name there), Colossians 1 does not myopically limit the efficacy of Christ's atonement to the individual or even to humanity. Without denying that the atonement suffices for individual people, the text applies the reconciliation effected by Christ's shed blood as comprehensively as possible, to "all things, whether on earth or in heaven."[97]

Important for new creationists is the inherent goodness of God's creation. For example, Moore writes, "In the beginning God created the heavens and the earth and declared it 'good.' God does not surrender this good creation to Satan but wins it back through the blood of Christ, which frees creation's rulers from the sentence of death for sin (Col. 1:19–21). God restores and recreates a world that vindicates his original creation purposes."[98] Wright notes the wisdom of God in his creative acts: "[Colossians 1:15–20] is the real cosmic Christology of the New Testament: not a kind of pantheism, . . . , but a retelling of the Jewish story of wisdom in

95. Moore, "Personal and Cosmic Eschatology," 912. Likewise, Wright: "What has happened in the death and resurrection of Jesus Christ . . . is by no means limited to its effects on those human beings who believe the gospel and thereby find the new life here and hereafter. It resonates out, in ways that we can't fully see or understand, into the vast recesses of the universe." Wright, *Surprised by Hope*, 97.

96. Snyder affirms the idea of renewal and healing but additionally argues that God's promises regarding redemption involve the concept of the creation thriving: "God's economy is more than salvation as commonly understood, more than creation healed. It is creation *flourishing* unendingly to God's glory. God's work is not just restorative; it is creative, generative, beautifully bountiful. Salvation is not just reversing the direction, not just returning to the starting point. The plan is to liberate all creation for God's original and unending project. Rather than just a return to square one, salvation means freeing creation to move and expand everlastingly in the opposite—that is, the right, good, beautiful, and bountiful—direction." Snyder, *Salvation Means Creation Healed*, 108.

97. Middleton, *A New Heaven and a New Earth*, 158.

98. Moore, "Personal and Cosmic Eschatology," 913.

terms of Jesus himself, focusing on the cross as the act whereby the good creation is brought back into harmony with the wise creator."[99] Snyder notes, "Jesus brings peace, not only in the sense of forgiveness of sins but in the full biblical richness of *shalom*."[100] In giving an extensive treatment of these verses, Moo concludes that the emphasis on the cosmic dimension of Christ's lordship is explicit and Colossians 1:20 teaches a restoration and renewal that includes all of nature.[101]

Another text that new creationists utilize to argue for the reconciliation of all things is 1 Corinthians 15:24–28. This text speaks of all things being put in subjection to Christ. For new creationists "all things" includes the created order as a whole, heaven and earth and all creatures. Wright states, "God *will be* all in all. The tense is future. Until the final victory over evil, and particularly death, this moment has not arrived. . . . God intends in the end to fill all creation with his own presence and love."[102] The idea that all of God's creation, including but not limited to humanity, will be in subjection to him implies that something has to be done to put them back into subjection. New creationists such as Moo argue that it is by the work of Christ that this is accomplished.[103] Relating 1 Corinthians 15:28 to Colossians 1:15–20, he writes, "Through the work of Christ on the cross, God has brought his entire rebellious creation back under the rule of his sovereign power. It is because of this work of universal pacification that

99. Wright, *Surprised By Hope*, 97. Wright treats Col 1 more fully in chapter 5 of his *Climax of the Covenant*.

100. Snyder, *Salvation Means Creation Healed*, 99.

101. Moo, "Nature in the New Creation," 469–74. Moo gives an overview of the various views of Col 1 and provides arguments why the reconciliation in the passage is cosmic and should not be limited to human beings.

102. Wright, *Surprised by Hope*, 101. Moore relates the subjection of all things to an intermediate millennial reign of Christ: "It seems that God's glorification of Christ entails a public vindication of his rule specifically in the presence of his enemies, a final, visible subjugation of the rivals of Christ's throne (Ps. 110; 1 Cor 15:24–28). Moore, "Personal and Cosmic Eschatology," 912.

103. The nature of this work does not allow for more to be said regarding the implications of this statement upon the relationship between Christ's sacrificial atonement and the reconciliation of the cosmos. It does seem that by emphasizing the cosmic purposes in Christ's atoning work, new creationists may have a contribution to the traditional debate regarding the extent of Christ's atonement. In his multiple-intentions approach of understanding the atonement, Bruce Ware has argued that in Christ's atoning work there is a cosmic triumph purpose. Ware's explanation of this purpose corresponds well to the new creation proponents understanding of cosmic redemption. Bruce Ware, "Extent of the Atonement."

God will one day indeed be 'all in all' (1 Cor 15:28) and that 'at the name of Jesus every knee should bow, in heaven and on earth and under the earth, and every tongue acknowledge that Jesus Christ is Lord, to the glory of God the Father' (Phil 2:10–11)."[104]

For some new creationists, personal regeneration is the individual picture of what will occur at a cosmic level. Moore writes,

> God demonstrates in individual lives what he one day plans to do with the entire universe, in the age of the Spirit. This is why Jesus speaks of the consummated kingdom in the age to come as the *regeneration* (Matt 19:28), and why he insists that personal regeneration is necessary to see the kingdom of God (John 3:3). God redeems individuals, transforming them through the Spirit because through redeemed human rulers, the sons of God, he will transform the creation itself, freeing it from its bondage to decay (Rom 8:18–23).[105]

For Moore, the continuity that exists between the individual before and after regeneration is "key to understanding God's plans for the earth and the heavens."[106] Paul's words in Colossians 1 promise cosmic recon-

104. Moo, "Nature in the New Creation," 472.

105. Moore, "Personal and Cosmic Eschatology," 913. Παλιγγενεςία (from which we get the term "regeneration"), occurring only twice in the NT, refers to the time "when the Son of Man will sit on His glorious throne" (Matt 19:28) and to individual salvation and renewal by the Holy Spirit (Tit 3:5). In addition to these texts, John 3:3–7 is normally included in systemic discussions of regeneration. In relating personal regeneration, specifically the new birth in John 3, to the consummated kingdom, Moore seems to be using the term regeneration in its proper biblical-theological sense as a New Covenant promise (Jer 31; Ezek 11:19; 36–37; cf. Isa 59:19–21) fulfilled only *following* the glorification of Jesus (John 7:37–39). In this sense, regeneration, at least in a biblical-theological sense, is neither the initial action of God to 'open the eyes' or 'quicken' sinners (a motivation in the Reformed tradition to see regeneration as preceding faith) nor is it a synonym for the broader systemic term salvation. Instead it is the new covenant gift of the indwelling presence of the Holy Spirit described throughout John's gospel as something that is happening for the first time (John 7:37–39; 14:16–17, 26; 15:26–27; 16:7, 13–14; and 17:25–26). This is not to deny that God changed hearts in the OT (e.g., Saul in 1 Sam 10:9–13), but to propose that what occurred at that time was not what is described as 'regeneration' or 'new birth' in the NT texts above.

106. This line of thought could be extended to argue against an annihilationist view of creation at judgment. Regeneration of the individual does not mean that he is a different 'person.' To say that the believer is a new creature (2 Cor 5:17; cf. Gal 6:15) is to say that *he* has experienced a radical transformation. If the regeneration of the universe is parallel to individual regeneration, then it seems that the creation *itself* will experience a radical transformation. Like in individual regeneration, the old has passed away and the

ciliation of all things by which the entire created order is put back into the subjection to him, "so that God may be all in all" (1 Cor 15:28). This reconciliation has implications for the original task of humans to subdue the earth and its creatures in a context of a transformed natural order (Rev 21–22) and animal kingdom (Isa 11:7–8; 65:25).

Conclusion

Time will reveal whether the recent rise in new creation eschatology will continue, but it seems that interest across ecclesial traditions is increasing. While the emphases vary from theologian to theologian, there are certain biblical themes which are emphasized, namely, the coming of God's kingdom, bodily resurrection, and the reconciliation of all things. A survey of the emphases of new creationism reveals that new creationists envision continuity between the materiality of the present earth and the materiality of the new earth. Yet, as argued in the following chapter, their conceptions imply more than continuity in the sense of a basic relationship. They imply a correspondence of identity between particular features in the present creation and the restored creation, respectively.

---

new has come (2 Cor 5:17), so also the "first heaven and the first earth passed away," and John sees a new heaven and a new earth (Rev 21:1).

2

The Concept of Continuity in New Creationism

The present creation is clearly material, and as such consists of a variety of types of matter.[1] There is inanimate matter that makes up the natural order and there is inanimate matter which has been fashioned from the natural materials created by God.[2] Animate life includes a variety of particular organisms. Finally, there is the human creation made in the image of God. Related to materiality is the concept of particularity. The term particularity can have a variety of meanings.[3] Two nuances of meaning are

1. I am using the term "matter" and "materiality" in a mathematical-quantitative sense as opposed to a metaphysical/ontological sense. The first has to do with the natural sciences while the second has to do with philosophical considerations. Max Jammer writes, "The quantitative concept of matter was . . . only elaborated with the development of classical mechanics, which emphasized quantities. The quantities in question were size (spatial extension), weight, and inertia (resistance to acceleration)." Jammer, "Matter: 1. Philosophy" and "Matter: 2. Natural Sciences."

2. Thomas Troeger notes that materiality includes states or phases of matter that cannot be seen. He describes materiality as "the weight of water, the thickness of air, the hardness of stone, the flesh and bone that untwine from the macramé of the DNA molecule, the pressure of blood in the veins, the body-ness of the aggregate of atoms that constitutes the universe." Troeger, "Spirituality of Materiality," 12.

3. *The Oxford English Dictionary* lists the following nine meanings: 1.a. The quality of being particular as opposed to general or universal; the fact of being or relating to one or some (not all) of a class; relation to an individual thing, individuality; *spec.* in *Theology*, with ref. to Christ as the incarnation of God as a particular human being at a particular time and place.; 1.b. A particular or individual matter or affair; a particular case or instance.; 2.a. The quality of being special or of a special kind; the fact of being in

especially important for the present discussion. The first has to do with making special distinctions among various types.[4] The emphasis in this meaning is upon the distinctiveness that each definite thing possesses rather than their general characteristics.[5]

Although related to the first meaning, the nuance of the second meaning is that of the relationship of the part to the whole or the concept of the partial in relation to the universal.[6] The point is that the whole is differentiated or particulate. In our experience and interaction with the created world, we encounter material objects in both senses of particularity—in their contradistinction from other material objects and as matter which is a portion of the whole of creation. New creationists appreciate the relationship between materiality and particularity in their conceptions and argue that at least some particular features of the present earth correspond to particular features that will be a part of the new earth. The basis of this

---

some way distinguished or noteworthy; speciality, peculiarity.; 2.b. Peculiarity such as to excite surprise, singularity, oddity; an instance of this, an odd action or characteristic.; 3. An attribute belonging to the thing in question; a special or distinctive quality or feature; a peculiarity.; 4. Personal interest or advantage.; 5. A particular point or circumstance, a detail.; 6. Minuteness or detailedness of description, statement, investigation, etc.; 7. Special attentiveness to a person; 8. Attentiveness to details of action; special carefulness; preciseness, fastidiousness.; 9. *in particularity*: In detail; individually; specially. Simpson and Weiner, *OED*, s.v. "particular."

4. The *Oxford English Dictionary* describes this meaning as follows: "Pertaining or relating to a single definite thing or person, or set of things or persons, as distinguished from others; of or belonging to some one thing (etc.) and not to any other, or to some and not to all; of one's (its, etc.) own; special; not general." Ibid.

5. One might think of material objects in a general sense. For example, he may conceptualize the boundaries and topography of a plot of land and even produce an illustration of a plot of land which in his estimation represents the concept of what land is—one might call this its land-ness. One could conceptualize any form of matter in this way and describe, illustrate, or simply meditate upon an object in its generality without consciously thinking of a particular object. However, the experience of material reality involves particular objects which are distinct from other objects. When one sees a particular plot of land, his experience does not conflict with his general idea of land-ness. Yet, he is actually seeing not land-ness in a general sense but a particular plot of land. The point is that the way we experience materiality in all its forms is by encountering that materiality in its distinct forms, i.e., in its particularity.

6. The nuance of the part to the whole is explained in *OED* as follows: "Belonging to, or affecting, a part, not the whole, of something; partial; not universal." Simpson and Weiner, *OED*, s.v. "particular." When one sees a plot of land, he sees the plot of land as matter that is distinct from creation as a whole. Particularity, in this sense of the term, means that one can experience a distinct portion of creation as opposed to the whole.

correspondence is new creationists' affirmation that the present earth is to be renewed.

The Affirmation of a Renewed/Restored Earth

Some new creationists argue that a primary reason for the aforementioned dominance of a spiritual conception of the final state is a denigrated view of materiality through church history.[7] The transience of space-time-matter, suffering, and death, according to Wright, have led "The Platonist, the Hindu, and, following Plato, the Gnostic, the Manichaean, and countless others within variants of the Christian and Jewish traditions" to conclude "that we are made for something quite different, a world not made of space, time, and matter, a world of pure spiritual existence where we shall happily have got rid of the shackles of mortality once and for all."[8] The assumption in this conclusion is that the material realm is at best inferior to the spiritual realm and at worst that matter is inherently evil.

As seen in the previous chapter, new creationists affirm the goodness of materiality.[9] For them, Scripture, instead of denigrating matter, upholds

---

7. See Wright's brief discussion of the "Platonic strain which entered Christian thinking early on." Wright, *Surprised by Hope*, 88–91. Regarding one of the troubling trends in the early church, Snyder states the following: "Despite the achievements of Irenaeus and others, Neo-Platonic conceptions of spirituality and doctrine began to drive a wedge between Christian understandings of spirit and matter, undermining the integrated wholism of the biblical worldview, and favoring the spiritual over the physical. The impact of such views on biblical interpretation was significant: Neo-Platonism began to distort the way in which the spirit/flesh distinction in Jesus' teachings and in Paul's writings (for example in John 3:6, 6:63; Rom 8:3 13) was understood." Snyder, *Salvation Means Creation Healed*, 8–9. Middleton discusses briefly "our dualistic philosophical inheritance from Plato." Middleton, "A New Heaven and a New Earth," 75. Moo states, "While the problem has been exaggerated, it is undeniable that generations of biblical interpreters have understated the place of the material world in the Bible because of the powerful current of dualism in the Western intellectual tradition." Moo, "Creation and New Creation," 40–41.

8. Wright, *Surprised by Hope*, 88.

9. The incarnation of Christ seems to be evidence of this goodness. The fact that the second person of the Trinity takes upon himself human form seems problematic if the material realm is inferior to the spiritual realm. Troeger writes, "The incarnation affirms that the meaning of life is not an abstract concept, not a vague ideal, not a collection of words and thoughts. Rather we find the meaning of life in the love and grace of God as embodied in a particular human being and in the community that gathers around him. Jesus, like us, had a heart that pumped blood and lungs that pumped air. He was not a spirit that floated above the earth but a body whose feet pounded the ground and whose

a certain God-given goodness in the material realm. If matter is not inherently sinful, then redemption from the curse of sin does not necessitate the end of materiality.[10] Still, there is a sense in which the nature of present materiality must be distinguished from that of future materiality. Noting that Paul sees "negativity inherent within the materiality of the present world" (e.g., mortality in Rom 8:21 and incompleteness in Rom 8:19), Charles Robinson concludes the following:

> Although Paul understands these negativities to be essential to the form of materiality in which we now live, his insight into the ultimate purposes of God for man as revealed in Jesus Christ leads him to the faith that the God who has created this present form of materiality has the power to re-create a new transformed mode of materiality. Thus, the negating futility of materiality as we now experience it is not to be understood as essential to materiality as such, but rather as manifesting God's loving purposes of creating a material mode of beginning (as the only appropriate beginning place for human life distorted by sin), which shall ultimately issue in a better, and indeed finitely perfect, End.[11]

Robinson's conception of the future sounds much like that of new creationists. He writes further, "The nature of that new world for which mankind is in Christ ultimately destined is understood to be a world characterized by materiality—not, as in Hellenistic and Gnostic notions, a realm of pure spirits. For in the Christian understanding, as true to its Hebraic rootage, God and God only can be as pure spirit."[12] Robinson concludes that the difference between the present material reality and the new mode of materiality for the redeemed has to do with a modification of the relationship between the material reality and the spiritual reality.[13] Ulti-

---

stomach growled when he was hungry." He goes on to state, "We need the spirituality of materiality that is rooted in a sound understanding of incarnation: finding the meaning of life through the bodily world in which we live as bodily creatures." Troeger, "Spirituality of Materiality," 12.

10. It should also be stated that the fact that matter is not inherently sinful has not inhibited man from forming matter into objects that are used primarily or solely for sinful acts.

11. Robinson, "Materiality and Eschatology," 112.

12. Ibid., 113.

13. Robinson writes, "With no presumption to have seen a blueprint or a geographical map of the world which is to be, we can nevertheless—following insights in the New Testament, especially in the Pauline epistles—sketch out some of the possible differences of life in that new mode of materiality as compared with life in our presently experienced

mately, materiality can and will be transformed so that it reflects the glory and goodness of God.

The idea of transformation of the present materiality is important to new creationists. Because matter is not understood as inherently sinful, it does not have to be utterly disposed of. However, because the curse of sin has affected all creation, the materiality of the creation must be freed from the curse. New creationists affirm that, instead of being annihilated, the present creation will be renewed or transformed. While implied in the overview offered in the previous chapter, new creationists' idea of the transformation of the present creation can be seen more clearly by surveying their respective views of two NT texts.

The "Destruction" of Creation in 2 Peter 3

In this text, Peter reminds his readers of the coming day of the Lord, a day in which the ungodly will be destroyed and for which fire is being reserved for the present heavens and earth (2 Pet 3:7).[14] In reference to the scoffers'

---

mode of materiality. The most important difference is the contrast between, on the one hand, a mode of materiality which fundamentally conditions spiritual reality and, on the other hand, a mode of materiality which is fundamentally conditioned by spiritual reality. In the first case (our present world) the basic direction of conditioning is from below upwards; in the second case (the world which is to be) the basic direction of conditioning will be from above downwards. In this world the existence and life-mode of spiritual beings is fundamentally dependent upon lower material orders of reality; in the re-created world the existence and modes of lower material orders of reality will be fundamentally dependent upon the will of spiritual beings—ultimately upon the will of the Spirit of God. Thus, whereas our present spiritual existence is sub-ordinated to the conditions of material reality, in the world to be revealed the order will be reversed and the material realm will be sub-ordinated to the conditioning of our spiritual existence and of God as spirit." Ibid.

14. In 2 Pet 3:12, Peter uses the phrase "day of God" instead of "day of the Lord." Schreiner writes, "We are surprised to see Peter speak of the coming of 'the day of God,' since that expression is unusual in the New Testament (Rev 16:14; cf. Jer 46:10). The word 'coming' (*parousia*) in 1:16 and 3:4 refers to the coming of Christ, but the day of God refers to the day of the Father, not the Son. Nonetheless, the coming of God's day is inseparable from the future coming of Christ." Schreiner, *1, 2 Peter, Jude*, 390. Referencing Starr, *Sharers in Divine Nature*, 3, Schreiner writes in a footnote, "The collocation of 'day of the Lord' and 'day of God' with the coming of Christ implies Christ's deity." Schreiner, *1, 2 Peter, Jude*, 390. In a parenthetical statement, Peter Davids writes, "(2 Peter 3:10 has called this 'the day of the Lord,' and here it is called "the day of God," so it looks as if 'the Lord' in the previous part of the chapter is God rather than Jesus, although in practice it makes little difference. What is clear is that 'the day of the Lord' and the 'day

doubt, Peter reminds his readers that the Lord's timing is different than man's and that the reason for the delay is God's patience (2 Pet 3:8–9). Returning to the description of the day, Peter writes the following in verses 10–13:

> But the day of the Lord will come like a thief, in which the heavens will pass away with a roar and the elements will be destroyed with intense heat, and the earth and its works will be burned up. Since all these things are to be destroyed in this way, what sort of people ought you to be in holy conduct and godliness, looking for and hastening the coming of the day of God, because of which the heavens will be destroyed by burning, and the elements will melt with intense heat! But according to His promise we are looking for new heavens and a new earth, in which righteousness dwells.

Peter clearly states that in the day of the Lord, the present heavens and earth will experience destruction, with the result that the heavens are burned and the elements are melted. What is not agreed upon is the exact nature of the destruction. The way in which one understands Peter's words regarding how the destruction affects the present heavens and earth has been a point of disagreement since the early church.[15] In recent decades, the discussion has revolved around the issue of textual variants, specifically the discovery of texts that use the verb εὑρεθήσεται.[16] Ultimately, the interpre-

of God' refer to the same eschatological event, which is also spoken of as the 'coming' or 'Parousia' of Christ [2 Pet 2:26; 3:4].) [sic] This overlapping terminology should make us extremely cautious in trying to separate these terms or in applying them to separate events. For our author they apply to a single event that we are to await.)" Davids, *Letters of 2 Peter and Jude*, 289. Bauckham simply states, "Whether 2 Peter intends a distinction between 'the Day of the Lord' (= Christ?) in v 10, and 'the Day of God' (= the Father) here, is very uncertain." Bauckham, *Jude, 2 Peter*, 325.

15. For a brief introduction to the early disagreement, see Heide, "What is New About the New Heaven and the New Earth?," 48–50, and Thiede, "A Pagan Reader of 2 Peter," 83–87. Also helpful in seeing elements of the disagreement throughout the first several centuries of the church is Daley, *Hope of the Early Church*.

16. Larry Overstreet states the reasons behind the recent textual disagreement as follows: "Second Peter 3:10–13 presents two major problems to the interpreter. The first of these is determining the text in the conclusion of verse 10, that is whether the text reads that the earth and its works 'shall be burned up' or 'shall be found.' The second problem is the actual interpretation of the passage." Overstreet, "A Study of 2 Peter 3:10–13," 354. The translation "shall be found" is of εὑρεθήσεται, a future passive indicative of the verb εὑρίσκω. The major variant reading substitutes κατακαίω for εὑρεθήσεται, which can be translated "burned up," so that the text would be rendered "the earth and its works will be burned up." For a discussion of the textual issues and the pros and cons of various translations, see, in addition to Overstreet, Bauckham, *Jude, 2 Peter*, 316–21 [additional

tive question is whether Peter is describing the new heavens and new earth as utterly new, coming into existence after the present heavens and earth have been reduced to nothing, or whether he is envisioning the new heavens and new earth as a renewed and purified present heavens and earth.[17]

New creationists have sided with those who argue that Peter envisions a renewed or purified cosmos. N. T. Wright calls 2 Peter 3:10 "the critical moment . . . upon which seems to hinge the worldview of the whole. . . . Is the writer saying that creation as a whole is to be thrown away and a new one, freshly made, to take its place?"[18] Arguing against a dualistic or Stoic interpretation, Wright approves of εὑρεθήσεται as the correct reading and believes the verb most likely should be translated "will be found."[19] Referencing Wolters, he notes a certain intriguing interpretation: "the writer wishes to stress continuity with discontinuity, a continuity in which the new world, and the new people who are to inhabit it, emerge tested, tried and purified from the crucible of suffering."[20] Despite his admission that the text is a difficult and obscure one, Wright makes the following conclusion: "[It] is not that of the dualist who hopes for creation to be abolished, but of one who, while continuing to believe in the goodness of creation, sees that the only way to the fulfillment of the creator's longing for a justice and goodness which will replace the present evil is for a process of fire, not simply to consume, but also to purge."[21]

Noting that Peter's argument is that the destruction to come is analogous to the destruction resulting from the Noahic flood and the judgment

---

arguments for Bauckham's preference of εὑρεθήσεται over other variant readings can be found in Wenham, "Being 'Found' on the Last Day," 477–79 and in Tresham, "A Test Case for Conjectural Emendation," 55–79]; Blaising, "Day of the Lord," 397–400; Rietkerk, *Millennium Fever*, 26–34; Schreiner, *1, 2 Peter, Jude*, 383–87; and Wolters, "WorldView and Textual Criticism," 405–13.

17. Heide describes the former position as follows: "The total-destruction viewpoint . . . takes this passage in its narrowest sense. The future destruction will be total obliteration. The burning will be complete. The melting of the elements will leave no trace of their former existence." Heide, "What is New About the New Heaven and the New Earth?," 50.

18. Wright, *Resurrection of the Son of God*, 462.

19. In addition to referencing Bauckham, *Jude, 2 Peter*; Wenham, "Being 'Found' on the Last Day"; and Wolters, "Worldview and Textual Criticism," Wright notes Neyrey, *2 Peter, Jude*, specifically the discussion starting on page 243.

20. Wright, *Resurrection of the Son of God*, 463. Cf. Wolters, "Worldview and Textual Criticism," 411–12.

21. Wright, *Resurrection of the Son of God*, 463.

of Sodom and Gomorrah, Moore concludes that the language in 2 Peter 3 describes a renewed present heavens and earth: "Peter compares the coming cosmic conflagration with the Genesis flood. Just as God destroyed the creation with water, bringing safely through the righteous remnant, he at the eschaton will destroy the creation with fire, bringing believers safely through to a new creation, a 'new heavens and a new earth in which righteousness dwells' (2 Pet. 3:13)."[22] Middleton is so convinced that 2 Peter 3 does not refer to an utter destruction of the present heavens and earth that he utilizes it as one his primary texts to articulate the NT's comprehensive scope of redemption. Regarding the language, specifically εὑρεθήσεται in verse 10, he writes, "The image is of the smelting of metal, where the dross is burned off so that the pure metal may be revealed (or 'laid bare')."[23] Instead of the disposing of that which needs purification, the text is describing an act in which the thing in need of purification is itself the object of the purification process. So, Middleton concludes, "While the text undoubtedly speaks of judgment and destruction (using the image of a cosmic conflagration), it describes the destruction, not of creation, but of *sin*, thus cleansing or purifying creation."[24]

In discussing what he believes to be a misreading of 2 Peter 3:10 and the unbiblical worldview that results, Snyder argues against the view that in using the language of burning up, Peter is implying an utter destruction of the present creation.[25] Snyder notes that particularly in the prophetic

22. Moore, "Personal and Cosmic Eschatology," 872. He writes elsewhere, "The new earth means the triumph of Christ *in the restoration of creation.* There really is no such thing as 'the end of the world.' God does promise to destroy this present creation, but he speaks of this destruction as analogous to a previous 'end of the world,' the flood— only this time with fire rather than water (2 Pet. 3:1–13). The pre-flood creation indeed was destroyed—the old order was wiped out. But God does not completely wipe out the earth. There is both continuity and discontinuity with the pre-flood order." Ibid., 913. Snyder makes a similar point about Peter's analogy to the destruction of the Flood, concluding that "the writer [of 2 Peter] says that in the flood the world was 'destroyed' (TNIV)—but, of course, it was not physically destroyed or annihilated; it was judged and cleansed." Snyder, *Salvation Means Creation Healed,* 60.

23. Middleton, "A New Heaven and a New Earth," 88. For an extensive treatment of Middleton's understanding of 2 Peter 3, including the meaning of "elements" in the passage, see his *A New Heaven and a New Earth,* 189–204.

24. Middleton, "A New Heaven and a New Earth," 89.

25. Snyder believes that premillennial dispensationalism is partly to blame for the unbiblical worldview that the present heavens and earth will be destroyed: "Premillennial dispensationalism undermines the biblical worldview by locating the renewal of creation exclusively after the return of Jesus Christ. Since the present world is headed

books, "fire is a key image of God's refining or purifying judgment."[26] He appeals to texts such as Malachi 3:2 ("For He is like a refiner's fire and like a fullers' soap") and Zechariah 13:9 ("And I will bring the third part through the fire, refine them as silver is refined, and test them as gold is tested"). Fire, he argues, represents God's power and holiness in Deuteronomy 4:24 ("For the Lord your God is a consuming fire"); Deuteronomy 9:3 ("the Lord your God who is crossing over before you as a consuming fire"); and Hebrews 12:29 ("for our God is a consuming fire"). The "fire" of God's power and holiness "can destroy if disregarded but is intended to cleanse all impurities so that people may experience and exhibit the pure love of God."[27] On the basis of these texts, Snyder concludes that "the heat and fire of 2 Pet 3:10 signify refining, revealing, and cleansing, not destruction or annihilation. . . . God is not in the destroying business; he is in the refining, recycling, and recreating business."[28]

Moo offers the most extended argument regarding 2 Peter 3. While discussing the discontinuity between the present creation and the new creation, he admits that the text stresses discontinuity, but concludes that it "does not require that this creation be annihilated before the new

---

for inevitable destruction, any concern with saving it is a distraction from rescuing souls before Jesus returns." He writes further, "Premillennial dispensationalism popularized the view that the earth and the whole material creation is destined to be destroyed. . . . [It] is a potent virus that worked its way, largely undetected, throughout the body of Christ over the past century and more. This disease makes the church's witness anemic, hampering its healing role in creation." Snyder, *Salvation Means Creation Healed*, 59–60. Snyder notes that the view that the creation would be destroyed was common prior to the rise of premillennial dispensationalism, writing that the movement "would probably never have caught on if the theological divorce between heaven and earth was not already in place." Ibid., 60. Perhaps Snyder is correct in this statement, but the notion of the present heavens and earth being utterly destroyed that appears among some within the dispensational tradition should be seen not as a necessary feature of premillennial dispensationalism per se but as an inherited concept. More importantly, Snyder's decrying of "premillenialist (or any other kind of) dispensationalism" is unfortunate in light of recent forms of dispensationalism that include the restoration of the present heavens and earth. For example see, Blaising and Bock, *Progressive Dispensationalism*, 242.

26. Snyder, *Salvation Means Creation Healed*, 59.

27. Ibid.

28. Ibid., 59–60. In support of his view, Snyder quotes approvingly from John Calvin's *Commentary on 2 Peter* and John Wesley's *Explanatory Notes New Testament*. While it is important to note that the context of Snyder's comment is in his discussion of God's plan for the future of the cosmos, his words may need to be nuanced to include the everlasting "destruction" of unbelievers (which John calls the second death in Rev. 20–21) which is not a refining, recycling, or recreating process.

is brought in."[29] Moo offers three reasons why Peter is not describing the utter destruction of the present universe. The first reason that he gives is the difficulty of variant translations that read that the earth and everything in it is "burned up."[30] The second reason that he offers is that the language of burning and melting in 2 Peter 3:7-12 should be informed by the OT metaphorical use of such language which referred primarily to judgment.[31] He adds, however, that "even if some reference to physical fire is present, the fire need not bring total destruction."[32] The third reason that Moo offers against an annihilationist understanding, and the one he believes to be the most important, is the sense of the various forms of the verb λύω in 2 Peter 3:10-12. Like the terms ἀπόλλυμι and ἀπώλεια, he argues, the verb λύω "does not necessarily mean total physical annihilation, but a dissolution or radical change in nature."[33] He also appeals to the fact that while these terms are "frequently used in the NT to refer to the ultimate fate of sinful human beings," most scholars do not believe that this usage implies the doctrine of annihilation of the individual.[34] Moo concludes, "Therefore, just as the 'destruction of the ungodly' in verse 7 need not mean the annihilation of these sinners, neither need the 'destruction' of the universe

---

29. Moo, "Creation and New Creation," 60, fn 67.

30. He writes that the English translations based on the variant readings that mean "burned up" are "almost certainly incorrect": "The text is notoriously difficult, but almost all modern versions and commentators assume that the reading 'will be found' (εὑρεθήσεται) is original. What it means is more difficult to determine, but perhaps the idea of being 'laid bare' before God for judgment is the best option." Moo, "Nature in the New Creation, 468. Like some of the other new creationists, Moo favors the arguments of Bauckham, 2 Peter, Jude, and Wenham, "Being 'Found' on the Last Day." He also cites as supportive of the "being found" language Danker, "2 Peter 3:10 and Psalm of Solomon 17:10," 82-86.

31. He cites as examples Isa 30:30; 64:1-2; 66:15-16; Nah 1:6; Zeph 1:18; 3:8; and Mic 1:3-4. Moo, "Nature in the New Creation," 468.

32. Ibid.

33. He gives several examples from the NT and the Septuagint: "The other NT words for 'destroy' and 'destruction' also often refer to much less than 'annihilation.' They can refer to land that has lost its fruitfulness (ὄλεθος in Ezek 6:14; 14:16); to ointment that is poured out wastefully and to no apparent purpose (ἀπώλεια in Matt 26:8; Mark 14:4); to wineskins that can no longer function because they have holes in them (ἀπόλλυμι in Matt 9:17; Mark 2:22; Luke 5:37); to a coin that is useless because it is 'lost' (ἀπόλλυμι in Luke 15:9); or to the entire world that 'perishes,' as an inhabited world, in the Flood (2 Pet 3:6). In none of these cases do the objects cease to exist; they cease to be useful or to exist in their original, intended state." Ibid., fn 77.

34. Ibid., 469.

in verses 10-12 mean that it is annihilated. The parallel with what God did when he 'destroyed' the first world in the Flood of Noah suggests that God will 'destroy' this world not by annihilating it but by radically transforming it into a place fit for resurrected saints to live in forever."[35] The consensus among new creationists, then, is that Peter is affirming the restoration of the present heavens and earth.

The Groaning of Creation in Romans 8

Another NT passage that is important for new creationists is Romans 8:19-22. Moo believes that this text is the most important passage concerning the eschatological expectation of cosmic renovation not only in Paul's writings but in the entire NT.[36] He writes, "The created world—probably the non-human created world—has, because of human sin, been subject to decay and frustration. But the revelation of God's children in glory will bring liberation to creation's degraded state."[37] Moo offers three primary reasons why Paul is arguing for cosmic renovation rather than simply the redemption of humans.[38] First, the background to the language of the creation being "frustrated" and in "bondage to decay" is the story of the Fall

35. Ibid. Moo references Russell, *"New Heavens and New Earth,"* 186-97, and Dyrness, *Let the Earth Rejoice*, 179.

36. Regarding Romans 8:19-22, Moo writes, "It is the clearest expression of future hope for the physical world in the NT." "Nature in the New Creation," 459.

37. Moo, "Creation and New Creation," 56. For Moo's argument for taking κτίσις, which appears once in each of the four verses in Rom 8:19-22, to refer to the non-human created order, see "Nature in the New Creation," 459-63. Essentially his argument proceeds as follows: 1) Paul's normal usage of κτίσις is to refer to the entire created universe; 2) Believers are excluded from the κτίσις in light of the transition from verse 22 to verse 23; and 3) All humanity is excluded because the κτίσις was subjected to futility unwillingly.

38. Moo notes that some interpreters attempt to show that Paul's language is a result of apocalyptic influence and that "his *real* point about the destiny of Christians ignores the degree to which apocalyptic categories are central to Paul's thought." Moo, "Creation and New Creation," 56 (He gives examples of interpreters who have argued this point in Moo, "Nature in the New Creation," 462, fn 45). While allowing for the influence of apocalyptic Judaism upon these verses (cf. Hahne, *Corruption and Redemption of Creation*), Moo concludes that it is reasonable to believe that Paul's use of new creation is analogous to the apocalyptic Jewish tradition in that it refers to renovation of the earth. In fact, he writes that "the way Paul introduces the idea, without explanation or defense, suggests that he may assume that his readers are already familiar with a standard early Christian eschatology that includes cosmic renovation." Moo, "Creation and New Creation," 56.

in Genesis 3, specifically God's curse upon the ground. The implication of Paul's language (including ματαιότητι, 8:20; δουλείας τῆς φθορᾶς, 8:21; and συστενάζει καὶ συνωδίνει, 8:22) is that "human sin led to some kind of change in the nature of the cosmos itself."[39] While admitting the difficulty of knowing with certainty the exact nature of the change resulting from the Fall, Moo concludes that the important point about the language in Romans 8:19-20 is that because of the Fall, the natural world is, like humanity, "no longer in its pristine created state."[40]

The second reason that Moo offers in favor of cosmic renovation is the implied analogy in the passage. The concept of the curse upon the cosmos and its reconciliation is analogous to humanity's sin and deliverance from that sin. While affirming the "anthropological focus of Romans 8," he argues that in verses 19-22 Paul is making a particular point about the whole created order, not just humanity:[41] "The reversal of the conditions of the Fall includes the created world along with the world of human beings. Indeed, the glory that humans will experience, involving as it does the resurrection of the body (8:9-11, 23), necessarily requires an appropriate environment for that embodiment."[42] Moo's third reason is that the language of Romans 8:18-25 has allusions to prophetic expectations, the most important of which is Isaiah 24:1-13.[43] More will be said about Moo's treatment of this and other prophetic texts in chapter 4. At this point, it is sufficient to say that Moo envisions cosmic reconciliation in Isaiah 24:1-13 and that the prophecy should inform one's interpretation of Paul's words in verses 19-22 of Romans 8.

In his discussion of Romans 8:19-23, Middleton emphasizes the Exodus imagery present in the text. He writes, "Paul draws on both the imagery of childbirth (labor pains) and the language of Exodus 2:23-24, which portrays the Israelites groaning in their bondage under Pharaoh (a different set of labor pains)."[44] Like Moo, Middleton sees the interweaving

39. Moo, "Nature in the New Creation," 461.

40. Ibid.

41. Ibid., 462.

42. Ibid.

43. Moo cites Keesmaat, *Paul and His Story*, 102-14 as having "noted that Paul's language in verses 18-25 reflects traditions about the exodus, which often provides the backdrop in Isaiah for the prediction of the new creation." Moo, "Nature in the New Creation," 462.

44. Middleton, "A New Heaven and a New Earth," 89. Middleton, like Moo, cites Keesmaat, *Paul and His Story*.

of individual redemption and cosmic redemption: "Utilizing the model of deliverance from Egyptian bondage, Paul here portrays salvation first (in verse 21) as *liberation* or *setting free* from bondage, and this is applied to *creation itself* and also to *humanity* (described as the sons/children of God). It is because the human race implicitly takes the place of Pharaoh in Paul's picture (subjecting creation to frustration) that non-human creatures await human liberation."[45]

Moore also understands Romans 8 as addressing the problem of the current state of the non-human created order. Humanity is not alone in its suffering in the present age and its expectation of deliverance from the suffering. Indeed, he asserts, "this longing for the coming of Christ, this agony in the face of present evil, is not limited to sentient creatures."[46] Creation itself is longing to be freed from its bondage to decay. The freedom from the bondage in which the present creation exists will come when redeemed humanity is freed from the bondage of sin.[47]

Wright connects the concept of liberation of the creation to the concept of resurrection and has strong words about the failure to recognize the connection in Romans 8:

> The marginalization of this part of Romans 8 in much exegesis down the years has robbed Christian imagination of this extraordinary picture of the future; only by restoring it to its rightful place – which is, after all, in Paul's build-up to the climax of the central section of his most important letter! – can we understand the larger picture within which his vision of resurrection makes sense. It is a picture in which the corruption and futility of creation itself, created good but doomed to decay, is seen as a kind of slavery, so that creation, too, needs to experience its exodus, its liberation.[48]

---

45. Middleton, "A New Heaven and a New Earth," 89.

46. Moore, "Personal and Cosmic Eschatology," 871.

47. Moore writes, "God redeems individuals, transforming them through the Spirit because through redeemed human rulers, the sons of God, he will transform the creation itself, freeing it from its bondage to decay (Rom. 8:18–23). This is why the redeemed groan along with the creation itself for the consummation of the kingdom (Rom. 8:23)." Ibid., 913.

48. Wright, Resurrection of the Son of God, 258. Elsewhere, he writes, "This passage [Romans 8] has routinely been marginalized for centuries by exegetes and theologians who have tried to turn Romans into a book simply about how individual sinners get individually saved." Wright, *Surprised by Hope*, 103.

Wright also focuses on the theme of new birth, first, like Moo and Middleton, in relation to the Exodus theme and, second, in relation to birth pangs. The Exodus language that Paul ascribes to the created order implies liberation. Just as the redeemed live in hopes of bodily resurrection, so does the entire creation. The birth pangs are "a well-known Jewish metaphor for the emergence of God's new age—not only of the church in verse 23 and of the Spirit a couple of verses later but also here in verse 22 of the creation itself."[49]

Like other new creationists, Snyder argues that a proper understanding of Romans 8 can be reached only by acknowledging a broader biblical worldview:

> Paul *simply assumes*, without elaborating, the Old Testament view of salvation as involving both people and the land. This is an important and often overlooked point. When Paul begins talking about the whole creation in verse 19, he is introducing no strange or alien subject. He expresses the biblical worldview, the biblical "all things" perspective. Since salvation is all about God, God's people, and God's land, *of course* one must speak of the liberation of all creation itself from its "bondage to decay," when we speak of salvation and Jesus' resurrection! How could salvation mean anything else?[50]

The bondage in which the creation now stands produces groaning from the creation itself. This groaning, along with the groaning of the redeemed (Rom 8:23) and the groaning of God the Spirit (Rom 8:26), further indicates the biblical picture of salvation as it is promised in the OT.[51] Regarding the extent of salvation, Snyder concludes the following: "Through Jesus and the Spirit, God is deeply engaged in salvation—a comprehensive healing of sin's disease. The good news of Jesus Christ is the complete cure for the disease of sin in all its ecological dimensions, all its cancerous fibers and filaments."[52] A cure is only a cure if it provides healing to that which is diseased. Any cure for the diseased present heavens and earth must deliver *it* from the disease. New creationists agree that, according to 2 Peter 3 and Romans 8, the way that this deliverance will take place is through a transformation of the present creation, a transformation that has implications

---

49. Ibid.
50. Snyder, *Salvation Means Creation Healed*, 103.
51. Snyder calls this a "threefold groaning." Ibid., 92.
52. Ibid.

for how one understands the relationship between the present state and the final state.

Continuity in New Creationism

The important point to be seen in the previous examination of new creationists' treatment of 2 Peter 3 and Romans 8 is the explicit affirmation that redemption upholds the existence of the present created order in its materiality. The overview in chapter 1 and the preceding pages in the current chapter show that, at a minimum, new creationists affirm that the present heavens and earth have an enduring role in God's plan of redemption. In this section we want to look more closely at the concept of continuity in new creationism.

John's vision in Revelation 21 describes the new heavens and new earth in ways that are radically discontinuous from the present heavens and earth. However, this radical discontinuity, according to new creationists, does not require that the present heavens and earth be obliterated. Wright relates the problem of continuity/discontinuity to the image of birthing labor:

> This is no smooth evolutionary transition, in which creation simply moves up another gear into a higher mode of life. This is traumatic, involving convulsions and contractions and the radical discontinuity in which mother and child are parted and become not one being but two. But neither is this a dualistic rejection of physicality as though, because the present creation is transient and full of decay and death, God must throw it away and start again from scratch. The very metaphor Paul chooses [in Romans 8] for this decisive moment shows that what he has in mind is not the unmaking of creation or simply its steady development, but the drastic and dramatic birth of new creation from the womb of the old.[53]

According to Middleton, in salvation God is not doing something completely new, but is *"re-doing* something, fixing or repairing what went wrong."[54] Snyder quotes approvingly David Field who writes, "Creation will

53. Wright, *Surprised by Hope*, 103-04.

54. Middleton, "A New Heaven and a New Earth," 91. The problem, Middleton argues, is that many readers of Scripture get lost or overwhelmed in the details and "tend to overlook the overall structure of the biblical plot (specifically its grounding in creation). But unless we have an understanding of the initial state (creation) and the nature of the

be cleansed and transformed, yet this new creation will stand in continuity with the old."[55]

For Snyder, the foundation of the continuity between the present creation and the future creation is the continuity between the testaments:

> The continuity from Old Testament to New Testament here is crucial. We stress this because Christian theology often over-spiritualizes God's saving plan . . . . The New Testament pictures not a divine rescue from earth but rather the reconciliation of earth and heaven—of "all things, whether on earth or in heaven," things both "visible and invisible." God is "making peace through [Jesus'] blood," shed on the cross (Col 1:16–21). God's plan in both the Old and New Testaments is to bring *shalom* to the whole creation. In this sense Christians are still "being saved," because ultimately no one experiences *shalom* in its fullness until the whole creation enjoys *shalom*.[56]

Moore writes that the Christian does not simply look forward to "a heavenly city of refuge for flown-away souls, but an entire universe of rocks and trees and quasars and waterfalls—everything created in which he [God] takes delight."[57] The reality of God's good design of creation, for Moore, necessitates continuity between the present cosmos and the future cosmos: "The material universe . . . was designed to declare the Creator's glory. In the new creation the heavens will declare this glory with unimagined brilliance, now freed from the bondage to decay."[58] For Moore, this even includes the existence of animals in the new heavens and earth.[59] In discussing the meaning of "new creation" in Galatians 6:15 and 2 Corinthians 5:17, Moo concludes the following: "Paul does not see 'new creation' as a simple replacement of this creation. The transition from this creation to

problem (fall), we will systematically misread the nature of this repair (redemption)—and thus the nature of the final fulfillment of God's purposes. Indeed, it will be difficult to see it as repair at all—that is, as fixing something that has gone wrong." Middleton, *A New Heaven and a New Earth*, 38.

55. Snyder, *Salvation Means Creation Healed*, 60. The source of the quote is Field, "Confessing Christ," 40.

56. Snyder, *Salvation Means Creation Healed*, 127–28.

57. Moore, "Personal and Cosmic Eschatology," 913.

58. Ibid., 914.

59. He writes, "The prophetic vision of Scripture is insistent, for instance, that non-human life is a part of God's eternal purposes, with Isaiah seeing a restoration of the original harmony of the animal order. . . . we must insist that the new earth will contain animals." Ibid., 913.

the next will be discontinuous to some extent, but Paul's language of 'liberation' and 'reconciliation' requires a basic continuity as well."[60] It is not that when describing the new creation, Paul is asserting that what happened as recorded in Genesis is to happen again. Instead, there is continuity between the present creation and the creation to come, such that it "is not a 'creation out of nothing' (*creation ex nihilo*) but a 'creation out of the old' (*creation ex vetere*)."[61]

Continuity between the present creation and the one to come is evident in Middleton's concept of the atonement of Christ. Regarding Colossians 1:19-20, he writes, "Paul does not myopically limit the efficacy of Christ's atonement to humanity. Rather, the reconciliation with God effected by Christ's shed blood is applied as comprehensively as possible to *all things, whether things on earth or things in heaven*."[62] After pointing out that Jesus is the first fruits as a result of his resurrection, Snyder concludes that "Jesus is the prototype as well as the redemptive basis of new creation. He is the point of coherence between the visible and invisible worlds (Col 1:17)."[63]

In addition to continuity in the areas related to the natural order of the cosmos, new creationists argue that there is continuity with regard to individual persons and with regard to human society. Moore's description of the final state of the redeemed in the new heavens and new earth includes certain societal features present during the current age. Life in the final state includes work. In addition, it includes a variety of other activities which, excepting the presence of sin, are somewhat continuous to the activities which humans perform in the present. Moore states, "The new earth is not simply a restoration of Eden but a glorious civilization with a *city*, and the glory of the nations redeemed and brought into it. One can expect that the new earth would be abuzz with culture—music, painting, literature, architecture, commerce, agriculture, and everything that expresses the creativity of human beings as the image of God. We can also expect in the eternal state, of all things, politics. Believers are promised a reigning function

---

60. Moo, "Creation and New Creation," 60.

61. Ibid. Moo references Moltmann, *Coming of God*, 265 and Polkinghorne, *God of Hope*, 31.

62. Middleton, "A New Heaven and a New Earth," 87-88. See chapter 1, fn 103 of the present work for a note on the possible implications of relating Christ's atonement to creation.

63. Snyder, *Salvation Means Creation Healed*, 107. After stating this, Snyder quotes approvingly from Wright's *Surprised by Hope*.

with Christ that is everlasting."[64] In this conception there is culture, work, and creativity. Affirming that the sphere of activities in the final state is not limited to the individual but extends to groups of individuals, Middleton writes, "The logic of biblical redemption, when combined with a biblical understanding of creation, requires the restoration and renewal of the full complexity of human life in our earthly environment, yet without sin. . . . eschatological redemption consists in the renewal of human cultural life on earth."[65] God promises that he will dwell in the midst of his people. The fulfillment of that promise, Moore says, "draws together the God-centered and relational human-centered aspects of Christian longing for eternity in Christ."[66] The goodness of the relational aspects of humanity's existence implies their endurance into the final state. So, Moore concludes, "Relationships begun in this life continue in the new creation . . . . We can expect to live life with friends, family members, mentors, and disciples forever; and we have forever to build new friendships as well."[67]

While one should be careful not to make hard conclusions about the level of continuity seen in new creation descriptions of the nature of the final state, it seems justified to conclude that, among new creationists, there is consensus that certain elements, both material and immaterial, that are a part of the present world will also be a part of the final state. This affirmation of continuity leads to the affirmation among new creationists

---

64. Moore, "Personal and Cosmic Eschatology," 914-15.

65. Middleton, "A New Heaven and a New Earth," 77. Middleton's argument regarding the renewal of human culture is related to his understanding of proper worship. He writes that "while various psalms (like 148 and 96) indeed call upon *all* creatures (humans included) to worship or serve God in the cosmic temple of creation (heaven and earth), the distinctive way *humans* worship or render service to the Creator is by the development of culture through interaction with our earthly environment (in a manner that glorifies God)." Ibid., 81. He develops his point in a corresponding footnote: "This [understanding of worship] is not meant to exclude what we call 'worship' from the appropriate human response to God. My point is twofold. First, the cultural development of the earth, rather than 'worship' narrowly conceived, is explicitly stated to be the human purpose in biblical texts recounting the creation of humanity. 'Worship' in the narrow sense may be understood as part of human cultural activity. Second, we should not reduce human worship/service of God to verbal, emotionally charged expressions of praise (which is what we usually mean by the term). Note that Paul in Romans 12:1-2 borrows language of sacrifice and liturgy from Israel's cult in order to describe the full-orbed bodily obedience (which, he says, is our true worship). This is the Bible's typical emphasis." Ibid. 81, fn 17.

66. Moore, "Personal and Cosmic Eschatology," 916.

67. Ibid.

that elements of the present material creation continue to exist in the new creation.

Correspondence of Identity in New Creation Views

In their affirmation of various points of continuity between the materiality of the present age and final state, new creationists are careful to point out that some particular objects that exist now will not necessarily exist in the final state.[68] However, regarding some particularities, new creationists see a correspondence of identity so that an identity exists between particular aspects of the present creation and particular aspects of the new creation. While the importance of the second nuance of particularity—the partial versus the universal—will become important in the critique in chapter 4, the first nuance—that of the distinctiveness of individual objects—is the primary focus here. In correspondence of identity, the point is that a single definite thing or person, or set of things or persons, as distinguished from others, maintains the same identity through the destruction of the present heavens and earth and all that entails to the establishment of the new heavens and earth.[69]

It has been shown that new creationists affirm that the present heavens and earth will be restored. The argument is that the particular materiality that makes up the heavens and earth that we experience today will endure into the final state. It will not be a new heavens and new earth that is distinct in its identity from the present heavens and earth. One can see from the survey in chapter 1 that new creationists affirm at least two examples of discontinuity. The first has to do with those elements which are taken

68. For example, after affirming the existence of animal life in the final state, Moore writes, "Christians do not believe that individual dogs or cats or other animals are resurrected from the dead since they do not bear the image of God." Ibid., 913.

69. The idea of correspondence of identity when referring to the enduring nature of the present creation can be seen in Eduard Thurneysen's bold description of the final state: "The world into which we shall enter in the Parousia of Jesus Christ is therefore not another world; it is this world, this heaven, this earth; both, however, passed away and renewed. It is these forests, these fields, these cities, these streets, these people, that will be the scene of redemption. At present they are battlefields, full of the strife and sorrow of the not yet accomplished consummation; then they will be fields of victory, fields of harvest, where out of seed that was sown with tears the everlasting sheaves will be reaped and brought home." Thurneysen, *Eternal Hope*, 204. In his discussion of the new earth, Hoekema approvingly quotes Thurneysen, a close colleague of Karl Barth. Hoekema, *Bible and the Future*, 281.

away or removed—i.e., sin, the wicked, etc. The second has to do with the addition of elements that are not a part of the present heavens and earth—i.e., peace, immortality, justice, etc. This addition may be understood as development, a development which allows for continuity through correspondence of identity.[70]

The correspondence between the present creation and the creation to come is seen at both the individual level as it relates to the resurrection of the body and at the cosmic level. In new creation conceptions these levels are intimately connected to one another. Regarding the connection between individual human identity and cosmic identity, Snyder writes the following: "If Jesus' body was recognizably the same after his resurrection, so also the earth will be recognizably the same after its renewal. To the degree that Jesus' resurrected body was and is physical, so also will be the earth and our bodies. To the degree that there was continuity in Jesus' body before and after his resurrection, so also there will be physical continuity between the old heaven and earth and the new."[71] In arguing for physical continuity, Snyder is arguing for what has been described here as correspondence of identity. The level of continuity that Snyder is implying accords with the definition of continuity with regard to material things: "The state or quality of being uninterrupted in extent or substance, of having no interstices or breaks; uninterrupted connexion of parts; connectedness, unbrokenness."[72]

Regarding the restoration of creation, Moore utilizes the analogy of Jesus' resurrection: "Jesus' resurrection body is glorified and transformed, but it is still *his body*, the same body that was placed in the tomb. A regenerate person is a 'new creation' in Christ, the old is pass away (2 Cor 5:17), but he is still the same man, just transformed and redeemed."[73] While

---

70. Middleton, for example, writes that "it is clear that redemption is not a simple return to primal origins. The Bible itself portrays the move from creation to eschaton as movement from a garden (in Genesis 2) to a city (in Revelation 21–22). Redemption does not reverse, but rather embraces, historical development. The transformation of the initial state of the earth into complex human societies is not part of the fall, but rather the legitimate creational mandate of humanity. Creation was never meant to be static, but was intended by God from the beginning to be developmental, moving toward a goal." Middleton, "A New Heaven and a New Earth," 76.

71. Snyder, *Salvation Means Creation Healed*, 107.

72. Simpson and Weiner, *OED*, s.v. "continuity."

73. Moore, "Personal and Cosmic Eschatology," 913. In his discussion of the resurrection, Wright states the following: "The point of the empty tomb stories always was that Jesus was alive again; the point of the appearance stories always was that the Jesus who was appearing was in bodily continuity with the corpse that had occupied the tomb.

acknowledging discontinuity, Middleton has a similar conclusion that "the resurrected Jesus is still recognizably the same person and even eats a meal of fish with his disciples on the beach."[74] Regarding Paul's metaphor in 1 Corinthians 15, Middleton writes, "[Paul] compares the mortal body to a seed, while the resurrection body is the plant (15:36–37). The one must die for the other to become a reality. But this is not a simple replacement. Paul is careful to stress the continuity of identity between the seed (mortal body) and the plant (resurrection body). In his terminology, the former is 'sown' perishable and 'raised' imperishable (15:42)."[75]

In his understanding of "renovation rather than replacement," Moo, while admitting the discontinuity apparent in Jesus' resurrection, argues that the doctrine of the resurrection demands a "significant continuity of some kind between this world and the next."[76] In reality, his conclusion implies correspondence of identity rather than simply relationship: "Yet there is continuity in the body: in some sense, the body that was in the grave is the same as the body that appears to the disciples after the resurrection."[77] The concept of correspondence of identity is also present in Wright, especially in *The Resurrection of the Son of God*. For example, in his explanation of 1 Corinthians 5–6, he states that "the argument of 6.12–20 depends

Neither, without the other, makes the sense that the early Christians believed they made." Wright, *The Resurrection of the Son of God*, 692. Regarding Paul's theology of resurrection, he states, "The continuity of the present Christian life (lived 'in the power of his resurrection') with the future resurrection itself shows that for Paul there was continuity as well as discontinuity between the Jesus who died and the Jesus who rose, and that this continuity was not a matter of spirit or soul, but of body." Ibid., 235–36. Wright also makes a statement as to how this continuity allows for an intermediate state, concluding that "belief in future resurrection *entails* some kind of post-mortem continuity, for which the word 'soul' can sometimes be used, but this does not of itself mean that the ontological basis of present or future existence has been radically altered." Ibid., 200, fn 304.

74. Middleton, "A New Heaven and a New Earth," 76. Regarding the discontinuity, he writes, "Indeed, there is good biblical evidence for significant discontinuity between creation and redemption. We may think of Paul's contrast in 1 Corinthians 15 between the present mortal body and the resurrection body, a contrast analogous to the difference between a seed and a fully-grown plant. Likewise, the resurrected Jesus is portrayed in the Gospels as being able to walk through walls and perhaps materialize at will." Ibid., 75–76.

75. Middleton, *A New Heaven and a New Earth*, 202.

76. Moo, "Nature in the New Creation," 469. In his resurrection body, Moo writes, Jesus has the ability "to dematerialize and materialize again; it is not always recognizable; it is, as Paul puts in respect to the resurrection body in general, a new kind of body, suited for existence in the spirit-dominated eternal kingdom (1 Cor 15:35–54)." Ibid.

77. Ibid.

on Paul's belief that what is done with the present body matters precisely because it is to be raised. The continuity between the present body and the future resurrection body is what gives the weight to the present ethical imperative."[78] The concept of correspondence of identity can be seen in Wright's discussion of Mark 9:43–48: "[It] speaks of 'entering into life'. . . at considerable personal cost. This assumes a standard Jewish dichotomy between the present age and the age to come, with a high degree of bodily continuity between the one and the other. Even assuming that Jesus intended the cutting off of feet and hands, and the plucking out of eyes, as vivid metaphors rather than literal advice, the point of the repeated explanation is that, whether the destination is Gehenna or 'life', it is the same person after as before."[79] Again, like other new creationists, Wright recognizes the discontinuity between the present body and the future one. However, he concludes, "despite the discontinuity between the present mode of corruptible physicality and the future world of non-corruptible physicality, there is an underlying continuity between present bodily life and future bodily life."[80] The idea of correspondence of identity also informs Moore's belief that human relationships endure into the final state because the persons involved in the various relationships have the same identity both prior to and in the new creation.[81]

The way in which the new creation proponents use the language of "restoration," "renewal," "transformation," and "redemption" to refer to various aspects of the present earthly existence (such as culture, society, work, government, etc.) also seems to imply the idea of correspondence of identity. The redemption of the cosmos, like the resurrection of the body, will improve but not replace the original good creation (e.g., Romans 8 and 2 Peter 3). As discussed in chapter 1, new creationists emphasize the coming of the kingdom of God, a kingdom which comes upon this particular earth, not one that is distinct from the present one. In the end we see, as

78. Wright, *Resurrection of the Son of God*, 289.

79. Ibid., 407.

80. Ibid., 359.

81. Akin to this affirmation of relationships is Wright's interpretation of 1 Cor 13. He states that "this exquisite chapter looks forward . . . to the final discussion [ch. 15], which will concern the resurrection, the new world that God will make, *and the continuity between the resurrection life and the life here and now*. The point of 13.8–13 is that the church must be working *in the present* on the things that will last *into God's future*. Faith, hope and love will do this; prophecy, tongues and knowledge, so highly prized in Corinth, will not." Wright, *Resurrection of the Son of God*, 296.

Wright states, "the new Jerusalem coming down from heaven to earth."[82] There is no indication in any of the new creationists surveyed in the present work that the "new earth" that is in view is distinct in its material identity from the present earth.

Conclusion

That the present earth will be restored rather than disposed of is a consistent affirmation among new creationists. This affirmation seems to be the basis for a variety of points of continuity between the present earth and the new earth. Regarding some particular elements, the relationship between the present state and the final state is understood as more than simple continuity. Rather, in the new creation conceptions, a correspondence of identity exists in which the identity of particular matter in the present age corresponds to matter in the final state. The foremost example of this correspondence of identity is the heavens and the earth. As will be seen in chapter 4, new creationists utilize a number of OT prophetical texts to inform their conception of the final state. A primary element of the materiality of the present earth that appears throughout many of these texts is the particular territory of Israel. In these texts, that territory is distinct from other lands (the first nuance of particularity discussed above) and is a distinct portion of the whole of creation (the second nuance of particularity discussed above). The presence of the territory of Israel in these OT restoration texts seems to demand treatment among new creationists who affirm the restoration of the present earth in its materiality. Before examining the utilization of the OT restoration texts in new creationism, I will offer an overview of the theological treatment of the theme of land. This background will provide a basis for evaluating the way in which new creationists envision the role of the particular territory of Israel.

---

82. Wright, *Surprised by Hope*, 19.

3

The Theme of Land in Recent Theology

In the pages to follow, I will survey the treatment of the land element within theological discussions. Because theological interest in the theme of land is relatively recent, I will focus on studies that have appeared in the last fifty years that emphasize the land as a predominant theme in Scripture. It is neither possible nor necessary to offer an extensive treatment of the various ways in which the land has been treated in Christian theology.[1] Therefore, I will survey what I see to be important theological contributions toward understanding the theme of land in Scripture. What will become evident in the following survey is that understanding the fulfillment of the land promise as metaphorical is common. At the end of the chapter, I will show that new creationists have affirmed various forms of the metaphorical view of the land.

Land—A Recent Interest?

In his essay "The Promised Land and Yahweh's Land in the Hexateuch," Gerhard von Rad states, "In the whole of the Hexateuch there is probably no more important idea than that expressed in terms of the land promised

---

1. A comprehensive treatment of the theme of land over the past fifty years is needed. In completing the present survey, I have found helpful the brief introductory survey in Martin, "Bound for the Kingdom," 7-16 and the introduction in Blanchard, "Changing Hermeneutical Perspectives," 1-4. As Martin points out, "most treatments of the land are embedded in works that cover much broader topics." Ibid., 8. The embedded nature of treatments of land makes comprehensiveness difficult to achieve.

and later granted by Yahweh, an idea found in all the sources, and indeed in every part of each of them."[2] After making the previous statement, von Rad laments, "Yet an examination of this conception which so evidently dominates the Hexateuch seems, oddly enough, never to have been made."[3] Elmer Martens's comment is in harmony with von Rad: "A little research will show that theological discussion about land is almost totally absent in the literature until recently. This scarcity of exposition is surprising because 'land' is the fourth most frequent noun or substantive in the Old Testament: it occurs 2504 times. Statistically land is a more dominant theme than covenant."[4] Likewise, David Frankel notes that since Eichrodt, there has been a "growing appreciation among Christian theologians and scholars of the centrality of the territorial orientation of the religion of the Hebrew Bible as more than just a passing phase in an evolutionary process leading to the New Testament."[5] While von Rad, Martens, and Frankel are certainly correct that scholarly interest in the land theme in Scripture is a recent phenomenon, it is difficult to pinpoint exactly why this is the case. It is probable that a combination of factors provided an environment in which such an interest arose.[6] It is to this interest that we now turn.

2. Rad, "The Promised Land and Yahweh's Land," 79. Von Rad actually wrote the essay in 1943. Not widely available, it was included in a set of essays which was published over twenty years later.

3. Ibid.

4. Martens, *God's Design*, 114. [The first edition was published in 1981 in England by Inter-Varsity and in America by Baker.] After admitting that many occurrences are not referring to the particular land of Israel, Martens concludes, "But even if these directive uses of 'land' are discounted, there is left a large number of occurrences of the word, and that in contexts where its theological significance is unquestioned." Ibid.

5. Frankel, *Land of Canaan*, 1.

6. While it would be impossible to trace out all of the causes behind the recent interest in the theme of land and it is difficult to make causal arguments, it seems that developments in the discipline of biblical theology and the renewed interest in the question of a future for ethnic Israel may have helped to provide the appropriate environment for the recent interest. For an introduction to the discipline of biblical theology, see Childs, *Biblical Theology*. Regarding the interest in a future for ethnic Israel, it does not seem like a coincidence that the recent theological interest in the land theme has occurred during a time of political unease about the land since the reconstitution of the political state of Israel in 1948, especially given that on various sides of the discussion there are appeals to what the Scripture says in regard to Israel and the land. In the preface to the second edition of *The Land*, Brueggemann notes another possible factor. He describes OT studies as in a state of unraveling in the 1970s at the hands of Gerhard von Rad and G. Ernest Wright and the diminishment of the accent on God's mighty deeds in history. This diminishment, he says, "entailed as well the end of the old dichotomies

Land as a Comprehensive Biblical Theme

In his brief essay, von Rad provides an introductory, yet helpful, argument for both the predominance and importance of the theme of land in the first six books of the Hebrew Bible. Concluding the essay, he states a problem for OT theology in general, not simply in the Hexateuch, regarding the theme of land: "Here we come face to face with one of the most interesting problems of Old Testament theology: promises which have been fulfilled in history are not thereby exhausted of their content, but remain as promises on a different level, although they are to some extent metamorphosed in the process. The promise of the land itself was proclaimed ever anew, even after its fulfilment [*sic*], as a future benefit of God's redemptive activity."[7] The "interesting problem," as von Rad describes it, has been taken up by others who have demonstrated the importance of the theme of land not only for OT theology but for the entire canon.

W. D. Davies

Davies wrote his seminal work *The Gospel and the Land: Early Christianity and Jewish Territorial Doctrine* in 1974.[8] At the outset of the work he proposes why there has been a lack of interest in the land element in Christian theology. He writes that Christians have been most interested in doctrine—"theological and metaphysical abstractions, that have been emphasized in attempts to understand how the Gospel emerged from and impinged upon Judaism."[9] As a result, he states, "Jewish faith came to be

---

that had been so prominent in the field between 'history and nature,' 'time and space.'" It was within this context, he states, that he began "to see that the Old Testament, in its theological articulation, was not all about 'deeds,' but was concerned with *place*, specific real estate that was invested with powerful *promises* and with strategic arrangements for presence in the place as well." Brueggemann, *The Land*, 2nd ed., xi.

7. Rad, "The Promised Land and Yahweh's Land," 93.

8. Davies, *Gospel and the Land*. William David Davies (1911–2001) was a Welsh Congregationalist minister. He taught first at Chestnut College in Cambridge before serving in the United States at Duke, Princeton, and Union Theological Seminary in New York. His expertise was in the area of Christian Origins and the NT. For a brief introduction to his life and work, see Hare, "Davies, W(illiam) D(avid)," 350–55.

9. Davies, *Gospel and the Land*, 4. At the beginning of part two of the work, Davies states his case more boldly: "Christians have usually understood Judaism in too theological and, therefore, too intellectual terms. And they have also usually looked at their own foundation document, the New Testament, in the same way. In their proper concern

understood largely as a body of ideas with which Christian doctrines could
be compared and contrasted: it came to be examined in terms of Christian
categories but seldom in terms native, or peculiar, to itself."[10] Once this occurred, "Any local or geographic particularistic elements in Judaism could
not but be regarded as insignificant or, at best, secondary, and could safely
be overlooked."[11] The irony of this neglect, he states, is that the theme of
the land in Judaism was "one of the most persistent and passionately held
doctrines with which the Early Church had to come to terms."[12]

Davies's goal in the work is to show that the lack of interest in the land
element, and ultimately in all the realia of Judaism, is justified based on
the proper reading of Scripture.[13] The work is divided into two main sections, the first of which is a comprehensive treatment of the land in Israelite
religion and Judaism while the second is an account of the historical and
theological process by which early Christianity gave a "spiritual" interpretation of the views of the land. At the outset of the work, he sets forth the
peculiarity of the particular land of Israel as it is described in the Hexateuch. The two-fold emphasis of the land being promised to Abraham and
his descendants and the fact that it is described as Yahweh's land "became
merged in the cultic life of Israel and in its transmission of various tradi-

---

to unravel theological developments and subtleties in primitive Christianity, they have
neglected to search for evidences of an encounter between it and the *realia* of Judaism
and for any possible resolutions of such an encounter. In particular, they have failed to
inquire after the place of the land in the thought and lives of early Christians." Ibid., 161.

10. Ibid., 4. In two appendices, entitled "Reflections on Judaism and Christianity:
Their Mutual Dependence," and "The Differences Between Judaism and Christianity Torah and Dogma: A Comment," respectively, Davies offers a brief excursus on the tension
he sees between the faith of Judaism and Christianity. See Appendix I (pp. 377–89) and
Appendix II (pp. 390–404) in *Gospel and the Land*.

11. *Gospel and the Land*, 4. Jewish or Rabbinic theology was not unaffected, since "in
reaction to and imitation of Christian Theology, from which it borrowed its philosophical tools and methods and by which it was stimulated, concentrated on themes dictated
to it by the need to defend itself against the specifically Christian challenges, and neglected such awkward, particular doctrines as that of the land. Rabbinic thinkers themselves, understanding Judaism in terms of or in reaction to Christianity, unconsciously
and consciously, asked what significance a particular place, Palestine, could have in their
Faith; and Christian scholars, naturally governed by their own doctrinal interests, easily
neglected the *realia* of Judaism and, in particular, its traditional concentration on the
land." Ibid.

12. Ibid., 5.

13. By "realia," Davies is referring to the objects of affection among Jews such as the
land, the temple, Jerusalem, and other holy places.

tional documents, so that, as the Old Testament now stands, they have to be carefully disentangled."[14] While the prophets speak clearly about the doom of the land, they promise ultimate restoration.[15] He writes, "There seems to be a paradoxical 'nationalism,' or rather attachment to Israel and her land, in the prophets, and, if we exclude Amos and Isaiah, they reveal a persistent yearning for the ingathering of the dispersed of Israel into one national entity in their own land."[16]

In the final sections of the first part of his work, Davies builds a foundation for his survey of the NT treatment of the peculiar land of Israel. He argues that outside the Pentateuch, the land begins to become a symbol of the transcendental. The beginning of the spiritualization of the realia (especially land and temple) of Israel sets the stage for the NT development of land theology. In the course of time, hope for restoration to and occupation of the land in history was by and large transformed into hope for an order beyond history.[17] Davies writes that this is the case even within Judaism: "Judaism survived and came to terms with the loss of the land in A.D. 70, catastrophic as it was, with dignity and comparative speed. It did so because Pharisaism, after A.D. 70, the dominant element in Judaism, was politically and otherwise prepared to adjust to the absence of the land, as to the loss of other symbols of its faith."[18] After admitting that in passages such

---

14. Davies, *Gospel and the Land*, 35. Davies writes that the promise to Abraham was "so reinterpreted from age to age that it became a living power in the life of the people of Israel." Ibid., 18. He states further, "However much the Prophets and the Writings gained in significance, in later ages the Pentateuch remained the bedrock of revelation for Jews, so that the references to the promise of land embedded in it must be accorded great weight in any assessment of Judaism." Ibid., 24. The notion that the land belongs to Yahweh, he writes, "persisted throughout the Old Testament and beyond it." Ibid., 27. This persistence was despite passages that suggest that the land truly belonged to the Canaanites.

15. Davies notes the important point that "alongside prophecies of doom against the land because of Israel's sin, there are promises of restoration." Ibid., 39.

16. Ibid., 40. Even in his discussion of Deutero-Isaiah, Davies notes the native concerns of Israel: "There is a core of particularism in the most universal of prophets." Ibid., 45. Davies includes a brief section in part one regarding extra-canonical sources. He concludes that while there is a scarcity of references to the land attributed to the fact that after the exile attention focused on Jerusalem and the temple, these two foci imply a concern for the land.

17. Davies attempts to show that in the writings of Philo and various Rabbinical teachings that the land was at times "spiritualized" or described in ways that transcend the physical land. Ibid., 121-26.

18. Ibid., 127. Part of the reason, he states, is the Pharisaic understanding of Judaism

as Isaiah 60:3, 5, 10, 13, "Jerusalem is envisaged as a very earthly city to which the wealth of the nations is brought," he counters with the following: "However, whether Jerusalem had already in the Old Testament gained a super-historical connotation or not, in later sources the duality of the city, if we may so put it, its earthly and 'heavenly' affinities, are evident although highly complex."[19] His conclusion about the seemingly contradictory messages regarding the land, especially following the exile, was that there "was no one doctrine of the land, clearly defined and normative, but, as is usual in Judaism, a multiplicity of ideas and expectations variously and unsystematically entertained."[20] He then makes a statement that foreshadows his argument in the second major section:

> Among many Jews the certainty of the ultimately indissoluble connection between Israel and the land was living and widespread in the world within which Christianity emerged. And, while the view that all Jewish eschatology was this-worldly cannot be accepted, because so many sources anticipate a transcendent order or supernatural changes "in the end of the days," this connection is not always to be "spiritualized," but accorded its full terrestrial or physical and historical actuality.[21]

In the second major section of *The Gospel and the Land* Davies surveys the land theme in the Pauline epistles, Mark and Matthew, Luke-Acts, and the Gospel of John, respectively. He argues that the marked absence of the land theme in Paul is the result of his christological logic which de-territorializes the promise and locates the sphere of its fulfillment in Christ, not the land.[22] This christological "fulfillment" involves replacing

---

which "placed Torah above political power and control of the land." Ibid., 128.

19. Ibid., 143. Davies seems to leave open the possibility that the belief in a heavenly Jerusalem appears in Isaiah 60:19–20.

20. Ibid., 157. Eight years after the publication of *The Gospel and the Land*, Davies wrote *The Territorial Dimension of Judaism*. While derivative of the *The Gospel and the Land*, this work is an attempt to answer a particular pressing question regarding perceptions of the land in Jewish history. In the book Davies goes beyond the perceptions among early Rabbinic writings to survey perceptions up to the time of the writing. His conclusion, much like that in *The Gospel and the Land*, is that, within Judaism, there is a wide range of thought regarding the land.

21. Davies, *Gospel and the Land*, 157.

22. Davies writes, for example, "In Galatians we can be fairly certain that Paul did not merely ignore the territorial aspect of the promise for political reasons: his silence points not merely to the absence of a conscious concern with it, but to his deliberate rejection of it. His interpretation of the promise is a-territorial." Ibid., 178–79.

the hope of the physical land with a hope that transcends that land: "Salvation was not now bound to the Jewish people centred [sic] in the land and living according to the Law: it was 'located' not in a place, but in persons in whom grace and faith had their writ. By personalizing the promise 'in Christ' Paul universalized it. For Paul, Christ had gathered up the promise into the singularity of his own person. In this way, 'the territory' promised was transformed into and fulfilled by the life 'in Christ.'"[23] Paul not only transcendentalized the element of the particular land, he implied that the other realia prominent in the faith of the OT had been transcended as well.[24] Davies admits that at times Paul seemed concerned with the realia, specifically the land.[25] However, Paul had made a complete break with the hope of the land:

> The moment the personal relationship with Christ became primary for Paul the process of his "disenlandisement," if we may use such a term, had begun. "Individualism" no less than "ecclesiology" would lead him to disconnect himself ultimately from the land. . . . the personal, theological, and ecclesiological factors . . . impinged upon Paul and led him not so much to look away from

23. Ibid., 179. Regarding the universalization of salvation, Davies writes further, "The logic of Paul's Christology and missionary practice, then, seems to demand that the people of Israel living in the land had been replaced as the people of God by a universal community which had no special territorial attachment." Ibid., 182.

24. Focusing on Paul's language of the church as the temple of God, for example, Davies writes that "holy space seems to have been 'transubstantiated' into a community of persons, the Body of Christ." Ibid., 185. Regarding the city of Jerusalem, he writes that "by the time we come to Romans, although the city remains the city of the End, Paul is no longer governed by concern with it as the ultimate centre [sic] of his activity. Rather, Jerusalem has become for him the place where the unity of the 'Israel of God,' not the end of history, is to be revealed." Ibid., 208.

25. In his treatment on Rom 9–11 in relation to the collection of Rom 15:22–29, Davies reasons that, contra Munck, by the time that he gets to Romans, Paul is no longer tied to the land. However, later he states, "It is arguable that he never completely and consciously and emotionally abandoned the geography of eschatology: it may have continued alongside his new awareness of the 'ecclesiological' eschatology inaugurated by Christ. For a long time Paul apparently felt no incongruity between retaining his apocalyptic geography, centred [sic] in Jerusalem, even though, since he was 'in Christ,' it had become otiose. Theologically he had no longer any need of it: his geographical identity was subordinated to that of being 'in Christ,' in whom was neither Jew nor Greek." Ibid., 220. For Munck's position, see his *Paul and the Salvation of Mankind*. In his earlier work, *Paul and Rabbinic Judaism*, Davies argues that, contra the history of religions school, Paul is better understood with the background of contemporary Rabbinic Judaism rather than that of the Hellenism of the day.

the land of his fathers as to discover his inheritance "in Christ"—
the land of Christians, the new creation, if we may so express the
matter.[26]

Moving to the theme of land in Matthew and Mark, Davies argues that
neither writer emphasizes the land. In Luke-Acts he sees an emphasis on Jerusalem but only to show continuity between the city as the center of Jewish
eschatological hope and the city as the birthplace of the Christian church.[27]
For Davies, John's gospel clearly spiritualized the fulfillment of the land
promise: "The fundamental spatial symbolism of the Fourth Gospel was
not horizontal but vertical. It does not lend itself easily to geographical concern so much as to the personal confrontation with the One from above,
whose Spirit bloweth where it listeth and is not subject to geographical
dimensions that had been dear to Judaism."[28] At the end of a brief chapter
on how Jesus deals with the land theme, Davies states that Jesus "paid little
attention to the relationship between Yahweh, and Israel and the land."[29]

Davies concludes that the overall witness of the NT both transcends
the realia of Judaism and is concerned with these realities in regards to
history and theology.[30] Although implied throughout the book, he states
his reconciling principle as follows: "The New Testament finds holy space

26. Davies, *Gospel and the Land*, 219.

27. Davies believes Luke's concentration on Jerusalem should be understood as only
the result of theological and political concerns. He writes, "For Luke to have discussed
the separation of the Gospel from the land directly would have undermined two of the
purposes which he dearly cherished, and which led him to concentrate so much on Jerusalem—first, the recognition of the theological continuity between Gentile Christianity
and Judaism, and, secondly, the political necessity to emphasize this. The same factors
which led him to give Jerusalem a full measure of attention would have led him to mini-
mize that given directly to the land." Ibid., 286-87.

28. Ibid., 335. While he does not discuss John 1:14 at length, Davies states that he
agrees with a "displacement motif" there and quotes approvingly R. E. Brown who states,
"When the Prologue proclaims that the Word made his dwelling among men, we are
being told that the flesh of Jesus Christ is the new localization of God's presence on earth,
and that Jesus is the replacement of the ancient Tabernacle." [from Brown, *Gospel According to John*, 321–22]. Davies, *Gospel and the Land*, 335, fn 98.

29. Ibid., 365.

30. So, alongside one another Davies can state 1) "It is justifiable to speak of the *realia*
of Judaism as being 'spiritualized' in the Christian dispensation," and 2) "The need to
remember the Jesus of History entailed the need to remember the Jesus of a particular
land. Jesus belonged not only to time, but to space; and the space and spaces which he
occupied took on significance, so that the *realia* of Judaism continued as *realia* in Christianity. History in the tradition demanded geography." Ibid., 366.

wherever Christ is or has been: it personalizes 'holy space' in Christ, who, as a figure of History, is rooted in the land; he cleansed the Temple and died in Jerusalem, and lends his glory to these and to the places where he was, but, as Living Lord, he is also free to move wherever he wills."[31] The peculiar or particular land of Israel, in addition to much of the other realia of Judaism, is taken over/replaced/fulfilled through the peculiar or particular person of Christ. As Davies puts it the land has been "Christified."[32] This "Christification" of the land—and of the realia in general—had a radical result for the early church's view of the land.[33]

Davies describes his book as a prolegomenon to the question of land and sets out to "offer some general suggestions, almost all exploratory rather than affirmative."[34] These descriptions of the work are interesting for at least two reasons. First, as seen in the brief survey offered here, there is present in the work a very strong affirmation that any enduring meaning for the peculiar or particular land of Israel as an object of faith has been transcended in the coming of Christ. Second, Davies's "general suggestions" appear to have framed subsequent Christian discussions of the land theme.

Walter Brueggemann

Three years after Davies's work appeared, Walter Brueggemann's *The Land: Place as Gift, Promise, and Challenge in Biblical Faith* was published.[35] Brueggemann's overarching thesis is that "Land is a central, if not *the central theme* of biblical faith."[36] Following the record of Israel's history from Genesis to the post-exilic community of Ezra, he organizes the work

31. Ibid., 367.

32. He writes, "In sum, for the holiness of place, Christianity has fundamentally, though not consistently, substituted the holiness of the Person; it has Christified holy space." Ibid., 368.

33. Davies explains the result as follows: "The overwhelming actuality and significance of Gentile Christianity soon swept away for many, if not most Christians, those patterns that had governed Jewish thinking on the land. This is why the question of the land so little occupies writers of the New Testament. In coming to grips with Gentile Christianity, early Christians had radically to assess the geographic *realia* of Judaism, and they either abandoned or transformed them or lent them a new perspective." Ibid., 373.

34. Ibid., 5.

35. Brueggemann, *The Land*.

36. Ibid., 3. emphasis in original. He even suggests "that land might be a way of organizing biblical theology." Ibid.

around three histories of land: 1) promise into land; 2) management into exile; and 3) a new history of promise that culminates in kingdom.[37] Each of these land histories, according to Brueggemann, is an experience in land manipulation and injustice. Brueggemann's interest is not in the history of Israel, per se, but in the history of Israel's view of and relationship to the land throughout her history.[38] So, while he is concerned with land as particular earthly matter in which people experience security and peace, his primary concern is to describe land symbolically as a condition of security and peace.[39] Land, specifically the combined losing and promising of it, gives hope for the hopeless that God will act:[40]

> The reversal of destiny is not some clever trick of human ingenu-
> ity, but it is the action of God himself when all human ingenuity

37. The first history includes the promise to the patriarchs, the time in Egypt and the Exodus, the wilderness wonderings, and Israel's reflections upon crossing the Jordan. The second history includes the kingly rulership of the lands and the prophets who remind Israel that they are in the process of losing the land. The third history includes the promises of restoration to the land.

38. For Brueggemann land is the essence of history. He writes that when Israel is incapable of calling upon and addressing God, land is lost, and when land is lost, "history is ended." Brueggemann, *The Land*, 121. He writes elsewhere, "history ended in landlessness" and "The landless have no history. It takes land to make history." Ibid., 125. Ultimately, "It is land that fully permits Israel to be Israel. It is land that fully permits Yahweh to be known as Yahweh. It is land that permits Yahweh and Israel to have history together." Ibid., 142. The land is so integral to God's covenant with Israel that "Israel never had a desire for a relation with Yahweh in a vacuum, but only in land." Ibid., 188.

39. In chapter 1, he states, "In what follows, 'land' will be used to refer to *actual earthly turf* where people can be safe and secure, where meaning and well-being are enjoyed without pressure or coercion. 'Land' will also be used in a *symbolic* sense, as the Bible itself uses it, to express the wholeness of joy and well-being characterized by social coherence and personal ease in prosperity, security, and freedom." Ibid., 2.

40. Although he speaks of God as the one who acts, Brueggemann, at times, comes close to personifying land so that it actually accomplishes various things throughout the respective histories. In discussing the way in which David is managing the land, Brueggemann concludes, "David had become a practitioner of one-way bureaucratic communication intended to cover the open, unresolved space between king and Torah. Surely something happened to this man who had gone so willingly into extremities with his fellows. What had happened to him was land! Land required and made possible a new form of communication which no longer communicated but only dispatched and commanded. The ones receiving the directives were not covenant members but functionaries in the ordering and retention of land." Ibid., 81. Regarding the forgetfulness of Israel as recorded in Hos 2:11–13, he writes that "the land has done something to Israel. The ones warned about forgetting (Deut. 8:11) remember nothing. Land has caused amnesia (Deut. 32:15–18)." Ibid., 106.

has failed. Nor is the reversal of destiny some psychological or spiritual change, but it is the radical transformation of an historical, political situation.

That is the good news, that God transforms those who are displaced and makes them a home, gives to them secure turf. And the good news is precisely to exile and precisely when no prospect of land is anywhere visible. Those are the only terms on which the new history could be initiated and that is the central thrust of a biblical understanding of land, that it is freely given gift to undeserving exiles in a context without expectation by a God who is able radically to reorientate the character of historical existence.[41]

The history of the land, and hence the history of Israel, ends where it began—landlessness. Contra Davies, Bruggemann does not believe that the theme of the land is disregarded in the NT.[42] Still, he devotes only one chapter to the NT view of the land. Also, contra Davies, Brueggemann denies that the land theme is displaced by the person of Christ and that it has been fully spiritualized in Christ.[43] However, Brueggemann does not affirm a future restoration of the particular land of Israel at some time in the future. Rather, he perceives the theme of landedness and landlessness throughout the NT.[44] He writes that "at the heart of the reversal of land/

41. Ibid., 134.

42. He writes, "It will be evident that I regard the interactions between the Old Testament and the New Testament on this theme as much more dialectical and complex than does W. D. Davies, *The Gospel and the Land* . . . . It will be equally evident that I have learned much from his study." Ibid., 167, fn 1. In discussing the reference to the stress on Abraham in Paul (esp. Rom 4 and Gal 3–4), he writes, "The Abraham imagery apart from the land promise is an empty form. No matter how spiritualized, transcendentalized, or existentialized, it has its primary focus undeniably on land. That is what is promised, not to the competent deserving or to the dutifully obedient, but freely given (as in the beginning) to one who had no claim and 'was as good as dead' (Heb. 11:12)." Brueggemann, *The Land*, 177. In another work he writes the following: "The great propensity of Christian theology has been in the spiritualizing direction, and therefore it must be accented that the initial promise is one of *materiality*, a bodily communal existence in the world, a conviction that is belatedly expressed in the Christian creed as 'communion of saint . . . the resurrection of the body.'" Brueggemann, *Old Testament Theology*, 270.

43. Regarding the theme of land in the NT, Brueggemann writes the following: "In order to try to sense the intention of the text, we must note that the promissory language is focused on land and surely cannot be understood apart from it. And no matter how much it has been spiritualized, it is probable that the image is never robbed of its original, historical referent." Brueggemann, *The Land*, 170.

44. For example, regarding Mary's song in Luke 1:51–55, he writes, "Quite clearly this is a vision of land-loss by the graspers of land and land-receipt by those who bear

landless is a scandal. It is not a new scandal, for it is precisely what the whole history of Israel evidences in terms of gift and grasp. But now [in the NT] that whole dialectic is encompassed in one person."[45] Bruggemann offers an alternative to either treating the NT as though it is uninterested in land or treating it as if it "contains a simple promise of land."[46] He writes, "Rather the New Testament has discerned how problematic land is; when the people are landless, the promise comes; but when the land is secured, it seduces and the people are turned toward loss. Thus the proclamation of Jesus is about graspers losing and those open to gifts as receiving."[47] He also states the following: "Those who gather around Jesus are heirs. Of course Davies is correct that the inheritance has been boldly redefined. But we cannot therefore deny the central and enduring referent which is land, unless we succumb to an otherworldly hermeneutic." Avoiding this requires the affirmation that the "heirs in Christ are not heirs to a new promise, but the one which abides, and that is centrally land."[48]

Brueggemann's position that the land theme is this-worldly is evident in his reflections on the implications of the theme upon socio-political and economic questions.[49] Yet, the land is not simply physical soil—"the Pauline question is about 'turf' and the gospel answer is that 'at-homeness' comes by the homelessness of trusting joyous obedience."[50] So, it seems that

---

promises but lack power." Ibid., 171. Other examples include Jesus' "concise but enigmatic statements which reject the world of grasping and affirm the world of gifts" (e.g., Luke 9:24; 13:30; 14:11) and the contrast of landedness and the landless in Luke 7:36–50 and Luke 16:19–31. Brueggemann sees a deliberate appeal to the theme in Jesus' words to Zacchaeus in Luke 19:9 and Jesus' actions of healing and cleansing (e.g., Mark 2:11; Mark 5:19; Luke 7:22). Ibid., 172–75.

45. Ibid., 175.

46. Ibid.

47. Ibid.

48. Ibid., 178.

49. See the final chapter of *The Land*, which is devoted to these hermeneutical reflections. In the revised and updated edition, the socio-political and economic overtones are further evidenced by the added chapter entitled "Land: Fertility and Justice." *The Land*, 2nd ed. In this chapter, Brueggemann suggests a connection between sexuality and land economics, modern practices of enclosure, displacement of individuals or groups as a result of land procurement, and land management. Ibid., 173–96. The preface to the second edition is nearly thirteen pages and traces significant developments in OT studies since the release of the first edition. Ibid., xi–xxiii.

50. Brueggemann, *The Land*, 178. He writes, "To argue that land is or is not a New Testament concern, literally or spiritually, misses the point. It is rather the history of *gift and grasp* which concerns the church. It is a radical affirmation in the New Testament,

Brueggemann does not deny "place" as earthly territory, but the materiality of the promised land fades into the background in his conception. Like Davies's work, Brueggemann's is relevant for subsequent treatments of the land theme. The significance of his work is evidenced in part by the six subsequent printings of the first edition and by the fact that a second edition was published twenty-five years after the first edition.

Christopher J. H. Wright

In *God's People in God's Land: Family, Land and Property in the Old Testament*, Christopher Wright focuses on the ethical implications of Israel's property laws, institutions, and customs.[51] Wright approaches the subject from a sociological perspective, seeking to bridge the biblical material on the subjects of land and property with contemporary social realities.[52] The work is divided into three parts. The first is concerned with the centrality of the family in Israel's social, economic and religious existence. God rests, he says, in "family-plus-land units." In part two, Wright surveys the rights and responsibilities of property owners in biblical laws. The third part deals with the concept of persons as property, such as in the case of wives, children, and slaves.

Most pertinent to the present work are Wright's conclusions to the first part of the book which have to do with the relationship of Israel's theology of land to the Israelites' understanding of family. According to Wright, the socio-economic emphasis of the eighth century prophets shows the link between the two, especially in the way the prophetical preaching condemns Israel's actions, actions which had a negative effect upon those

---

but an affirmation which Israel surely learned . . . It is not what one would expect. It is not how it seems with land. But it is the case nevertheless. Coveting yields nothing but anxiety. The meek, the ones claiming no home and living with homelessness, do indeed inherit the land." Ibid., 183.

51. Wright, *God's People in God's Land.* The book is a revised and updated edition of Wright's 1977 doctoral dissertation submitted at Cambridge. It also has as its foundation the earlier survey work by Wright, *Eye for an Eye* which was published in England as *Living as the People of God.*

52. The socio-ethical relevance for today is primarily seen in Wright's conclusions to the three respective parts: Wright, *God's People in God's Land,* 104–14; 174–80; and 260–65. Examples of the implications for contemporary social realities include enfranchisement, fighting against slavery, the discouragement of the unnecessary accumulation of land, and helping the poor (especially those in third-world countries) work toward self-sufficiency.

households owning land:[53] "The theological status of Israel was earthed and rooted in the socio-economic fabric of their kinship structure and their land tenure, and it was this fabric which was being dissolved by the acids of debt, dispossession, and latifundism. The prophetic protest against these evils, therefore, must be illumined by the fact that there was an essential link between the social and economic facts of life and the theological self-understanding of Israel. That link was the family."[54] The "family-plus-land" concept, intrinsic to an OT understanding of Yaweh's relationship to Israel, weakened over time according to Wright. Having recognized and argued that Israel's relationship with God was "grounded in" and "experienced through" land and family, Wright asserts that even in the prophets there is indication that the relationship transcended "that realm and was not permanently or exclusively bound to it."[55]

More importantly for Wright, however, is that "in later Israelite prophecy there can be discerned a 'loosening' of—almost a dispensing with—the ancient family land basis."[56] This waning of the land basis, he argues, signals a change in the relationship between God and his people. This change "is entailed in the descriptions of its all-inclusiveness, which will bring into full and assured relationship with God categories of people whose position, on a family-land criterion, would have been ambiguous and insecure."[57] The NT records the realization of the eschatological expectation in the inclusion of the Gentiles. Wright focuses on Ephesians 2:11—3:6 as evidence.[58] There, the Gentiles are described in such terms as "joint heirs" (συγκληρονόμα), a "joint-body" (συσσωμα), and "joint sharers" (συμμέτοχα) with Israel through Jesus the Messiah. This inheritance

53. Wright affirms that the prophets understood Israel's primary problem to be a religious one resulting from their disobedience which is in contrast to the view that the prophets were "social heroes" and religious or ethical concerns were secondary to the social struggle. For a brief discussion of these competing views, see Wright, *God's People in God's Land*, 107–09.

54. Ibid., 109.

55. Ibid., 110. He cites as evidence Israel's sonship—the fact that, despite the total loss of land, Israel did not utterly lose her status as the people of Yahweh, and Amos describing as righteous those who did not possess land or family.

56. Ibid.

57. Ibid. He offers the example of the foreigner's doubts in Isa 56:3–7, the barren woman in Isa 54:1, and the inclusion of the "aliens" (גרים) in Ezek 47:22.

58. Wright discusses the passage in slightly more detail in his *Eye for an Eye*, 96–98.

language, "evokes the triangular pattern of relationships between God, Israel, and the land."[59] However, what becomes clear is that the territorial promise was simply a type for the relationship with Christ that Paul describes. Wright states, "So then, by incorporation into the Messiah, all nations are enabled to enter upon the privileges and responsibilities of God's people. Christ himself takes over the significance and function of the land kinship qualification. 'In Christ,' answering to 'in the land,' denotes a status and a relationship, a position of inclusion and security, a privilege with attendant responsibilities."[60] Interestingly, Wright denies that the socio-economic dimensions evident in Israel's history cease to have import.[61] Instead, they have an ongoing paradigmatic function.[62] The function of the territory of Israel as a feature of the relationship between God and his people, however, no longer exists. Wright states, "There are so many similarities which show that the experience of fellowship in its full, rich New Testament sense fulfills analogous theological functions for the Christian as the possession of land did for Old Testament Israelites."[63] Possession of the particular territory of

---

59. Wright, *God's People in God's Land*, 111.

60. Ibid.

61. He writes, "But what then has become of the socio-economic dimension of the land which we found to have been of such importance in Old Testament Israel? Has it simply been transcended, as spiritualized and forgotten? By no means." Ibid. Actually, Wright concludes, "Christianity *has* a social basis, which has transcended the land and kinship structure of Old Testament Israel—but not in such a way as to make that original structure irrelevant. In this, as in so many other ways, Christ and all that flows from Christ 'fulfills' the Old Testament, taking it up and transforming it into something that can be the experience of everyman—everyman in Christ." Ibid., 114.

62. Wright notes the two major ways—typological and paradigmatic—in the introduction. Regarding the typological, he writes, "In New Testament theology the Christian Church, as the community of the Messiah, is the organic continuation of Israel. It is heir to the names and privileges of Israel, and therefore also falls under the same ethical responsibilities—though now transformed in Christ." Ibid., xvii–xviii. The paradigmatic (he also calls it "exemplary") function means that the socio-economic reality of Israel serves as a model "within a particular cultural context of principles of justice, humaneness, equality, responsibility, and so forth which are applicable, *mutatis mutandis*, to all people in subsequent cultural contexts." Ibid., xviii.

63. Ibid., 113. Wright continues, "The explicit purpose of the Exodus was the enjoyment of the rich blessing of God in his 'good land'; the goal of redemption through Christ is 'for a sincere love of the brethren' (1 Pet. 1:22), with all its practical implications. Both are linked to the status of sonship and the related themes of inheritance and promise. Both thereby constitute a proof of an authentic relationship with God as part of his redeemed community. For fellowship, like the land, has limits, so that the person who departs permanently from it—or refuses to accept it—shows that he has no real part in

Israel has, in the Christian dispensation, been replaced by possession of a particular relationship open to any person who becomes united to Christ.

Wright's understanding of Jesus as the fulfillment of OT prophecies of the restoration of Israel can also be seen in his essay "A Christian Approach to Old Testament Prophecy Concerning Israel."[64] In discussing the way in which the NT writers interpret the fulfillment of OT prophecy, he writes the following: "Both Jesus himself and his immediate interpreters tell us that in the events of his arrival, life, death, resurrection and exaltation, God had acted decisively for the redemption and restoration of his people Israel in fulfillment of the whole range of Old Testament prophecy that he would do so. To this they were called urgently to respond there and then as a present reality, not as some still future hope. 'The time is fulfilled. . .'"[65] Again, for Wright, the fulfillment that occurs in Christ is for Jew and Gentile alike, each receiving the full blessing promised in the OT, but in a different way.[66] Wright concludes that "it is not a case of abolishing and 'replacing' the realities of Israel and the Old Testament, but of taking them up into a *greater reality* in the Messiah."[67]

Norman Habel

Norman Habel boldly states that land "is such a comprehensive symbol in the Old Testament that it could be ranked next to God in importance."[68] Appearing nearly twenty years after Brueggemann's work, Habel's *The Land is Mine: Six Biblical Land Ideologies* is also part of the Fortress Press series Overtures to Biblical Theology. Habel refers to his work as "a sequel [to Brueggemann's work] that takes into account recent approaches and findings in biblical research."[69] What is especially important for Habel is

God's people (cf. 1 John 2:19; Matt. 18:15–17)." Ibid.

64. Wright, "Christian Approach to Old Testament Prophecy Concerning Israel," 1–19.

65. Ibid., 14–15.

66. Wright states, "Christ does not *deprive* the believing Jew of anything that belonged to Israel as God's people; nor does he give to the believing Gentile anything *less* than the full covenantal blessing and promise that was Israel's. On the contrary, we share together in all of it and more—in him, and for ever." Ibid., 19.

67. Ibid. [emphasis mine]

68. Habel, *The Land is Mine*, 6.

69. Ibid., xi. Habel's use of the word "sequel" in describing his work to that of Brueggemann's could be somewhat misleading since the two have their own distinct approaches

the advance of socio-critical scholarship since the time of Brueggemann's contribution.[70] In the preface to the work, Habel states his purpose: "My volume identifies and analyzes six discrete land ideologies found in the Hebrew Scriptures. These ideologies are not reconstructions of historical movements in Israel, but positions that are promoted in the texts chosen for analysis. As such, they are the ideologies that have influenced readers of these texts over the centuries."[71]

In laying the foundation for the work, Habel addresses the common understanding of land in terms of physical reality but moves quickly to an alternative meaning of land, specifically land as a social construction or symbol. Rather than attempting to reconstruct the historical and social reality behind the texts which he has chosen, Habel seeks to mine "the specific set of beliefs the texts espouse and the corresponding social force of those beliefs as they are reflected within the rhetoric and wording of the texts."[72] Expressing doubt as to the feasibility of certainty regarding the specific historical audience, Habel concentrates on the literary power of the texts themselves.[73] Through the texts, Habel writes, one can gain a biblical ideology which refers to a wide "complex of images and ideas that may employ theological doctrines, traditions, or symbols to justify and promote the social, economic, and political interests of a group within society."[74]

to the investigation of the land theme.

70. Regarding his work, Habel states the following: "Although my analysis of these ideologies has intrinsic value as an academic exercise, the findings of this study should prove a useful resource for those who wish to explore the implications of biblical land ideologies for contemporary land issues and land claims." Ibid., xii.

71. Ibid.

72. Ibid., 5. Habel's disinterest in the particular land of Israel as manifested in the history of the Bible can be seen in the following statement: "I do not examine the text of the book of Joshua, for example, to ascertain its contribution to the discussion of how the Israelites emerged historically or socially as a people. Rather, my concern is to ascertain the set of beliefs located by a given literary complex that promulgates a social and political ideology of Israel. It is the ideology of that text, rather than the actual social history behind it, that has had, and continues to have, an influence on generations of readers of that text." Ibid., 5–6.

73. He writes, "We can only guess at the specific historical audience to which a given text may have been addressed at any particular stage of its development. Yet we can discern something of the ideas, doctrines, polemics, symbols, allusions—and, indeed, the ideologies—that are being promoted within the world of the text to the implied audience within the text." Ibid., 9.

74. Ibid., 10. The interrelated concept of biblical theology, according to Habel, is "the doctrine and discourse about God expressed within a biblical literary unit that reflect the

The various images, ideas, values, symbols in a particular text have the purpose of persuading "the implied audience within that text of the truth of a given ideology."[75] At the heart of the ideology is a struggle about land, either upholding the dominant group in a society or contesting the dominant group.[76] Ultimately, the ideology "is promoted in the biblical texts as 'the way things should be' in society, whether as nostalgia for the past, a justification of the status quo, a vision for the future, or an intricate combination of these."[77] The six main chapters of Habel's work examine the respective six land ideologies that he sees reflected in the OT.[78] Upon completing his examination, Habel offers the following conclusion: "[T]hese studies make it abundantly clear that there is no monolithic concept of land in the Hebrew Scriptures. There is, rather, a spectrum of land ideologies with diverse images and doctrines of land. These ideologies, moreover, are promoted by particular social groups with vested interests in promoting a given ideology to gain, regain, or maintain land."[79] Habel admits that in most of the ideologies, "the land of Canaan is depicted in appealing material terms as good, pleasant, and fertile, replete with grain fields, vineyards, and olive orchards."[80] The images, though, "go beyond these physical portraits to indicate the social and political relationships among YHWH, the land, and the people of the land."[81] In his investigation of the six themes Habel, then, is interested in the particular land territory of Israel in so far as it promotes a theology of land control and ownership.[82]

---

living faith of a given community." Ibid.

75. Ibid., 11.

76. Habel writes, "An ideology . . . incorporates the factor of contestation, the text being the literary product of the struggle. The purpose of the text is to persuade the thinking of that audience or, alternatively, to condemn the thinking of that audience as alien to the true ideology of the speaker in the text." Ibid., 11–12.

77. Ibid., 13.

78. The six discrete land theologies that Habel analyzes include 1) Land as the Source of Wealth: A Royal Ideology; 2) Land as a Conditional Grant: A Theocratic Ideology; 3) Land as Family Lots: An Ancestral Household Ideology; 5) Land as Sabbath Bound: An Agrarian Ideology; and 6) Land as Host Country: An Immigrant Ideology. For a summary of the six ideologies, see Habel's chart summary in *The Land is Mine*, 147–57.

79. Ibid., 148.

80. Ibid., 135.

81. Ibid.

82. He writes, "It also needs to be recognized that the doctrine of YHWH's promise of Canaan, which justifies Israel's entitlement to the land and which is common to all six ideologies, is not a theological axiom that stands alone. Rather, this doctrine is

P. W. L. Walker

In *Jesus and the Holy City: New Testament Perspectives on Jerusalem*, P. W. L. Walker analyzes the NT treatment of not only Jerusalem, but the territory of Israel and the physical temple.[83] The majority of the book (chs. 1–7) is an inductive survey of NT authors' distinct attitude towards the three interconnected entities of the city, temple, and in the case of Paul, John, and Hebrews, the land.[84] His conclusion is that the NT authors "came to view the city in a new way" and "in almost every instance there is evidence of some re-evaluation of Jerusalem's significance in the light of the coming of him whom they believed was the Messiah."[85] Mark, while emphasizing Jerusalem's pivotal role in the story of Jesus, gives no indications that there will be a physical replacement of the temple. Instead, he focuses on the identity of Jesus as Messiah and "that the significance that previously had been located in the Temple had now been transferred to him. *He* was the new Temple."[86] Matthew's gospel, possessing both positive and negative comments on Jerusalem and the temple, emphasizes the importance of the presence of God.[87] Regarding the temple, "Jesus himself must be identified personally with the 'one who dwells in it.'"[88] Regarding Jerusalem, it "has

appropriated and adapted by specific power groups who use it to promote their claims for control or ownership of all or parts of the land." Ibid., 143.

83. Walker, *Jesus and the Holy City*. At the outset, Walker acknowledges the historical debate on the issue of the land and Jerusalem. In earlier works, he examines the competing views of Eusebius and Cyril on the significance of land, Jerusalem, and other holy places. See Walker, *Holy City, Holy Places?*; Walker, "Gospel Sites and 'Holy Places,'" 89–108; Walker, "Jerusalem and the Holy Land in the Fourth Century," 22–34; and Walker, "Jerusalem in the Early Christian Centuries," 79–97.

84. The first seven chapters are concerned with the theologies of Mark, Matthew, Luke-Acts, Paul, John, Hebrews, and Revelation, respectively. Regarding the distinct attitudes of each writer and the benefit of examining each on his own terms, Walker writes, "Not unnaturally their different vantage-points result in our being presented with different 'landscapes' of the city. One of the fruits of our study is therefore a new appreciation of the rich diversity of the New Testament writings as each author sketches Jerusalem from his own distinctive angle. In the midst of this diversity, however, there is also a profound unity." Walker, *Jesus and the Holy City*, xii.

85. Ibid., xi.

86. Ibid., 24.

87. Regarding the positive and negative elements in Matthew, Walker writes, "In regard to his long-cherished commitments to Israel, the Temple and Jerusalem, Matthew pursued a policy both of affirmation and denial simultaneously, or (in his own terms) of seeking to balance the 'new' and the 'old' (*cf.* 13:52)." Ibid., 27.

88. Ibid., 31.

effectively, through the coming of Jesus, been left behind. Jesus is the new Zion."[89] Further, Jesus is the "true embodiment of Israel."[90] Walker quotes Davies approvingly: "there is in Matthew the awareness that the geographic dimensions of Jewish expectation . . . have been *shattered*."[91]

Walker also sees in Luke-Acts an emphasis on the temple, but the emphasis is on the fall of the temple which signifies a denial of any future status. In addition, the exodus theme is present, but in Luke-Acts the movement is away from land. Likewise, the city of Jerusalem was no longer a focus of God's plan: "Luke presented Jerusalem as a city which had mysteriously lost its destiny. The place which had been at the centre [sic] of God's purposes had missed its 'hour.'"[92] The city of Jerusalem and the land remain important in the ministry of Jesus and the Apostles, but only because of their history: "Jerusalem and the land are important as the scene of the beginning and they continue important [*sic*] to preserve the historical roots of the gospel and its continuity with the ministry of Jesus. But the gospel is not tied to them."[93] While there are both positive and negative strands regarding Jerusalem in Paul's theology, the period of coming judgment demanded a new theology.[94] Paul's new theology no longer had room for a physical place. Walker argues, "Paul's conversion-experience (which not coincidentally occurred away from Jerusalem) had instilled within him a whole new sense of what constituted the heart of God's purposes. Those

89. Ibid., 41. Additionally, Walker states, "Matthew's readers were not to hanker after a restoration of Jerusalem, a resumption of the previous *status quo* (or even something far better). Instead they were to focus upon Jesus, the one who through his death and resurrection had brought about the restoration predicted by Jeremiah and the prophets. God had now transferred onto Jesus the future restoration promises which previously had related to Jerusalem; no physical restoration of the city was therefore to be expected." Ibid., 47.

90. Ibid., 45.

91. Ibid., 54. Cf. Davies, *Gospel and the Land*, 242.

92. Walker, *Jesus and the Holy City*, 103. For Walker, Israel's rebellion and the judgment for that rebellion was the reason behind the change of focus from Jerusalem and the temple. He writes, "Jesus had pronounced judgement on the city, while simultaneously offering an alternative; but Jerusalem's response (culminating in Jesus' death) made the judgement all but inevitable. In Acts the issue became focused upon the Temple, the inner heart of the city; but when that institution endorsed its rejection of Jesus' apostles (thereby effectively rejecting Jesus a second time), all hope for both city and Temple finally disappeared." Ibid., 104.

93. Ibid., 104.

94. While references to Davies are present throughout Walker's analysis, his reliance on Davies is clearly evident in his section on Paul. See especially pages 116–19.

purposes were focused on Christ—the One who called those who were 'in him' to have a foretaste even now of the 'Jerusalem that is above'. The physical city of Jerusalem, for all its previous significance, could no longer serve as the centre [*sic*] of God's people. There was now a new centre [*sic*]—not Jerusalem, but Jesus."[95]

John highlights the theme of Jesus as a new tabernacle and temple, while de-emphasizing any particular focus on land.[96] The particularity had become universalized: "Despite the necessary focus upon Jerusalem, the ultimate direction of his [John] Gospel was outwards, and any particularities were subsumed in a comprehensive emphasis upon the universal implications of what had taken place in Palestine."[97] The author of Hebrews, according to Walker, argues that, since the OT tabernacle pointed to Christ, there are repercussions for the temple as well as Jerusalem and the land. Christians were faced with a conflict and had to make a choice. The writer of Hebrews made the choice clear: "Christian believers had a new calling—to identify with Jesus, not with Jerusalem."[98] In line with his Gospel, John's vision in the book of Revelation identified both the church and Jesus himself as the true temple (Rev 11:1–2 and 21:22, respectively). In addition, the biblical imagery previously associated with the earthly Jerusalem is applied to the heavenly city. According to Walker, "The focus on the earthly city has given way to a concentration on the eschatological new Jerusalem; this alone will prove the true fulfillment of the motifs in Old Testament prophecy concerning Jerusalem. . . . Christians, even if like John of a Jewish background, are not to look back nostalgically to the physical Jerusalem, but instead to look forward to the revelation of the new Jerusalem."[99]

The final three chapters of Walker's *Jesus and the Holy City* move beyond the distinct contributions of each NT writer to make some broader conclusions about the theology of the NT and the whole Bible. The

---

95. Ibid., 160.

96. Walker states, "John would not have accorded any ongoing significance to the Jerusalem of his own day. Not only had he played down Jerusalem's significance in the past; he had also given ample indication that Jesus' concentration on Jerusalem, while necessary in its time, was now eclipsed by the universal nature of his message. The Temple had been replaced and Jerusalem eclipsed." Ibid., 186.

97. Ibid., 199.

98. Ibid., 234.

99. Ibid., 262. Interestingly, Walker allows for a premillennial return of Christ but argues that this return has nothing to do with the physical city of Jerusalem. Ibid., 259–62.

transformation of Jerusalem (and, in extension, the temple and the land) as seen in the writers of the NT can be traced to Jesus, Walker argues. The theme of the whole NT is that the focus on the realia of Judaism has been replaced with a focus on Jesus:

> Christians' experience was now to be centred [*sic*] on Christ himself and their focus for the future was to be on the 'heavenly Jerusalem', not the 'Jerusalem below'. Moreover, when focusing on the return of Christ, those future expectations did not include some end-time rebuilding of the Temple or a 'restoration' of Jerusalem, precisely because in Jesus that Temple has been revealed and that restoration accomplished. Jerusalem therefore had lost its distinctively 'sacred' character—though for reasons of historical and religious association it would be forever 'special'. No other city had been so central in God's purposes, but those days were now past.[100]

In his final chapter, Walker utilizes the argument of 1 Peter as evidence that a proper biblical theology "requires that the Old Testament material be interpreted through the prism of the New," concluding that Peter is providing "a first-century example of how a biblical theology of Jerusalem might be developed."[101] For him, this means that Jerusalem, the temple, and the land, while having enduring historical and theological significance in the plan of God, have no enduring material geographical significance.

Gary M. Burge

A more recent contribution to the theme of land in Scripture is Gary Burge's *Jesus and the Land: The New Testament Challenge to "Holy Land" Theology*.[102] In the preface, after summarizing the claims of both Jews and Arabs to the land of Palestine, Burge states that the aim of the book is to investigate

100. Ibid., 308. This is an all-encompassing statement of Walker's view and argument in the work. He acknowledges the following two writers who previously argued along similar lines: Deyoung, *Jerusalem in the New Testament* and Beagley, 'Sitz im Leben'.

101. Walker, *Jesus and the Holy City*, 309. He writes further, "Although this denies to Jerusalem some of the significance associated with it both in the Old Testament and even by some today, the Jerusalem-theme is one of the vital interpretive keys for understanding the dynamic flow of the scriptural revelation." Ibid.

102. Burge, *Jesus and the Land*. Burge is known widely for his work on John [see Burge, *Anointed Community*; Burge, *Interpreting the Fourth Gospel*; and Burge, *Letters of John*. However, for many years prior to the writing of *Jesus and the Land*, Burge expressed interest in how Christians should understand the complex land crisis in the Middle East. See Burge, *Who are God's People in the Middle East?* and Burge, *Whose Land?*

the question of "how Christians should understand these competing land claims."[103] While the book is written primarily as a response to evangelical Christian Zionism, it is also a challenge to any theological system which affirms future territorial promises for ethnic Israel. Burge's appreciation for Brueggemann is expressed in the first words of the book: "Walter Brueggemann is correct when he suggests that *land* might be the central theme of biblical faith."[104] However, instead of focusing on Brueggemann's three trajectories of land promised, land possessed, and land lost as respective symbolic histories of land, Burge emphasizes the particular territory of land referenced throughout the OT: "The interest of the Old Testament . . . falls on one land, 'the land,' the 'promised land,' which is different from every other land. Ezekiel refers to it as the center of the earth (38.12) and Jerusalem as the center of this center (5.5). Hence in all of creation, this land is set apart, for as we shall see, God has unique purposes for it and will describe it as his own."[105]

In the opening chapters Burge offers a brief overview of the OT view of land and the view of land in extra-biblical writings, notably those of Philo and Josephus. He affirms the promise of a particular land to Abraham in Genesis 17:7–9 (cf. Gen 26:2–4; 28:13–15).[106] He writes, "The land is central to Jewish identity; the promise of the land is anchored to the covenant; and life in the land is contingent on upholding the righteousness expected by God."[107] The territorial feature of Jewish identity continued in Jewish writings until the NT.[108] However, in the diaspora, the affirmation of the territorial feature became less clear. Burge utilizes the writings of Philo and Josephus as evidence that "Judaism's 'Land Theology' has been

---

103. Burge, *Jesus and the Land*, xxi.

104. Ibid., 1.

105. Ibid.

106. Burge notes that four themes are clear in these passages: "(a) Abraham will receive land as an everlasting possession; (b) Abraham's posterity will become a great nation in this place; (c) this promise is directly tied to the covenant; and (d) all of the people of the earth will be blessed by this promise. This promise of land and progeny is held up in the Old Testament as a remarkable gift of grace to Abraham and his descendants." Ibid., 2.

107. Ibid., 11.

108. Here, Burge approvingly references Davies's *Gospel and the Land* and *Territorial Dimension of Judaism*, specifically Davies's discussion on the continuing presence of the land theme among rabbinical writers during the Hellenistic period, and Davies's point that possession of the land is contingent on obedience. Burge, *Jesus and the Land*, 10.

entirely redefined."[109] This redefinition, Burge writes, "will deeply influence the formation of Christian thinking in the New Testament."[110]

The later chapters of Burge's book develop the theme of his subtitle, that the NT challenges the belief that territorial promises remain unchanged after Jesus appears. As he works his way through the various parts of the NT, Burge argues that the heart of the challenge for a territorial theology is the NT's relative silence when it comes to the subject of land. Jesus, aware of the political environment into which he came, spoke of the land in veiled and nuanced ways in order to not "be drawn into the competing agendas of the activists of his day."[111] Nonetheless, Jesus acknowledged that Israel possessed a unique location and that "both Judea and its great city Jerusalem were sacred locales with unparalleled theological roles to play in history."[112] At the same time, Burge concludes that Jesus neither sustained nor advanced the territorial land theme: "Jesus is reticent with regard to debates about the land. He expresses no *overt* affirmation of first-century territorial theologies. He does not repeat Judaism's call to land ownership nor does he express criticism of the foreign occupation. He never elevates Jerusalem to such a degree that it becomes a focal point of Jewish nationalism. He even anchors his work in Galilee, a region looked upon with scorn by Judeans."[113] Burge understands Jesus as changing the meaning of land from that of the particular land of Israel which Jews had longed to possess to that of blessing that extends only to the poor and landless—hence Jesus' words in Matthew 5:5 that the meek or the gentle will inherit the earth.[114]

---

109. Burge, *Jesus and the Land*, 24. He writes, "In both Philo and Josephus the Jewish people now have become an esteemed cultural or religious 'nationality' in the Roman world." Ibid., 23.

110. Ibid., 24.

111. Ibid., 40.

112. Ibid.

113. Ibid.

114. Burge argues that the alteration of the meaning of land can be seen in seven passages: the meekness theme in Matt 5:5; the necessity of righteousness—and hence the judgment of Israel—in Luke 13:6–9 and Mark 11:12–14, 20–22 (Matt 21:18–19), respectively; God's ownership of the land and his prerogative as to who inhabits it in Mark 12:1–12 (Matt 21:33–46; Luke 20:9–19); the transformation of the land implied in Matt 19:28 (Luke 22:30); the preservationist instinct in Matt 25:14–30; and the foolishness of fighting over a temporal inheritance in Luke 12:13–20. It should be noted that Burge holds as tenuous the interpretation that in the parable of the talents in Matt 25:14–30, Jesus is rebuking the Jewish instinct to place hope in the possession of the land. He writes, "Such an interpretation is far from certain since it requires an allegorizing of the story

Burge does not hide his fondness of Brueggemann's "scandal" of the land/ landless theme. He approvingly writes, "Those who possess the most and who have the most to lose by a revision of Jewish territorialism resist Jesus forcefully. Jesus in this respect is the great 'rearranger' of the land."[115]

Although echoing and reinforcing the synoptic portrayal of Jesus' relationship to the land, John's gospel, according to Burge, develops the theme of land fulfillment in Christ: "For John, the importance of location is how it serves to reveal the identity of Jesus."[116] Burge recognizes, and even affirms, that materiality is important in John's narrative. However, the materiality within the narrative is symbolic for deeper spiritual meaning.[117] Christ's incarnation has altered the religious system of Judaism.[118] Burge calls John's theological agenda a "messianic replacement (or fulfillment) motif."[119] Instead of the temple, Christ becomes the holy *place* where worship should take place.[120] Burge writes, "*Divine space is now no longer located in a place but in a person.*"[121] In the metaphor of the vine and vinedresser (John 15:1–

that is foreign and arbitrary to the story itself. This may be an innocent account of a man putting money in the ground." Ibid., 39.

115. Ibid., 41. Continuing his affirmation of Brueggemann, specifically that, contra Davies, the theme of land that is so prevalent in the OT continues to be a theme in the NT, Burge writes, "The land itself presented Israel with a devastating challenge to faith. One could *grasp with courage* or one could *wait in confidence* for the gift of land. One could seize the land or one could wait for land." Ibid.

116. Ibid. 44.

117. He writes, "The land . . . exists as a means to another end. Without denying the realities of Jesus' historical life and ministry, John invites locations to evolve into iconic placeholders that bear more meaning than the characters in the story could know." Ibid., 45. Burge also notes Davies in his affirmation that John's gospel is laden with the materiality inherent in Judaism.

118. Burge states, "John views the incarnation not simply as a revelation of light to the world (1.9), although this is vital. John also views the incarnation as having a vital impact on the established religious systems of first-century Judaism." Ibid., 46.

119. Ibid.

120. Ibid., 51. Burge writes, "John understands the deep Jewish commitment to holy space. And the Temple was the premier example of this. However, this is where John's own Christology enters the picture. In Christ, the Temple had been eclipsed. In Christ, the holiest of all Judaism's places had found their fulfillment." Ibid., 52. Burge's understanding of the Temple is in line with that of Beale, *Temple and the Church's Mission* and Perrin, *Jesus and the Temple*. In another work, Burge states, "Christ brought an eschatological fulfillment to Jewish Temple practice and for the early church, there was no going back. I have simply taken this deep trajectory of the NT and applied it to the Land." Burge, "Rejoinder to Boyd Luter," 77.

121. Burge, *Jesus and the Land*, 52.

6), Burge sees "the Fourth Gospel's most profound theological relocation of Israel's 'holy space.'"[122] Jesus himself, for Burge, is the spiritualization of the land: "In John 15 we are given a completely new metaphor: God the vine-dresser now has one vine growing in his vineyard. And the only means of attachment to the land is through this one vine, Jesus Christ. . . . The Fourth Gospel is transferring spatial, earthbound gifts from God and connecting them to a living person, Jesus Christ. . . . He alone is the way to God's Holy Space, to God's Holy Land. 'The way' is not territorial. It is spiritual. It is to be in the Father's presence (John 14.1–11)."[123] God's people should no longer be concerned with material land or place, or festivals and institutions for that matter, as a source of life or hope in the future. Christ has become "the new avenue to God, the unexpected nexus between the Father and his people, the exclusive place of revelation and glory."[124]

In subsequent chapters Burge argues that the book of Acts, Paul's letters, the book of Hebrews, and Revelation, respectively, are relatively silent on the issue of territory and, therefore, uphold the replacement/fulfillment motif demonstrated in the gospels.[125] In a separate essay, Burge summarizes the effect of the NT on territorial theology: "_Simply put: Christian identity could abandon an allegiance to 'the Holy Land theology' because God's arena for work and revelation was now the entire world._"[126] In light of his conclu-

---

122. Ibid., 53. He further describes John 15 as "a careful critique of the territorial religion of Judaism." Ibid. 56.

123. Ibid., 55.

124. Ibid., 57. Burge goes on to suggest that among John's earliest hearers/readers there were few who possessed a territorial theology and that the lack of a territorial theology explains why the early community consisting of Jews and Gentiles had neither need nor desire to live in the land and had no reason to fight for the land in AD 66–70 or during the Bar Kokhba rebellion of AD 132–35. Ibid.

125. Regarding Acts, Burge concludes, "Thoughtful Christians in the early Church—Luke, Stephen, Paul among them—were formed by the Diaspora and were reflecting on the extra-territorial dimensions of God's new work." Ibid., 71. One example Burge highlights is the ethnically diverse church in Syrian Antioch. In his letters, Paul "moved away from ethnicity and regionalism and focused on personal appropriation of faith and attachment to Christ . . . Paul _inevitably_ had to abandon a Christian commitment to Jewish territorialism." Ibid., 92. Burge, however, affirms that in Rom 9–11 Paul has in mind ethnic Jews when he looks forward to a future hope, only in reference to salvation and not to territorial promises. Ibid., 87–91. The writer of Hebrews, through the images of the city of God, a better country than Abraham could possess, and rest, counters a territorial theology while John's vision as recorded in Revelation is concerned "for the world, not the land, and what God has determined to do for it." Ibid., 109.

126. Burge, "Rejoinder to Boyd Luter," 77.

sions about the demise of the territorial feature in the NT, Burge devotes the majority of the final chapter of *Jesus and the Land* to a critique of Christian Zionism, especially the territorial dimension present in its theology.[127]

The Physical Land of Israel as Metaphor

As the previous survey demonstrates, it is common to view the physical territory promised to Israel as a metaphor for something other than that territory, something that is perceived as greater and more far-reaching. While divergent positions regarding the land can be seen in the above survey, and while not all of the theologians surveyed would be comfortable describing their conception as a metaphor, each would argue that in the NT the land comes to have an entirely different meaning.[128] While this meaning is believed to have importance for Christians, the importance has nothing to do with a restoration of the particular geographical territory promised to Israel.

The common practice of understanding the particular land promised to Israel as a metaphor is evident in a variety of other studies not covered above. Colin Chapman's *Whose Promised Land?* interprets the fulfillment of land prophecies in a metaphorical manner.[129] His argument against a literal fulfillment of the land promise is most apparent in part three which is entitled "The Land Before and After Jesus Christ." The implication in the title is that a definite change takes place through the person of Jesus regarding the interpretation of the land. He states his conclusion without equivocation:

> [T]he New Testament writers showed no interest in a literal interpretation. Since they were silent about the future of the land and at the same time interpreted the concept of the land in the light of Jesus and his kingdom, they must have believed that this was

127. Luter argues that Burge wrongly implies that those who see biblical significance in the modern state of Israel are, necessarily, Christian Zionists. See Luter, "Review of Gary M. Burge," 217–20.

128. Regarding the positions of Davies and Brueggemann, for example, Lilburne writes that they "agree that the issue of land must be pursued in relation to the New Testament texts, but their opinions diverge sharply as to how that should be done and what results may be drawn from the inquiry. Brueggemann turns to a 'land hermeneutic,' while Davies offers a 'Christocentric reading.'" Lilburne, *A Sense of Place*, 65–66. He then proceeds to describe both positions in metaphorical terms. Ibid., 66–70.

129. Chapman, *Whose Promised Land?*

the only possible interpretation of the significance of the land for the Christian, whether Jew or Gentile. Once the New Testament writers had seen the significance of the land and the nation in the context of the kingdom of God which had come into being in Jesus of Nazareth, they ceased to look forward to a literal fulfillment of Old Testament prophecies of a return to the land and a restored Jewish state. The one and only fulfillment of all the promises and prophecies was already there before their eyes in the person of Jesus. The way they interpreted the Old Testament must be the norm for the Christian interpretation of the Old Testament today.[130]

In his brief work, *A Sense of Place: A Christian Theology of the Land*, Geoffrey Lilburne argues against spiritualizing the particular land of the OT so that the land becomes an abstract concept.[131] Lilburne argues that the theme of land is developed eschatologically through the OT.[132] The de-

130. Ibid., 153. Chapman writes further, "[The] land was intended to the be the scene of God's gradual revelation of himself, which would lead eventually to the coming of Jesus, and so to blessing for all peoples of the world. Since the New Testament speaks of all followers of Jesus as 'Abrahams seed and heirs according to the promise' (Galatians 3:29), it must mean that all four aspects of the covenant—the land, the nation, the covenant relationship between God and his people, and the blessing for all peoples of the world—find their fulfillment in Jesus and in those who put their faith in him." Ibid., 226. Chapman also has pointed words regarding interpreting the contemporary state of Israel as fulfillment of prophecy: "[F]or Christians to interpret these events simply as the fulfillment of prophecy represents a kind of regression. It is a return to a way of thinking which the disciples abandoned once for all when they grasped the kind of kingdom that Jesus had inaugurated through his death and resurrection. Instead of helping the Jew to come nearer to believing in Jesus as the Messiah, it may have the opposite effect and harden him in his unbelief." Ibid., 227.

131. Interestingly, in describing Brueggemann's position on the land, Lilburne writes, "By seeing the land as a metaphor for political realities and by using it as a hermeneutical concept for interpreting the New Testament, Brueggemann comes close to turning land into an abstract principle. In his concern to avoid theological spiritualization he runs the risk of a hermeneutical spiritualization. In doing this, Brueggemann passes over the concrete center of the New Testament witness and an important continuity between the two Testaments." Lilburne, *A Sense of Place*, 66–67.

132. Lilburne states that in the development of the theme of land through the OT, "we see the spiritual genius of the Hebrew people. The stress upon the landed experience of preexilic Israel is a way of proclaiming that the notion of the eternal inheritance still has power and effect. All these traditions, of covenant and creation, speak of the free gift of land to Yahweh's covenant partner, Israel and this is now understood eschatologically. The language is kept alive, even as it is transformed into a new language of hope and promise for the future. In the new language of apocalyptic land is again seen as gift, the arena for divine holy intervention and transformation. Standing over against the experiences of land loss, of dispossession, this language asserts the reality of God's rule and the

velopment leads to the incarnation of Christ who fulfills the land promise in his bodily existence.[133] Lilburn writes, "The presence of God's kingdom can mean no less than that the blessings of the promised land find their fulfillment in Jesus Christ. . . . all the blessings associated with land—security, peace, and plenty in the presence of God—are now directly connected with the presence of Jesus Christ. In other words, in Jesus Christ all the promises of God come to their fulfillment. . . . All the expectation for holy space, for the blessings of the land, are concentrated in Jesus Christ."[134] Lilburne concludes that understanding the fulfillment of the land promise as the incarnation of Christ avoids spiritualization: "The christification of holy space does not in any way spiritualize or dilute the concrete focus of Israel's hopes. On the contrary, it provides them with an even more concrete locus, namely the body of Christ, understood first in terms of the earthly presence of Jesus but second as the designation for the Christian community."[135] Ultimately, however, the particular land of Israel in its materiality is a metaphor for the particular person of Christ in his materiality and, therefore, the fulfillment of the land promise can still be understood as metaphorical.

O. Palmer Robertson, relying considerably on the work of both Davies and Walker, argues that "any transfer from the old covenant to the new covenant involves a movement from shadow to reality."[136] Specifically regarding the land, he states, "The land of the Bible served in a typological role as a model of the consummate realization of the purposes of God for his redeemed people that encompasses the whole of the cosmos. Because of the inherently limited scope of the land of the Bible, it is not to be regarded

---

closeness of God's intervention to restore God's own people to their heritage." Ibid., 53.

133. For Lilburne, "the engagement of the God of the Hebrews with the space and time of their history in the land comes to a fitting climax in the entry of that God into space and time in the person of Jesus Christ." Ibid., 54. In discussing the concept of the kingdom of God, he states that "just as the kingdom had a present and a future reference, so the location of the kingdom had both an immediate and a more distant location. Just as the kingdom is exclusively related to the presence of Jesus Christ in both its present and its future modalities, so in its spatial implications the kingdom was to center in the very flesh of Jesus." Ibid., 101.

134. Ibid., 103.

135. Ibid.

136. Robertson, *Israel of God*, 25. Robertson writes, "The old covenant appealed to the human longing for a sure and settled land; yet it could not compare with the realities of the new covenant fulfillment." Ibid. Elsewhere he describes the "move" as a shift "from type to reality; from shadow to substance." Ibid., 30–31. Cf. Robertson, "Land of the Bible," 109–32.

as having continuing significance in the realm of redemption other than its function as a teaching model."[137] The reality of the land, according to Robertson, must be understood in light of "the newly recreated cosmos."[138] In a process of universalization, "the land has expanded to encompass the whole world."[139] So, for Robertson, in the case of the land, the shadow seems to be the particular territory of Israel and the reality is the whole earth.

In addition to his distinct work on the topic of land, P. W. L. Walker was involved in three additional works consisting of essays on the topics of Jerusalem and the land: *Jerusalem Past and Present in the Purposes of God* (1994); *The Land of Promise: Biblical, Theological, and Contemporary Perspectives* (2000); and *The Gospel and the Land of Promise: Christian Approaches to the Land of the Bible* (2011).[140] The respective studies are born out of their distinct contexts and pose their own distinct questions.[141] However, in each work, the majority view is that the land promised has been fulfilled in either an inaugurated or complete manner in the person and work of Christ. Ultimately, the focus is not on physical land, but on a universal vision that involves the whole earth (a particular geographical territory is metaphorical for the universal cosmos) and rest with God in the new creation.

William Dumbrell's eschatological vision includes a metaphorical understanding of the particular land of the OT.[142] In his discussion of the promised land in Deuteronomy, for example, he concludes that the intimate relationship between land and rest in the book finds its place in the NT in "the notions of a heavenly Canaan and a heavenly Jerusalem. . . . the people

---

137. Robertson, *Israel of God*, 194.

138. Ibid., 26. Examples of Robertson's argument include Paul's language regarding Abraham being the heir of the "world" (Rom 4:13), the earth groaning in travail (Rom 8:22–23), and Jesus' words regarding the meek inheriting the earth (Matt 5:5). Ibid.

139. Ibid., 31.

140. Walker, *Jerusalem Past and Present*; Johnston and Walker, *Land of Promise*; Church et al., *Gospel and the Land*.

141. For example, Johnston and Walker, *Land of Promise* is a collection of essays from the annual conference of the Tyndale Fellowship Biblical Theology Study Group (1999) and the majority of the essays in Church, et al, *Gospel and the Land* originated from a one-day colloquim at the Laidlaw-Carey Graduate School in Auckland, New Zealand (July 9, 2009). The primary concern of *The Land of Promise* and again in *Gospel and the Land* is to repudiate the "Christian Zionism" of dispensationalism and to show that the physical land promise has been fulfilled in Christ.

142. Dumbrell, *Search for Order*.

of God must worship God continually in the place of *God's* appointment, finally fulfilling the role projected for Israel in Canaan."[143]

In his *From Eden to the New Jerusalem*, T. D. Alexander emphasizes divine presence as a major subject of the Bible moving from Eden, echoed in the tabernacle and the temple, and fulfilled in the person of Jesus who tabernacles among his people (John 1:14).[144] In the movement from the OT to the NT, "the theocracy of Israel is replaced by the kingdom of God, which is inaugurated through the coming of Jesus."[145] The kingdom that the NT describes "is not restricted by national boundaries, but is gradually expanding to fill the whole earth."[146] Ultimately, Alexander concludes, the "international dimension" of the fulfillment of God's promise to Abraham "looks beyond the merely national dimension associated with Israel/Judah in the Old Testament and anticipates something that will have universal significance: the creation of the church and ultimately the New Jerusalem."[147]

While Craig Bartholomew focuses less on the particular land of Israel in his argument for a Christian view of place, he also employs a metaphorical approach in articulating his understanding of the fulfillment of the OT

---

143. Ibid., 55. Dumbrell states that in light of the NT fulfillment of the rest, "Israel did not surrender the theology of the Promised Land. . . . Since the ideal of Eden recaptured, which the Old Testament theology of the Promised Land incorporates, is integral to the divine purpose for the people of God, the hope could not be surrendered." Ibid., 54-55. He also concludes, "The advent of the New Jerusalem [in Rev 21] fulfils the eschatological expectation associated with Zion in the Old Testament—that of the world united in redemption and of the saved community as the one new people of God undivided by the consequences of Genesis 3-11. That God will henceforth permanently dwell in the midst of his people (Rev. 21:3) also fulfils the temple theology of both Testaments." Ibid., 344.

144. Alexander, *From Eden to New Jerusalem*. Alexander argues that "the New Jerusalem of Revelation 21—22 represents the fulfilment [sic] of God's original blueprint for the earth. From the outset of creation, God intended that the earth would become a holy garden-city in which he would dwell alongside human beings. . . In the process of recovering the earth as his dwelling place, God progressively established the tabernacle, the Jerusalem temple and the church. In differing ways each of these functioned as a model resembling God's ultimate ambition for the world. Additionally, all three herald new stages in the process by which God himself gradually begins to inhabit the earth." Ibid., 74. Alexander's understanding of the fulfilment [sic] of the land promises also can be seen in his treatment on the major themes of the Pentateuch in *Paradise to Promised Land*, especially in the sections on the application to the NT (e.g., 171-72), and in his brief essay "Beyond Borders," 35-50.

145. Ibid., 89.

146. Ibid., 96.

147. Ibid., 190.

territorial promise.[148] Though not a focused study on the theme of land, Gentry and Wellum's work *Kingdom through Covenant: A Biblical-Theological Understanding of the Covenants*, addresses the land theme in light of the overall argument of the book.[149] The authors attempt an alternative to covenant theology and dispensationalism termed "progressive covenantalism."[150] They argue that covenant theologians and dispensationalists, respectively, fail to do justice to the fulfillment of the Abrahamic covenant which takes place in Christ. The bulk of their argument comes in the explanations of six covenants: Adamic, Noahic, Abrahamic, Mosaic, Davidic, and New. The Adamic typology within the covenants finds its apex in the New Covenant in which certain expectations of the previous covenants are transcended or "fulfilled." Gentry and Wellum argue that the land "functions as a type/pattern in the Old Testament context" and "cannot be understood apart from a backward and forward look: backward to the archetype reality of Eden and the entire creation, and forward, through the covenants, to its antitypical fulfilment [*sic*] in the new creation that Jesus has inaugurated in the new covenant."[151] They go on to state their view of the land even more clearly:

148. Bartholomew, *Where Mortals Dwell*. Bartholomew's understanding of the move from the particular to the universal comes out, for example, in his understanding of the kingdom of God in the NT. He writes that "the universal perspective of the kingdom is precisely what gives poignance and density to the local and the particular." Ibid., 117. Then, affirming Bauckham, he writes, "I would say for a theology of place, we need a hermeneutic of the kingdom which does justice to its particularity and universality. Such a hermeneutic will take account of 1. the temporal movement of the biblical story from creation through fall to redemption and consummation; 2. the placial movement of the biblical story from 'one place to every place, from the center to the periphery, from Jerusalem to the ends of the earth.'" Ibid. Bartholomew's quote of Bauckham is from Bauckham, *Bible and Mission*, 14. Bartholomew's conception can also be seen in Goheen and Bartholomew, *Drama of Scripture*.

149. Gentry and Wellum, *Kingdom through Covenant*. For their application of the kingdom through covenant idea to the land theme, see especially pages 703–16. While it is a section on Eschatology, the authors focus primarily on the concept of land.

150. Ibid., 24. Gentry and Wellum also call it "a species of 'new covenant theology.'" By these terms, they stress two points: "First, it is a *via media* between dispensational and covenant theology. It neither completely fits nor totally disagrees with either system. Second, it stresses the *unity* of God's plan which is discovered as we trace God's redemptive work through the biblical covenants." Ibid.

151. Ibid., 607. Arguing against Kaiser's view [see Kaiser, "Israel and Its Land," 249], Gentry and Wellum state "that there are exegetical grounds both in the immediate context and across the entire Canon to argue that the 'land' was never intended by the biblical authors to be understood *merely* within the limited confines of specific geographical boundaries. In other words, 'land,' when placed within the biblical covenants and viewed

> In the New Testament, it is our contention that the land promise does not find its fulfillment in the future in terms of a specific piece of real estate given to the ethnic nation of Israel; rather it is fulfilled in Jesus, who is the true Israel and the last Adam, who by his triumphant work wins for us the new creation. That new creation has "already" arrived in the dawning of the new covenant in individual Christians (2 Cor. 5:17; Eph. 2:8–10) and the church (Eph. 2:11–21) and it will be consummated when Christ returns and ushers in the new creation in its fullness (Revelation 21–22).[152]

According to Gentry and Wellum, the move to the new creation which is fulfilled in Christ excludes any promise for "a specific piece of land given to national Israel."[153]

Oren Rhea Martin's work *Bound for the Promised Land* offers a canonical interpretation of the land.[154] Martin's framework for understanding the land is the kingdom of God. Tracing the theme of land as it unfolds across the canon, Martin notes the partial and preparatory fulfillment of the land promise resulting from Israel's repeated covenant failure. The promise of something fuller, greater, and permanent is anticipated in the prophets. This fulfillment, Martin argues, is inaugurated in the person and

diachronically, was intended by God to function as a 'type' or 'pattern' of something greater, i.e., creation, which is precisely how it is understood in light of the coming of Christ and the inauguration of the new covenant." Gentry and Wellum, *Kingdom through Covenant*, 706.

152. Gentry and Wellum, *Kingdom through Covenant*, 607. It has been noted by several that, while the book is presented as a whole-Bible theology, there is a noticeable lack of extended interaction with and discussion of NT passages, especially those which demand explanation in light of the authors proposed metanarrative. Examples of such a critique include Bock, "Kingdom through Covenant: A Review,"; Moo, "Kingdom through Covenant: A Review,"; and Vlach, "Have They Found a Better Way?" The issue was also addressed at the Dispensational Study Group meeting at the Evangelical Theological Society in San Diego, 2014: "A Review of *Kingdom Through Covenant: A Biblical Understanding of the Covenants* by Peter Gentry and Stephen Wellum," San Diego, California, November 19–21, 2014. The session included critiques by Craig Blaising, Michael A. Grisanti, and Darryl Bock, and a rejoinder by Gentry and Wellum.

153. Gentry and Wellum, *Kingdom through Covenant*, 714.

154. Martin, *Bound for the Promised Land*. The work is a revision of Martin's dissertation entitled "Bound for the Kingdom." Just before the completion of Martin's dissertation, Gentry and Wellum's *Kingdom through Covenant* was published. Martin states, "While this dissertation is in substantial agreement with *Kingdom through Covenant*, it aims to go in much greater depth by restricting its focus to the theme of land." Martin, "Bound for the Kingdom," 15.

work of Christ. For Martin, the land becomes a symbol for all of the blessings received by those who are united to Christ.[155]

At least two dissertations have been written in the last few decades on the theme of land. William Blanchard's "Changing Hermeneutical Perspectives on 'The Land' in Biblical Theology" examines the hermeneutical shift that takes place from the OT to the NT in regards to the de-emphasis of the land.[156] After identifying six factors that explain why early Christians abandoned the territorial dimension of Judaism, Blanchard concludes that the hermeneutical shift that he has outlined is a legitimate one.[157] The "complex matrix" of factors "prepared the way for the earliest Christians (Jews themselves!) to accept a faith that was not restricted to The Land and its structures but which, at the same time, was firmly rooted in basic tenants of the Old Testament faith."[158] The acceptance was valid, Blanchard argues, because holy space, typified by the land in the OT, is fulfilled in the person of Christ.[159]

Joon-Sik Kim's dissertation is concerned with the interpretation of land in the Gospel of Matthew.[160] Dating the book from 80-90 C.E., Kim argues that the Matthean community was struggling to find itself in light of its relationship to Judaism and the Gentile mission. One of the viable elements from the transitioning community's past was that of the particular

155. Martin concludes, "People enter God's rest through faith in the true and greater Son, Jesus Christ, and look for a better country. Though Old Testament believers looked through the land of promise to God's greater eschatological rest and city, by virtue of Christ and his work, new covenant believers now look to Jesus and confidently await their arrival in the new Jerusalem, homeland, unshakable kingdom, and abiding city that is to come, which is described in the letters of Peter and Revelation as the new heaven and new earth. In short, the land, which served as a type of this greater reality, now reaches its *telos*. And the covenant relationship for which we were created is realized in the new heaven and new earth, where our glorious triune God will dwell with us, and we will be his people, and God himself will be with us as our God (Rev. 21:3)." Martin, *Bound for the Promised Land*, 159.

156. Blanchard, "Changing Hermeneutical Perspectives."

157. The six factors served as a "complex matrix" which provided the environment in which the transformation of the land took place. They include 1) the terror of the exile; 2) the emergence of synagogue worship; 3) the dispersion; 4) Hellenistic and Roman influences; 5) the Christifying of space; and 6) the universal and expanding nature of the Christian movement. Ibid., 57–88.

158. Ibid., 88.

159. In his explanation of "Christifying space" Blanchard acknowledges his approval of and reliance upon Davies's *Gospel and the Land*. Ibid., 80–82.

160. Kim, " 'Your Kingdom Come on Earth.' "

land that was promised to Israel. Matthew, Kim argues, shows little concern for the loss of land after 70 C.E., distancing himself from the question of the fulfillment of the promised land. According to Kim, Matthew understands the loss of the land as God's judgment upon Israel for its rejection of Christ. Ultimately, Kim argues, Matthew reinterprets the promise of a particular land as a symbol or metaphor for the kingdom of God. In addition, he argues that Matthew presents Christ as the realized fulfillment of the OT promise of land.

The metaphorical approach also can be seen in broader works on OT theology. While he does not discuss the nature of land fulfillment in depth, Bernhard Anderson seems to argue for a metaphorical view. In universalizing the narrative of Israel's history through theological concepts that transcend Israel's historical situation and speak to man's relationship to God, he leaves no room for the land.[161] In his OT theology, Bruce Waltke also employs a metaphorical approach to understanding the land.[162] He argues "that the New Testament redefines the Land in three ways: first, *spiritually*, as a reference to Christ's person; second, *transcendentally*, as a reference to heavenly Jerusalem; and third, *eschatologically*, as a reference to the new Jerusalem after Christ's second coming."[163] He proceeds to explain his use of the term "redefine" as meaning "that whereas 'Land' in the Old Testament refers to Israel's life in Canaan, in the New Testament 'Land' is transmuted to refer to life in Christ."[164] In Christ, Waltke claims, the land promise is *literally* fulfilled.[165] Waltke even utilizes the term metaphor for his understanding: "the promise that Israel will inherit a land flowing with milk and honey becomes a metaphor for the milk and honey of life in Christ,

---

161. Anderson, *Understanding the Old Testament*. C.f., Anderson, "Biblical Theology," 292–306; and Anderson, *Creation to New Creation*.

162. Waltke, *Old Testament Theology*. Waltke devotes three chapters to the gift of land in Joshua, the OT, and the NT, respectively (512–87).

163. Ibid., 560.

164. Ibid. Waltke utilizes an odd analogy: "[T]he New Testament skins like a banana the Old Testament references to the Land as real estate in order to expose its spiritual food." Ibid. The result is a "redefinition of holy space from a reference to holy geopolitical territory to the holy body of the incarnate Son of God and those baptized into Christ, and to the eschaton that uniquely unites territory and the Spirit." Ibid., 576.

165. Waltke writes, "Old Testament promises and prophecies regarding the essentials of the gospel of Jesus of Nazareth—his life, death, and resurrection—necessarily find their literal fulfillment in the Land." Ibid., 584 (cf. 563–65).

a participation in heaven itself and in a world that is beyond what saints could imagine or think."[166]

Ari Leder's recent work, while not a theology of the entire OT, moves beyond the Pentateuch to offer a theology for the church that sees the land as metaphorical for God's presence.[167] He argues that in the Pentateuch the presence of God is primary over land ownership: "As a whole . . . the Pentateuch declares to God's people of every generation that the presence of God *already* is, but that the land is *not yet*, a present reality."[168] For Leder the land is symbolic for God's presence, or at least being in a right place to anticipate God's presence.[169]

Elmer Martens concludes that the central theme in the OT is God's "design" or "purpose."[170] God's design, he argues, consists of four parts, one of which is the land.[171] While Martens claims that the land "is more than acreage or territory," he warns against spiritualizing it so as to make it an "ethereal thing."[172] Yet, in tracing the theme throughout Israel's history, Martens makes the turf and soil of the physical land a metaphor for something that transcends that physical land—abundant life or, as Martens states, "a high quality of life defined biblically."[173]

166. Ibid., 586.

167. Leder, *Waiting for the Land.*

168. Ibid., 196.

169. Leder states, "The entire biblical narrative . . . develops the problem of humanity's refusal of divine instruction and exile from the presence of God and emplots [sic] a sequence of events, complications, and conflicts that brings about life in God's presence again." Ibid., 25. He writes further, "The Pentateuch moves the reader from the expulsion from one place to the waiting for entry into another. . . . by the end of the Pentateuch Israel is in a place that anticipates the land: the camp where she enjoys the *reality* of God's presence." Ibid., 28–29. Leder terms his understanding as "desert theology" which concludes "this world is not the church's home, . . . she is waiting for the fullness of Christ's presence and the descent of the heavenly Jerusalem." Ibid., 210.

170. Martens, *God's Design.*

171. The three other parts include 1) salvation/deliverance, 2) covenant community, and 3) knowing/experiencing God.

172. Martens, *God's Design*, 136.

173. Ibid., 236. Martens writes, "The relationship of 'life' to land and wisdom materials is not at first obvious. Land is turf, but very early it acquires a symbolic meaning. For Israel land is the promised land, the good land, and as such is symbolic of a rich quality of life. To be in the land is to be the recipient of the blessings of God. For the land is a 'land flowing with milk and honey' (Deut 26:9), a land with blessings of security, a land free from molestation, and above all a land with the blessing of God's presence. It is almost axiomatic that the prospect of dwelling in the land involved more than substituting

Although NT theologies have not been as concerned with the land promise (perhaps because the NT refers to land much less than the OT), G. K. Beale, in his recent NT theology posits that the land promise receives inaugural fulfillment in a spiritual sense and then is ultimately fulfilled in a physical new heaven and new earth.[174] Beale writes, "All the explicit references to Israel's promised land in the NT refer in various ways to the final consummation of these promises in a new cosmos."[175] Still, he believes that in Christ and in the church, the land promises are even now beginning to be fulfilled.[176]

New Creationists and the Land

The view that the land promise should be interpreted metaphorically can be seen in various degrees and nuances among new creationists. As noted in chapter 1, Anthony Hoekema seems to be the forerunner for contemporary evangelical affirmations of new creation eschatology. Hoekema ultimately views the territory of Israel as a metaphor for the entire earth. He understands the "widening of the scope of the [Abrahamic] covenant" as a movement from the particular to the universal.[177] According to Hoekema,

---

a Palestinian address for an Egyptian address. At stake was the quality of life, so that the word 'I will bring you into the land' is only partially fulfilled when the people pass through the Jordan and set foot on the land." Ibid., 217-18. He also states that by the post-exilic period, the land was viewed by Israel as "a cipher for a gift, a promise, a blessing, a lifestyle, and even revelation." Ibid., 305. Still, it should be noted that Martens seems to leave open the possibility that the particular territory of Israel may figure into the future of Jewish history. Ibid., 313.

174. Beale, *New Testament Biblical Theology*, 751. Earlier development of Beale's new creationism can be seen in his "Eschatological Conception," 11-52; "New Testament and New Creation," 53-65; "Eden, the Temple, and the Church's Mission," 5-31; and more fully in *Temple and the Church's Mission*. Beale's conception also can be seen in the recent work which he co-authored with Mitchell Kim, *God Dwells Among Us*.

175. Ibid., 756. Elaborating on Waltke's view, Beale concludes that "the land was a type of the new creation in that its true design was for Israel (as a corporate Adam) to be faithful and expand the land's borders to encompass the whole earth. Since Israel failed in this, its old land still pointed to this unfulfilled universal consummated expansion into a new creation at some point in the future." Ibid., 769.

176. Ibid., 769-70.

177. Hoekema, *Bible and the Future*, 278. He writes, "In the matter of the inheritance of the land, we have a similar situation: a temporary narrowing of the promise is followed by a later widening. In other words, just as the people of God in the Old Testament era were restricted mostly to Israelites but in the New Testament era are gathered from all

the "sabbath rest" in Hebrews 4 for which the earthly land of Canaan was a type points to the new earth which is to come.[178] In a similar manner new creationists have understood the fulfillment of the promise of the territory of Israel as a metaphor for something other than its original referent.

N. T. Wright believes that Jesus embodies Yahweh's return to Zion.[179] One of the implications of this embodiment is the beginning of a new history. Jesus "is the climax of Israel's history and the launch of a new history."[180] Further, he states that when one properly understands the resurrection of Christ, he sees "that Israel's history is full of partial and preparatory analogies for this moment."[181] Once the resurrection of Jesus has occurred, "the entire story of God and Israel, and God and the world, must be told in a new way."[182] In this new telling of the story, the element of the particular land of Israel is expanded to include the entire earth.[183] The promises, including that of a particular territory, which were made to Abraham, Moses, David, and the prophets turn out to be "promises not only for Israel but also

---

the nations, so in Old Testament times the inheritance of the land was limited to Canaan, whereas in New Testament times the inheritance is expanded to include the entire earth." Ibid. In his argument toward universalization of the promise of land, Hoekema utilizes passages such as Ps 37:11; Matt 5:5; and Rom 4:13. Ibid., 281.

178. Ibid., 279.

179. An example of Wright's argument can be seen in his interpretation of the parable of the talents which he calls "a key explanatory riddle" for understanding Yahweh's return to Zion in the person of Jesus. For an analysis of Wright's treatment see James, "Has Yahweh Come to Zion?."

180. Wright, *Surprised by Hope*, 71.

181. Ibid. Wright notes that "Luke insists that since Jesus really was raised from the dead, the ancient scriptures of Israel must be read as a story that reaches its climax in Jesus and will then produce its proper fruit not only in Israel but also in Jesus's followers and, through them, in all the world." Ibid., 237. Wright's use of "climax" here is used to suggest that the promises and prophecies are fulfilled in Jesus and therefore take on new meaning.

182. Ibid., 236. Wright states, "The resurrection isn't just a surprise happy ending for one person; it is instead the turning point for everything else. It is the point at which all the old promises come true at last: the promises of David's unshakable kingdom; the promises of Israel's return from the greatest exile of them all; and behind that again, quite explicit in Matthew, Luke, and John, the promise that all the nations will now be blessed through the seed of Abraham." Ibid.

183. Wright stops short of completely separating the new story from the OT promises to Israel. He writes that Jesus' commission in Luke 24 that repentance and forgiveness be proclaimed to all nations "is not something other than the Jewish hope. It is woven into the scriptures from very early on that when God finally does for Israel what he's going to do, then the nations of the world will come to share in the blessing." Ibid., 237.

for the whole world."[184] The expansion of the territory of Israel to include the entire earth is the natural result of Wright's conception: "The whole world is now God's holy land."[185]

This movement from a particular land to the whole world in Wright can also be seen in his understanding of Jesus' response to the disciples in Acts 1.[186] Wright rejects the common belief that Jesus rebukes his disciples in verse 7. Instead, he says Jesus' reply is an affirmation with a twist: "I suggest that if we understand what the kingdom and Israel mean, and what Jesus's reply is about, we can see that his answer is actually, 'Yes!—but it won't look like you imagine; it will look like something very different instead.'"[187] The resurrection of Jesus had changed things dramatically:

> The question of god lay at the heart of second-Temple Jewish life. Each affirmation, each act of worship, contained the question: not Who? (they knew the answer to that), nor yet Why? (again, they knew because he was the creator, the covenant god), or particularly Where? (land and Temple remained the focus), but How? What? and, above all, When? How, they wanted to know, would YHWH deliver them? What did he want them to be doing in the meantime? And, *When would it happen*? The resurrection of Jesus of Nazareth provided the early Christians with a new, unexpected and crystal clear answer to these three questions; and, by doing so, it raised the first three in a quite new way.[188]

---

184. Ibid.

185. Ibid., 266.

186. Ibid., 242.

187. Ibid. He writes elsewhere, "What happened, it seems, was this. The early Christians had lived within and breathed and prayed that old Jewish story line. In the resurrection and ascension of Jesus, shocking and unexpected though they were, they grasped the fact that in this way Israel's God had indeed done what he'd always intended, though it hadn't looked like they thought it would. Through this they came to see that Jesus, as Israel's Messiah, was already the world's true Lord and that his secret presence by his Spirit in the present time was only a hint of what was still to come, when he would finally be revealed as the one whose power would trump all other powers both earthly and heavenly. The Jesus story thus created a radical intensification and transformation from within the Jewish story, and the language that results in describing the Jesus event that is yet to come is the language that says, in relation to the future: Jesus is Lord and Caesar isn't." Ibid., 130.

188. Wright, *Resurrection of the Son of God*, 724-25.

As a result of Jesus' work, the focal point of the particular territory of Israel had expanded to include the whole earth.[189]

The land as metaphor is also present, though in a slightly different way, in Wright's understanding of inheritance language about the Spirit in Ephesians 1. He states, "Clearly Paul sees both continuity and discontinuity between present Christian experience and final Christian hope; there is still an 'inheritance', which speaks of this future hope not now in terms of the Christian's own *state of being*, but of *possession and responsibility*. Those who 'inherit' the age to come will do so after the manner of Israelites 'inheriting' the promised land. Ephesians 1.13-14 is, among other things, a retelling of the exodus story."[190] Ultimately, for Wright the particular territory promised to Israel in the OT is a metaphor for the whole earth but it also seems that he believes it to be a metaphor for spiritual blessings of salvation.

In Middleton's conception there is no place for the particular land of Israel as a portion of the renewed earth. The OT expectation that Israel will possess a particular territory has expanded to—or been replaced with—an expectation that all of the redeemed will possess the entire earth. In discussing Isaiah 65 and 66, for example, Middleton states, "The this-worldly prophetic expectation in Isaiah is universalized to the entire cosmos and human society generally in late Second Temple Judaism and in the New Testament."[191] After discussing the earthly salvation described in the OT, including its interest in mundane matters such as a particular land, Middleton concludes that God's interest is no longer in that land: "And while God's salvific purpose narrows for a while to one elect nation in their own land, this 'initially exclusive move' is, as Old Testament scholar Terence Fretheim puts it, in the service of 'a maximally inclusive end', the redemption of all nations and ultimately the entire created order."[192] The death and

---

189. He writes, "The disciples are assuming that for the kingdom to be restored to Israel will mean some kind of national superiority, perhaps a military defeat of Israel's enemies. But what Jesus has in mind is every bit as much the fulfillment of God's long-delayed plan for Israel and the kingdom. Jesus has now been raised from the dead as Israel's Messiah, and Israel's Messiah, as the psalms and prophets insist, is the world's true Lord. 'His dominion shall be from one sea to the other, from the River to the ends of the earth.'" Ibid., 242.

190. Wright, *Resurrection of the Son of God*, 236.

191. Middleton, *A New Heaven and a New Earth*, 24.

192. Ibid., 25. Cf. Fretheim, *God and World*, 29; also 103.

resurrection of Jesus and the mission to the Gentiles had resulted in a new understanding of the land promise for Israel.[193]

Regarding the land, Moore speaks more explicitly than Middleton. Jesus, he states, "applies the inheritance language of Israel (the meek inheriting the land, Ps. 37:11,22) directly to his followers now (the meek shall inherit the earth, Matt. 5:5).[194] This application is possible, Moore argues, because Jesus embodies "the remnant of Israel."[195] Without equivocation, he states,

> Israel is Jesus of Nazareth, who, as promised to Israel, is raised
> from the dead and marked out with the Spirit (Ezek. 37:13-14;
> Rom. 1:2-4). *All* the promises of God "find their Yes in him" (2
> Cor. 1:20), as Paul puts it, and this yes establishes a Jew like Paul
> with Gentiles like the Corinthians "in Christ, and has anointed
> us, and who has also put his seal on us and given us his Spirit in
> our hearts as a guarantee" (2 Cor. 1:21-22). The Spirit guarantees
> what? It guarantees that all who share the Spirit of Christ are "joint
> heirs with Christ" of his promised inheritance (Rom. 8:17 NKJV).[196]

Ultimately, all Christians, both Jew and Gentile, experience the blessings of the promises, including the promise of land, as a result of being united to the true Israelite.[197] However, the land that is inherited is no longer the particular territory which was promised to Abraham and his descendants. The inheritance has become the whole earth. Moore writes,

> We share his [Jesus] inheritance because we are the branches,
> united to him by faith (John 15:1-11). Is there a future for Israel?
> Yes. Does this future mean material and political blessings? Yes.
> Docs this mean the granting of all the land promised to Abraham
> in Canaan? Yes, along with the entire rest of the cosmos (Rom.
> 4:13). Does this promise apply to ethnic Jews? Yes, one ethnic Jew

193. Middleton believes that as a result of the Gentile mission, OT texts such as Exod 19 are applied to the church. He understands 1 Pet 2:9, for example, as "a continuation of the Abrahamic calling. God's redeemed people are called to mediate blessing to the world." Middleton, "A New Heaven and a New Earth," 85.

194. Moore, "Personal and Cosmic Eschatology," 865.

195. Ibid., 907.

196. Ibid.

197. Moore states, "Jesus fulfilled both the hopes embedded in human psyches everywhere and, more specifically, the kingdom promises God made to the people of Israel. He applied that nation's imagery—of temple, vine, shepherd, light of the nations, and so forth—to himself first, and then to those who are found in him." Moore, "A Purpose Driven Cosmos," 32.

whose name is Jesus. Do Gentile believers share in this inheritance? Yes, if they are in Christ, one-flesh with him through faith (Eph. 5:22–23), they receive the inheritance that belongs to him (Eph. 1:11).[198]

The land is simply an element of what Moore sees as a metaphor for the life of Christ, and in extension the blessings received through Christ by all of the redeemed: "The structure of the universe, the covenants to Israel, and the kings, prophets, and institutions of God's people all picture ahead of time, in some way, the life of Christ Jesus. The life of the church pictures the same life, after the fact."[199]

Moo also perceives that as one moves from the OT to the NT a change takes place regarding the land promise. After the return from exile, there was to be fruitfulness in the land. However, Moo states, "it quickly became clear that this return fell far short of what the prophets had promised. And so a new deliverance was still anticipated."[200] The new deliverance, according to Moo, takes place in the person of Christ.[201] Even though Moo argues that the consummation of the deliverance is still to come, he envisions no place in that consummation for the particular territory of Israel because the fulfillment of the territorial promise has been expanded to include the whole earth. As evidence, he offers Romans 4:13 in which Paul states that Abraham would be "heir of the world," concluding that Paul "clearly universalizes" Abraham's initial inheritance "of one particular land, Palestine" in the book of Genesis.[202]

Additionally, Moo argues that, according to Colossians 1:20, the peace that is promised in the OT of ethnic Jews living in the territory promised to them, "has now been established in Christ and enables God's new covenant people to live in a still dangerous and hostile world with new confidence and freedom from anxiety."[203] Again, Moo is clear that "universal peace is

---

198. Moore, "Personal and Cosmic Eschatology," 907.

199. Moore, "Purpose Driven Cosmos," 32.

200. Moo, "Nature in the New Creation," 457.

201. Moo states, "The NT claims that this deliverance has taken place in and through the coming of Jesus the Messiah. He, the second Adam, the true and ultimate image of God, obeys where Adam had disobeyed and through his death and resurrection inaugurates the last days that the prophets had longed for. The true 'return from exile' has finally taken place." Ibid., 457–58.

202. Ibid., 463.

203. Ibid., 473.

not yet established."[204] Still, when the consummation of the peace has been established, the particular land is universalized: "the eschatological fulfillment of God's promises continues, according to the NT witness, to include the 'land,' expanded to the entire cosmos."[205]

Snyder's ecological perspective seems to drive his theology of the land, so that his concern is with the whole earth instead of a particular territory of it. He writes, "The biblical theology of land, from the Old Testament to the New, 'grounds' (literally) salvation in God's plan for the whole earth. The theme of the earth as God's habitation implies human respect for and care of nature."[206] Snyder concludes that the particular land is subsumed under God's plan to restore creation through Israel. While affirming that the focus in the OT is on the relationship between God, Israel, and Israel's land, he concludes that this three-fold relationship is the background for the "God-intended relationship between God, humankind, and the created order. . . . In the Old Testament, we learn that through Israel God begins a plan to restore creation. God intends *shalom*, a harmonious, reconciled interrelationship between himself, his people, and the land."[207] By choosing a particular people who are to be a blessing to all other peoples and promising that particular people a particular land, God is working "to restore harmony to creation."[208] Even though the subjects of the relationship change, the "fundamental actions" are constant: "(1) God *gives the land* to the people; (2) the land *provides food for* or nourishes the people; and (3) the people are to *praise* or worship the Lord."[209] Pervading Snyder's understanding of the unfolding of God's plan of salvation, seen in the OT and supported by the NT, is the development from the particular to the general.[210] According to Snyder, as a result of this development, the particular territory of Israel plays no role in the new creation.

204. Ibid.

205. Ibid.

206. Snyder, "Salvation Means Creation Healed," 31.

207. Snyder, *Salvation Means Creation Healed*, 125. Part of Snyder's justification for widening the intended relationship is that 'land' and 'earth' are the same word in Hebrew. For problems regarding making theological conclusions based upon terminology alone, see Uemura, *Land or Earth?*.

208. Ibid., 124.

209. Ibid., 125.

210. Snyder writes, "As the plan of salvation unfolds in the Old Testament, we come to understand four essential things: 1. The Lord God is God of all peoples, not just of Israel. 2. God's plan includes the whole earth, not just the land of Israel. 3. God's plan

Conclusion

In the recent theological interest on the theme of land, a common conclusion is that the particular territory of Israel referenced throughout the OT becomes a metaphor for something revealed more fully in the NT. The survey in the current chapter of recent theological treatments of land reveals this dominance. The common conclusion is that the OT promise of a particular territory to a particular people is fulfilled in some manner other than the giving of the territory of Israel to ethnic Jews. The multiplicity of interpretations surveyed above reveals two primary ways of understanding the particular land promises within contemporary theological thought. These two ways could be classified as spiritualized (or Christified) and universalized (or expanded), respectively.[211] The spiritualized view understands the particular territorial promise as foreshadowing spiritual blessings received by those who have been united to Christ. The universalized view upholds a material fulfillment of the territorial promise but not in its particularity. Instead, the universalized view generalizes the fulfillment of the promise, expanding it to include the whole earth. Both the spiritualized and universalized views can be said to be metaphorical in that the particular territorial promise to Israel finds its fulfillment in each view in something other than in the giving of the particular land to a particular people. Whether it refers to an aspect of the Christian life as a result of christological and spiritual fulfillment or it comes to mean the entire earth, the common conclusion is that the original thing that is promised is replaced by something else. It seems ironic that those who are emphasizing the regeneration or renewal of the present earth in its materiality are interpreting promises regarding a particular territory of that earth in a metaphorical way. What I aim to show in the following chapter is that a metaphorical understanding of the particular land of promise is inconsistent with a new creation conception that envisions a renewed earth.

---

includes all nations and peoples, not just the Hebrews. 4. God has chosen Israel in order to bring *shalom* to the whole creation." Ibid., 127. It should be noted that agreement with these four essentials does not necessarily make the particularities of Israel and the land irrelevant.

211. The two ways of understanding do not seem to be mutually exclusive as some affirm a spiritual fulfillment in Christ (extending to all of the redeemed) while also affirming a universalized fulfillment in which the particular land promise is fulfilled (or replaced) by the restoration of the territory of the whole earth.

4

Territorial Particularity
in New Creationism

As seen in the previous pages, new creationists have expressed affirmation of a metaphorical fulfillment of the promise of the particular territory of Israel. In the pages to follow, I argue that this affirmation results in a logical inconsistency for new creationism. At the heart of the inconsistency—and a consensus among new creationists—is the belief that the present earth will be renewed as a part of the renewal of all creation. In arguing for continuity—and in some instances correspondence of identity—between the present earth and the new earth, new creationists utilize OT prophetic texts which include language referencing the particular territory of Israel. These OT prophetic texts include passages that reference God creating new heavens and a new earth (e.g., Isa 65-66) and those that employ the language of restoration and cosmic peace in the context of Zion and Jerusalem and the effect that this has upon other nations (e.g., Isa 2:2-4 [cf. Mic 4:2-3]; 11; 32; Ezek 36-37; Zech 2, 9). In examining the manner in which these texts are utilized by new creationists, a logical inconsistency arises between the new creation conceptions and a metaphorical fulfillment of the promise of the particular territory of Israel. The inconsistency involves the practice of new creationists affirming a new earth that corresponds in identity to the present earth while denying an enduring role for the particular portion of territorial Israel as a part of that earth.

95

The Logical Inconsistency of New Creationists

In an essay on supersessionist hermeneutics, Craig Blaising writes that supersessionists "believe that a *reality shift* takes place in the overall story of the Bible when one moves from *promise* in the Old Testament to *fulfillment* in the New."[1] The resulting "alternate reality" of the supersessionist hermeneutic has no place for a territorial restoration of Israel. The shift, Blaising writes, "is from the material, the earthly, the ethnic, to a heavenly, a spiritual, a non-ethnic reality. It moves from a political, national reality to a non-political, universal reality. The focus changes from the particular to the universal."[2]

The practice of new creationists does not correspond well to the traditional supersessionist hermeneutic. On the one hand, as evidenced from the examination in chapter 1, new creationists argue vigorously for a continued material and this-worldly reality for the final state, a reality in which time and particularity play a part. This final state which takes place upon a restored "new" earth is inhabited by the redeemed who have either died and been subsequently raised from the dead or are transformed upon entering the final state. The new earth, though changed in a multitude of ways, corresponds in material identity (particularity) to the present earth just as the redeemed person, in his identity, corresponds in material identity (particularity) to his identity prior to death or glorification. In this way, new creationists deny a reality shift to the heavenly and spiritual by

---

1. Blaising, "Israel and Hermeneutics," 155. Blaising defines supersessionists as "those who believe that the church has replaced ethnic and national Israel in the plan of God so that there is no future for the latter." Ibid., 152. Another commonly-used term for this belief is replacement theology. For more extensive definitions of supersessionism and re-placement theology, see Soulen, *God of Israel*; Diprose, *Israel in the Development of Christian Thought*; and Vlach, *Has the Church Replaced Israel?*. Blaising offers a brief synthesis of contemporary evangelical hermeneutics, which traditionally has been referred to as the historical, grammatical, and literary approach to the interpretation of the Bible. He explains several terms that help to describe the approach: historical, lexical, grammatical, syntactical, literary/formal, conventions, genre, performative, thematic, canonical, and narratological. Then, he concludes, "This list of categories, methods, and practices would generally be accepted by most evangelical biblical scholars, including supersessionists and non-supersessionists alike." Blaising, "Israel and Hermeneutics," 155.

2. Ibid., 156. As examples of this type of interpretation, Blaising references several scholars included in the discussion of the land theme in the previous chapter of the present work such as W. D. Davies, Colin Chapman, Gary Burge, Peter Walker, Palmer Robertson, William Dumbrell, and T. Desmond Alexander.

affirming the reality of earthly life in its temporality and materiality upon a renewed earth.[3]

On the other hand, however, new creationists argue that while the new earth is restored so that there is a correspondence of identity between the old earth and the new earth, there is no necessary corresponding identity for the particular territory of Israel as a portion of the whole earth. It seems that in these conceptions the particularity ends with the earth as a whole, with a particular part of the whole being neglected, specifically the part that is the territory of Israel. In their affirmation of the common practice of viewing the particular land promise as metaphorical, new creationists imply that a reality shift takes place in regards to that particular land. In its fulfillment, they argue, the promise no longer refers to that particular part of the earth, but that it either has been fulfilled in a spiritual way, or that it will be fulfilled through the restoration of the whole earth. It seems that new creationists are operating under an inconsistent hermeneutic. Ultimately, what seems to be both an affirmation and a denial of the reality shift does not fit neatly with what Blaising describes as the evangelical supersessionist hermeneutic. As Blaising argues, there is inconsistency and incoherence in new creation conceptions that affirm a restored or regenerated earth while neglecting the particular territory of Israel.[4] Noting N. T. Wright as an example of a new creationist who understands the land as Christified, Blaising poses the following questions: "Are these views consistent or coherent? So let's just imagine traversing the new earth, crossing its various and particular geographical features, and coming to the Middle East. What do we find there? A void? A spatial anomaly?"[5] Then, he concludes, "Maintaining

---

3. This affirmation relates to the new creationists' critique of spiritual vision conceptions of the final state. Interestingly, Wright's critique of "heaven" as the final destiny of the redeemed seems to be a critique of certain kinds of replacement theology that see a transition as one moves from the OT to the NT from a focus on the realia of Judaism to a focus on Jesus (e.g., Peter Walker's language regarding the spiritual fulfillment of the 'heavenly Jerusalem' taking place in Jesus himself who represents the Temple. Walker, *Jesus and the Holy City*, 308).

4. The consistency and coherency to which Blaising refers is tested at the canonical narratological level of interpretation. By "canonical . . . interpretation," he means that the whole canon is the ultimate context of interpretation while the "narratological" element refers to the understanding that Scripture, while containing various genres, is itself a unifed and coherent story. Blaising, "Israel and Hermeneutics," 155.

5. Blaising, "Israel and Hermeneutics," 163–64.

new creation eschatology while arguing that the territory of Israel has been spiritualized or 'Christified' is not a consistent or coherent view."[6]

The dynamic of the affirmation of the reality shift on the one hand regarding the land and the denial of the shift on the other hand regarding the earth can be seen clearly in an article by Moo in which he argues for the inclusion of the idea of cosmic renewal in the NT language of "new creation."[7] Moo states the following:

> If "new creation" does, indeed, signify in Paul the "new world of re-creation," does it therefore include cosmic renovation? This question is often answered with a "no," because Paul applies the concept in both texts where it appears to the present stage of salvation history—a time in which we do not see and are not told to expect evidence of cosmic renovation. Paul's use of "new creation" would then fall into a familiar hermeneutical pattern, according to which physical things—land of Israel, temple, return from exile—are applied to new covenant spiritual realities—church, Christ's spiritual presence, salvation. Without denying this pattern, which is, indeed, central to the NT interpretation of the old, I want to argue that new creation does not fit this pattern and that the concept does, indeed, include reference to cosmic renovation.[8]

This quote is further evidence of the logical inconsistency of new creationists, namely, that they maintain the affirmation of a renewed earth while spiritualizing or universalizing the physical territory of Israel. The inconsistency also can be seen in Wright's description of language that appears in apocalyptic writings and has its basis in prophecy. He states that "complex, many-layered and often biblical imagery is used and re-used to invest the space-time events of Israel's past, present, and future with their full theological significance."[9] Jesus, Wright believes, explained the full theological significance by redefining the imagery: "[Jesus] had not come to rehabilitate the symbol of holy land, but to subsume it within a different fulfilment [sic] of the kingdom, which would embrace the whole creation."[10] Further, Wright claims, "Jesus spent his whole ministry *redefining* what the kingdom meant. He refused to give up the symbolic language of the king-

---

6. Ibid., 164.

7. Moo, "Creation and New Creation."

8. Ibid., 55.

9. Wright, *New Testament and the People of God*, 286.

10. Wright, *Jesus and the Victory of God*, 446.

dom, but filled it with such new content that, as we have seen, he powerfully subverted Jewish expectations."[11] The question is whether Wright's new creation conception allows the particular space-time events (and places) of Israel's past and present to be replaced by other space-time events. The answer to the question seems to be no, in that Wright argues that the particular space-time events and places of Israel's history have no enduring role, as they have been fulfilled in a spiritual manner.[12]

The concern in the following pages is to examine one practice among new creationists that manifests the inconsistency. This practice has to do with how new creationists utilize certain restoration passages in the OT to inform their understanding of the new earth. The inconsistency becomes evident by examining the way in which new creationists utilize OT restoration texts to inform their understanding of the restoration of the earth in its materiality and the way in which they discard the territory of Israel in those texts. Following the examination, I show the inconsistency of the common practice among new creationists of utilizing the OT restoration texts to inform their conception of the new earth while universalizing—or alternatively, Christifying—the particular territory of Israel in those texts. The argument here could be seen as advancing Moo's argument referenced in the quote above. He argues that the affirmation of cosmic renovation within the concept of new creation is proper and, therefore, does not fit the pattern of physical things being applied to new covenant spiritual realities. I am arguing that OT prophetic texts connect the promise of a restoration of the particular territory of Israel to the promise of a renewed earth. Like cosmic renovation, the affirmation that the particular land will be restored does not fit the familiar hermeneutical pattern which Moo describes. In other words, a consistent treatment of the prophetical texts by new creationists should include the affirmation of territorial restoration of Israel as a part of the renewed earth instead of that territorial particularity being subsumed conceptually under cosmic reconciliation.

11. Ibid., 471. By Jewish expectations, Wright is referring to the physical "symbols" of land, temple, city, etc.

12. Again, Wright's critique of conceptions of a spiritual existence in 'heaven' as the final destiny of the redeemed seems to belie his explanation of the fulfillment of the territorial promise in the person of Christ.

Utilization of OT Restoration Texts in New Creationism

As seen in earlier chapters, new creationists believe that the present earth is to be renewed or restored rather than being annihilated and replaced by an utterly new earth. OT texts that speak prophetically about a new heavens and earth or that speak in some way of a restoration are taken as referring to future reality that takes place upon the present earth. It makes sense, then, that new creation proponents would utilize these OT texts to inform their conception of the new earth. While none of the selected new creationists provide an extensive analysis of the passages in their explanation of new creation eschatology, they clearly utilize the passages to inform their conception of the final state.

While Moo focuses on the NT evidence for his conception of the final state, he also relies on OT prophetic language. After noting the scholarly disagreement on the "degree of direct referentiality" in Isaiah, he concludes that "the nature of the continuity between this world and the one to come is not clear from Isaiah."[13] Despite this hesitancy regarding the clarity with which Isaiah speaks, Moo, in a discussion of 2 Peter 3:10-12 and Revelation 21, refers to Isaiah 65:17 and 66:22-24 as "the ultimate source of new heaven and new earth language."[14] He also states that "while the phrase 'new creation' is not found in the OT, it is generally agreed that Paul's phrase refers to the hope of a world-wide, even cosmic, renewal that is so widespread in the last part of Isaiah."[15] In these latter chapters of Isaiah, according to Moo, the singular hopes of Israel are "given a more explicitly cosmic orientation: the return will mean nothing less than 'a new heaven and new earth,' centered on a 'new Jerusalem,' and where 'the wolf and the

---

13. Moo, "Nature in the New Creation," 465. Moo describes the disagreement by asking the following questions: "Is the prophet describing rather straightforwardly the conditions of the new world, as they will exist in the millennium or in the eternal state? Or is he using language drawn from this world to describe in a series of metaphors an experience that simply has no direct analog to our experience in this world?" Ibid.

14. Ibid.

15. Ibid., 475. Elsewhere, Moo writes that "in his familiar prophecies about a 'new heavens and new earth,' Isaiah envisages an ultimate salvation that extends beyond the people of Israel or even the land of Israel to include the entire comos [sic]: a 'new heavens and new earth' (Isa 65:17-22; cf. 66:22-24)." Moo, "Creation and New Creation," 45. In reference to 2 Cor 5:17, one of only two occurrences of the phrase "new creation" in the NT [the other one being Gal 6:15], Moo makes the following observation: "The pervasiveness of creation language in Isa 40-55 is probably one of the reasons that Paul chooses to use creation language to describe the 'new things' that God is doing among his new covenant people." Moo, "Creation and New Creation," 54.

lamb will feed together, and the lion will eat straw like the ox' (65:17-25; 66:22-24)."[16]

Regarding the role of the prophets in general, as related to the affirmation of the renewal of the cosmos, Moo notes both the return to the land and the blessing of the land.[17] In his treatment of Romans 8:19-22, he describes Isaiah 24-27 as "the single most important prophetic text echoed in these verses."[18] He quotes approvingly Jonathan Moo, who writes that Isaiah the prophet looks

> to a time when the Lord will reign as king on Mount Zion (24:23) and the glory of the Lord (δόξα κυρίου) will be praised (24:14, 15) and manifested (25:1). On that day, the Lord will destroy "the covering that is cast on all peoples, the veil that is spread over all nations. He will swallow up death for ever, and the Lord God will wipe tears from all faces, and the reproach of his people he will take away from all the earth" (25:7-8). This is the day that God's people have waited and yearned for as they have sought him in their distress (25:9, 26:8, 9, 26:16). Indeed, they have been suffering as in birth pains (ωδίνω) but they have not been able to bring about deliverance in the earth (26:17-18). But despite their seemingly fruitless labor, "the dead shall live, their bodies shall rise" and the "dwellers in the dust awake" (26:19) and, in the days to come, "Israel shall blossom and put forth shoots, and fill the whole world with fruit" (27:6).[19]

In discussing Colossians 1:20, Moo connects the peace in the OT prophets which "would bring security and blessing to Israel as the people live in the land God gave them" to the peace that believers have in Christ and which will be fully established universally in the future.[20]

---

16. Moo, "Nature in the New Creation," 476.

17. Ibid., 458.

18. Ibid., 462. Moo writes, "Isaiah 24:1-13 describes the effects of sin in cosmic terms: 'the heavens languish with the earth' (v. 4), 'a curse consumes the earth' (v. 6). And why is the earth in this condition? Because 'the earth is defiled by its people; they have disobeyed the laws, violated the statutes, and broken the everlasting covenant' (v. 5). Isaiah goes on in these chapters to describe how that situation will be reversed." Ibid., 462-63. For an extended treatment of Moo's interpretation of Rom 8:19-22, see Moo, *Epistle to the Romans*, 513-18.

19. "Nature in the New Creation," 463. The quote is from a paper written by Moo's son Jonathan while he was a student at Gordon-Conwell Theological Seminary.

20. Ibid., 473. Cf. Moo, "Creation and New Creation," 56.

It is clear upon an examination of Snyder that his conception, like Moo's, is primarily informed by the NT. Yet he also utilizes OT prophetic texts when discussing the final age to come. He states that although "the comprehensive picture of salvation is most fully elaborated in Paul's writings, it is also the larger biblical view. All the promises of cosmic restoration in the Old Testament apply here, reaching their climax in Isaiah's sublime vision (Isa 11:6–9; 35:1–10; 65:17–25)."[21] Snyder argues that God's promises in the OT prophets are evidence that the broad concept of salvation includes the future healing of all creation.[22] Referencing Isaiah 65:17 and 66:22, in addition to 2 Peter 3:13 and Revelation 21:1, Snyder concludes, "The testimony of Scripture is consistent: the same God who created the universe perfect, and sustains it in its fallen condition (Heb 1:3), will restore all things through the work of Jesus in the power of the Spirit."[23] More explicitly, Snyder argues that OT passages such as Isaiah 11 promise that in the final state there will be neither death nor predation. Though he understands the passage to inform how we are to live in the present age, it is clear that he believes that the passage should inform one's conception of the physical reality of the age to come. He writes,

> The Bible explicitly teaches that God's purpose is to put an end to
> *all* predation. "The wolf shall live with the lamb, the leopard shall
> lie down with the kid, the calf and the lion and the fatling together,
> and a little child shall lead them. . . . They will not hurt or destroy
> on all my holy mountain" (Isa 11:6, 9). If the created order will
> indeed be "liberated from its bondage to decay," then this promise
> in Isaiah is not just metaphor or allegory. It is a picture of the new
> creation; the promise of deliverance from earth's bondage to decay
> and predation—and a signpost for how we are to live today.[24]

---

21. Snyder, *Salvation Means Creation Healed*, 100.

22. Snyder writes, "The great concern of the church is *salvation* and, biblically speaking, salvation ultimately means *creation healed*. God promises to hear humanity's cries 'and heal them' (Isa 19:22). God pronounces 'Peace, peace, to the far and near' and pledges, 'I will heal them' (Isa 57:19). 'Return, O faithless children, I will heal your faithlessness' (Jer 3:22). When God's people truly turn to him, he promises to 'heal their land' (2 Chr 7:14). In fact, the Bible promises a healed, restored 'new heavens and a new earth' (Isa 65:17; 66:22; 2 Pet 3:13). We recall that the Old Testament word for peace, *shalom*, means comprehensive well-being—healthy people in a flourishing land." Ibid., xiv.

23. Ibid.

24. Ibid., 102.

The end to predation is brought about by one who would bring about the promise of Isaiah: "Israel's prophets promised that God would in time send a special servant-king, the Messiah, who would actually accomplish God's healing plan. Through the Messiah, God would himself bring perfect *shalom*, as pictured so beautifully in Isaiah 11 and many other passages."[25] Referencing several of these texts, Snyder offers a summary of the shalom:

> Both the Old and New Testaments prophesy a renewed earth community, "new heavens and a new earth, where righteousness is at home" (2 Pet 3:13; cf. Isa 65:17; 66:22; Rev 21:1). Here is universal *shalom* with all peoples and the whole earth: "they shall all sit under their own vines and under their own fig trees, and no one shall make them afraid" (Mic 4:4; cf. 2 Kgs 18:31; Isa 36:16). Eschatologically speaking, Christian community is restored earth community, refined and purified by God's judgment and renewal.[26]

Snyder clearly is utilizing these OT prophetic texts to inform his conception of the final state, a state which comes about in space (upon the present earth) and in time (at some point in the future) and a state which continues to exist in space (upon a renewed earth) and in time (an everlasting sequence of events).

Middleton argues that law, wisdom, and prophecy establish that the goal for salvation is that the earth be renewed. Though he admits "the critique of injustice that pervades the prophetic literature," he affirms that the expectation of restoration that pervades both law/wisdom and the prophets indicates "the inescapable connection between the moral and cosmic orders" and "a profound and comprehensive vision of earthly flourishing."[27] This emphasis in law/wisdom and the prophets continues the movement toward earthly flourishing seen in God's work on behalf of Israel during

---

25. Ibid., 127. Referencing John Wesley, Snyder writes the following: "Referring . . . to Revelation 21, Wesley notes that the promised destruction of death, evil, and pain is not limited to humans. Rather, we may expect that the 'whole brute creation will then undoubtedly be restored, not only to the vigour, strength, and swiftness which they had at their creation, but to a far higher degree of each than they ever enjoyed'—each creature 'according to its capacity.' Then will be fulfilled the great promise of Isa 11:6—9, the *peaceable kingdom*." Ibid., 154. The quote from Wesley can be found in John Wesley, Sermon 60, 449. Snyder makes reference to the picture of peace in Isa 61:1-4 when discussing the Sabbath principle and "the biblical promise of ultimate Jubilee, healing, and *shalom*." Snyder, *Salvation Means Creation Healed*, 199.

26. Snyder, *Salvation Means Creation Healed*, 215.

27. Middleton, *A New Heaven and a New Earth*, 96.

the exile.[28] Middleton writes, "Thankfully, the prophets do not leave Israel in judgment. Beyond exile there is the hope of restoration. Many prophetic texts promise a renewal of people and land after their expulsion from the land."[29] It is these prophetic texts that Middleton utilizes to argue that the OT envisions holistic salvation which includes earthly restoration.[30] Referencing a number of prophetical texts, Middleton sketches seven components that "together testify to God's purpose for earthly flourishing."[31] These seven components include: 1) *Return to the Land*; 2) *Restoration and healing of God's people in society*; 3) *Flourishing of the natural world, including peace among animals*; 4) *New relationship with the nations, centered in Zion*; 5) *Forgiveness of sin and new heart, enabling God's people to keep Torah*; 6) *Restoration of righteous leadership for Israel*; and 7) *God's presence among the people in the renewed land.*[32] The prophetic texts that Middleton utilizes in describing each of these components envision an earthly situation in which each of these components of flourishing takes place.

28. Regarding the pattern in Exodus, Middleton concludes, "This paradigmatic work of YHWH on behalf of Israel establishes a movement toward this-worldly flourishing as the goal of salvation. The exodus pattern begins when God's original intent for his people's well-being and blessing has been disrupted, and its epicenter is God's intervention to deliver those in need and to restore them to a life of shalom in their concrete earthly environment." Ibid., 95.

29. Ibid., 105.

30. Regarding the prophetic texts that promise a renewal or restoration, Middleton writes, "A sketch of the major components of this renewal sheds light on the Old Testament's vision of holistic salvation." Ibid.

31. Ibid.

32. Ibid., 105–07. The numerous references that Middleton uses to argue for the seven respective components include 1) *Return to the Land*: Isa. 11:10–12, 16; 35:8–10; 55:12–13; 60:4; Jer. 32:37; Ezek. 34:27; 36:8–11; 37:11–14; Amos 9:15; Zeph. 3:19–20; Zech. 8:7–8; 2) *Restoration and healing of God's people in society*: Isa. 35:5–6, 10; 60:1–2, 18–22; 61:1–4, 7, 9; 62:4–7, 12; 65:18–24; Jer. 31:4–6, 11–14; Ezek. 34:25–31; 36:33–36; 37:5–6, 12, 14; Amos 9:14; Zeph. 3:11–18; Zech. 8:1–5, 11–15; 3) *Flourishing of the natural world, including peace among animals*: Isa. 11:6–9; 35:1–2, 6–7; 55:12–13; 65:25; Ezek. 34:25–29; 36:8–11, 34–35; 47:1–12; Joel 2:23–24; 3:18; Amos 9:13; Zech. 8:12; 14:8; 4) *New relationship with the nations, centered in Zion*: Isa. 2:2–4; 19:23–25; 60:5–16; 61:5–6, 9, 11; Jer. 3:17; Mic. 4:1–4; Zech. 2:11; 8:20–23; 5) *Forgiveness of sin and new heart, enabling God's people to keep Torah*: Isa. 30:20–21; 59:20–21; Jer. 31:31–34; 32:40; 50:20; Ezek. 11:19; 36:26; 37:23; Joel 2:28–29; 6) *Restoration of righteous leadership for Israel*: Isa. 11:1–5; 32:1; Jer. 3:15; 23:5–6; 30:9; Ezek. 34:23–24; 37:22–25; Hosea 3:5; Amos 9:11–12; Mic. 5:2–4; Zech. 9:9–10; and 7) *God's presence among the people in the renewed land*: Isa. 11:9; Jer. 32:37–41; Ezek. 34:25–31; 37:24–28; Hab. 2:14; Zech. 2:11; 8:7–8; 14:9 (cf. 10:9).

Most important for the present discussion are those elements in Middleton's explanation which speak directly to land promises. He writes that "a return to the land is key to Israel's renewal" and "The Old Testament simply cannot conceive of full salvation or flourishing without earthly, landed existence."[33] The return to land not only signals restoration of a people, but also the flourishing of the natural world.[34] Middleton's vision of earthly flourishing in the prophets also includes a change in the relationship between Israel and other nations.[35] The dynamic of the relationship includes the place of Zion to which the nations stream, seeking God and his law and offering elements of their respective cultures.[36] Middleton sees an additional feature in certain restoration texts of just leadership for the nation of Israel which replaces "the corrupt leadership of the past, that the people may be led into righteousness."[37] He also understands Isaiah 65:17 and 66:22 as envisioning "a healed world with a redeemed community in rebuilt Jerusalem, where life is restored to flourishing and shalom."[38] The prophet Zechariah "envisions God dwelling in the midst of Israel along with the 'many nations' that will have joined God's people (2:11) and speaks of the day when YHWH will become king over all the earth (14:9; cf. 10:9)."[39] The ultimate result of the promises of restoration and renewal is "God's permanent presence among the redeemed people in the context of the flourishing,

---

33. Ibid., 105.

34. Essentially connecting the return to land and the flourishing of the natural order, Middleton writes, "Some prophetic visions of restoration depict the flourishing of nature as Israel returns home, both during the return journey from Babylon and when the people resettle the land. . . . Some texts portray a new harmony with the animal kingdom, such that people and animals will live in peace." Ibid., 106.

35. He writes that "the prophets promise a new relationship with the nations, in which enmity is transformed into service." Ibid., 106. Elsewhere, he states, "According to Isaiah 60, the nations that formerly oppressed Israel will now contribute to Zion's glory. In particular, we are told that the temple will be rebuilt with lumber from the trees of Lebanon (v. 13), and that the ships of Tarshish will bring the exiles home (v. 9)." Ibid., 124.

36. Middleton states that "some texts envision the fulfillment of Israel's vocation of mediating God's blessing to the world as the nations stream to Zion to seek God and his ways . . . . Isaiah 60 even has the best cultural contributions of the nations being brought to Jerusalem to be transformed and used for Israel's benefit and YHWH's glory . . . , while Isaiah 19 predicts a future parity between Israel, Egypt, and Assyria, in which all of them will be YHWH's people (vv. 23–25)." Ibid., 106.

37. Ibid.

38. Ibid., 24.

39. Ibid., 107.

bountiful land."[40] Regarding the OT, specifically the vision of the prophets, Middleton concludes, "In the end, the Old Testament anticipates that salvation will be as wide as creation."[41]

N. T. Wright also utilizes OT restoration prophecies in his argument for a restored earth. He writes that the events involved in the age to come, "including the ones that were expected to come as the climax of YHWH's restoration of Israel, remained within (what we think of as) the this-worldly ambit."[42] He writes further, "The 'kingdom of god' has nothing to do with the world itself coming to an end. That makes no sense either of the basic Jewish worldview or of the texts in which the Jewish hope is expressed."[43] Wright argues that the affirmation that the world is to be renewed can be seen in the great prophetic promises of Isaiah 2:2-4 (cf. Mic 4:1-3); 11:1-9; 42:1, 4; 61:1, 3f, 11; and 65:17-25.[44] Although he ultimately interprets these expressions in a universalizing manner (as seen in the previous chapter), Wright allows these texts to inform his understanding of the material reality of the final state. For example, after quoting Isaiah 11:1-9, he adds, "The promise of a new and non-violent creation is expanded in 65.17-25."[45] Wright seems to take the language of Isaiah 11 concerning the cohabitation

---

40. Ibid. Middleton writes further, "This is the fulfillment of the ancient and often reiterated claim that it is God's intent to dwell among the redeemed in the context of a divine-human relationship, where he would be their God and they would be his people . . . . This intent is rooted, ultimately, in God's purpose from the beginning to manifest his presence on earth through the mediating role of humanity as the authorized image of God in the cosmic temple." Ibid.

41. Ibid. An important element in Middleton's argument is that the judgment from God envisioned in the prophets is ultimately redemptive in nature. He offers as an example Isaiah 24 "which speaks of the violent shaking of the earth (both people and environment [vv.1-13, 17-20]) and the punishing of the host of heaven, along with the shaming of sun and moon (vv. 21-23a). This vision of destruction is punctuated by the songs of praise of the redeemed from the ends of the earth (vv. 14-16a) and concludes with the glory of YHWH reigning on Mount Zion (v. 23b)." Ibid., 121-22. He also argues that "the language of apocalyptic destruction in the Old Testament intends not the annihilation of the cosmos, but rather a new world cleansed of evil. Judgment is real because sin is a serious matter, and extreme language is often used to emphasize the radical nature of the purging required for salvation. While judgment is an inescapable reality for those who resist God's will, God's ultimate purpose is to accomplish his original intent for the flourishing of humanity (Israel and the nations) and the nonhuman world." Ibid., 125-26.

42. Wright, *New Testament and the People of God*, 285.

43. Ibid.

44. Wright, *Resurrection of the Son of God*, 100-02.

45. Ibid., 101.

of the wolf and the lamb as a literal vision of the reality of the world to come.[46] Arguing against "a theology in which human beings are set free from space-time existence" which "is detached from the created world," Wright utilizes Isaiah 40-55 as evidence that all the creation will rejoice and the wilderness and the barren land will celebrate.[47]

Even though he concludes that prophecies regarding national Israel have been given a "fresh use within early Christianity," Wright utilizes prophetic passages to argue that second-Temple Judaism does not abandon Jewish earthly, material, and socio-political categories.[48] Further, throughout his argument for the restoration of the present creation, Wright utilizes OT restoration texts.[49] Fulfilling the covenant, according to Wright, meant that God would re-establish "the divinely intended order in all the world."[50] He states further,

> Isaiah and Micah speak of Zion as the place to which the nations would come, and of Israel's task as being their light. The prophets

46. Wright states, "In Isaiah 11 the Messiah's judgment creates a world where the wolf and the lamb lie down side by side." Wright, *Surprised by Hope*, 138.

47. Wright, *New Heavens, New Earth*, 12.

48. Wright, *Resurrection of the Son of God*, 565. After citing Ps 2:7-12; 72:1f, 8-12, 17; 89:20, 22f, 25-27; Isa 11:1, 4, 10; 42:1, 6 (cf. 49:1-6); and Dan 7:13f, Wright states the following propositions: "(1) these texts all bear witness to a biblically rooted belief in a coming king who would be master not only of Israel but also of the whole world; (2) these are the passages drawn on by the early Christians to speak about Jesus not only as Israel's Messiah (albeit in a redefined sense) but also as the world's true lord, again in a sense which was redefined but never abandoned; (3) we must therefore understand the early Christian belief in Jesus as lord, not as a part of an abandonment of Jewish categories and an embracing of Greek ones, nor as part of an abandonment of the hope for god's kingdom and a turning instead to 'religious experience', nor yet as an abandonment of the political meaning of this universal sovereignty and a re-expression of it in terms of 'religious' loyalty, but as a fresh statement of the Jewish hope that the one true god, the creator, would become lord of the whole world." Ibid., 565-66. Thus, concerning the coming age in which there would be a new exodus (and a final return from exile) and a return to Zion, Wright sees in various prophetic texts the "proper and historically appropriate context in which to understand Jesus' sayings about the kingdom, or kingship, of Israel's god." Wright, *Jesus and the Victory of God*, 209.

49. Wright's view of OT prophetic hope regarding Israel is earthly. In Jewish expectation of salvation, he states that "there can be little thought of the rescue of Israel consisting of the end of the space-time universe, and/or of Israel's future enjoyment of a non-physical, 'spiritual' bliss. That would simply contradict creational monotheism, implying that the created order was residually evil, and to be simply destroyed." Wright, *New Testament and the People of God*, 300.

50. Ibid., 271.

who look ahead to the restoration of Jerusalem and the rebuilding of the temple see in this event the refounding of the Garden of Eden; Ezekiel envisages rivers flowing out to water and heal the rest of the world, Zephaniah imagines the nations looking on in admiration as YHWH restores the fortunes of his people, and Zechariah (who imitates Ezekiel's idea of the rivers) sees the restoration of Jerusalem as the signal for YHWH to become king over all the world, so that the nations will come to Jerusalem to keep the Jewish festivals. Thus, in the literature which urged the exiled people to look forward to the coming age when all would be restored, the future glory of the land is described in terms borrowed from paradise-imagery; Israel after restoration will be like a new creation, with the people once again being fruitful and multiplying in her own land.[51]

Like other new creationists, Moore utilizes OT prophetic promises concerning the restoration of Israel to inform his conception of the final state as an earthly reality. The basis of Moore's conclusion that the hope that the OT promises "is not of an eschatological flight from creation but the restoration and redemption of creation" is the picture of the final order seen throughout the prophets.[52] In this final order, "animal predation is no more (Isa. 11:6-9), nature itself will be in harmony with humanity (Isa. 60:19-22), the demonic order is crushed (Isa. 27:1; Hab. 3:13), and all the nations stream to Israel bringing their wealth into her gates (Isa. 60:1-14; Micah 4:1-5)."[53] Regarding the end to death, Moore writes, "The prophetic Scriptures point to the day when death itself, human and animal, is wiped away from the cosmos (Isa. 25:6-9; Ezek. 37:1-14)."[54] He also utilizes prophetic texts in his argument that there will be a restoration of the animal order in the final state, concluding that the animals present there "will be under the dominion of human beings, chiefly the Son of man himself, and will be restored to their original nonpredatory vegetarian diets (Isa. 11:7; 65:25).[55] Moore is clearly utilizing prophetical texts in such a way that the

---

51. Ibid., 264. For justification, Wright references the following passages in a footnote: Isa 2:2-5; 11:1f; 42:6; 45:8; 49:6; 51:4; Jer 3:16; 23:3; Ezek 36:11; 40-47, esp. 47:7-12; Mic 4:1-5; Zeph 3:20; Zech 10:8; and 14:8-19.

52. Moore, "Personal and Cosmic Eschatology," 859.

53. Ibid.

54. Ibid., 860.

55. Ibid., 864.

reality described in the texts (including material existence and even na-tional distinctions) informs the way in which he conceives the final state.

Moore notes that there are certain events that take place before this fi-nal order becomes reality, events related to Day of the Lord prophecies. He describes this Day as "a time of cosmic disturbance in which the heavens and the earth are tossed about and come under the fearful judgment of Is-rael's God (Joel 3:14-16). The Prophet Elijah will return to point the nation of Israel toward her king, before the 'great and awesome day of the Lord' (Mal. 4:5-6). Then—and only then—comes the peace of the final messianic order."[56] Similarly, when discussing the eschatological implications of God's covenantal promises, Moore notes that a number of prophetic passages look forward to the territorial restoration of Israel. Referencing Jeremiah's prophecy, for example, he writes, "In the prophesied new covenant God promises to unite the fractured nations of Israel and Judah into one people, a people who all know Yahweh, are forgiven of their sins, and are restored as a nation in the promised land (Jer. 31:31-40)."[57] In an extended para-graph, Moore summarizes the prophetical promises for Israel:

> The covenants look forward—past Israel's then-present disobedi-ence—to the day when the vine of God bears fruit (Ps. 80:8-19; Isa. 5:1-7; 27:6; Ezek. 15:1-8; 17:1-24; 19:10-14; Hos. 10:1-2), the harlot of God's people is a faithful bride washed of all unclean-ness (Isa. 54:5-6; Jer. 3:20; Ezek. 16:1-63; Hos. 2:1-23), the exiled refuges are returned to a secure homeland, and the flock of God is united under one Davidic shepherd who will feed them and divide them from the goats (Jer. 3:15-19; 23:1-8; Ezek. 34:1-31; Micah 5:2-4; 7:14-17). In this coming future Israel will be what she is called to be, the light of the world, a light that the darkness cannot overcome (Isa. 60:1-3). In this future God's favor on Israel is clear to the nations because he is present with his people. The repeated promise of the covenant is: "I will be your God and you will be my people." As Joel prophesies: "You shall know that I am in the midst of Israel, that I am the Lord your God and there is none else" (Joel 2:27). . . . the covenants picture their fulfillment not just in terms of inheritance blessings but also in terms of restoration of Eden (Ezek. 36:33-36; 37:22-23), the building of a glorious temple (2 Sam. 7:13; Ezek. 40:1-47:12), the return of a remnant from ex-ile (Isa. 11:12-16), and the construction of a holy city of Zion in

56. Ibid., 860.
57. Ibid., 861.

which Yahweh dwells with his people in splendor (Pss. 48:1–14; 74:2; Isa. 18:7; Lam. 5:17–22; Ezek. 48:30–35).[58]

The important point here is the earthly reality in which these prophecies will be fulfilled. God's reign will be "through his human mediator-king over a world in submission to his righteous rule."[59] Christ will possess "wisdom to judge the people of God and power to defeat the enemies of God (Isa. 11:1–5; 42:1–2; 61:1–11)."[60] The Spirit will be poured out on all flesh (Joel 2:28–32).[61] The rule of the messianic king "will extend to the ends of the earth (Zech. 9:9–10)" and he will "rule the earth in justice and with permanence (Isa. 9:1–7)" and this kingdom "will remain forever (Dan. 7:14)."[62] Though he ultimately understands the fulfillment of the territorial promise to Israel as metaphorical, Moore is comfortable to utilize OT restoration texts which speak vividly about the territorial restoration of Israel to inform his conception of the final state.

The Land as a Portion of the Whole

The first observation from the analysis in the previous paragraphs is that new creationists utilize OT prophetical texts not only to affirm the concept that the earth is to be renewed but also to inform the nature of that renewal.[63] According to these texts, for example, new creationists argue that animal predation will not be a part of the new earth. There will be no more sorrow and pain. The dead will be raised to immortality and death will be no more. Peace, security, and blessing will fill the earth. The cultures and societies of the nations will bring glory to the Lord. Nature will be healed from the curse and the earth will flourish and be bountiful.

58. Ibid., 861–62.

59. Ibid., 862.

60. Ibid., 863.

61. Ibid.

62. Ibid., 864.

63. It is conceivable that one could question the validity of the use of these passages to inform the nature of the final state in its materiality. After all, none of the new creation proponents seem to offer an apologetic for the practice. Instead, it seems that the practice is a natural move for the new creationist who affirms a renewed earth as a part of the renewed cosmos. For the purposes of arguing the logical inconsistency within new creationists' usage of the passages, the point only needs to be made that the new creation proponents utilize the passages to inform their conception of the final state.

The second observation from the analysis is the presence of particular territorial references in the new creationists' descriptions of the new earth. These references are present despite the already established fact that new creationists deny the role of the territory of Israel as part of the new earth. The question is whether the texts themselves offer any indication regarding the validity of the common practice of discarding the territorial particularity of Israel. Is the particular territory of Israel a necessary element to the restoration described in the passages? Or, alternatively, is it a disposable element that can be redefined in a spiritual manner or universalized so that it becomes the whole earth?

The territorial restoration of Israel seems to be an inherent feature of the promised restoration in those texts. One might think of a building whose infrastructure includes lighting for all of its respective rooms being controlled by one switch.[64] If one turns the switch to "on," the lights in each distinct room shine. Alternatively, if one turns the switch to "off," the lights in each room turn off. One may desire to have a light on in one or more of the rooms only. However, it would be impossible to do so with the existing infrastructure. What would be required is a change of the infrastructure so that each room can be controlled individually. What I am suggesting is that new creationists' practice of discarding land particularity is not allowed by the framework (i.e., the infrastructure) of the OT texts. Because they utilize the texts to inform their conception of the material reality of the restored new earth, discarding the particularity of territorial Israel in those texts is logically inconsistent.

The reason that it is logically inconsistent for new creationists to discard the particularity of the territory of Israel is that in the prophetical texts that are utilized the particular land of Israel is presented as a portion of the whole. For example, in Isaiah 2:2–4, a vision that is said to concern the particular places of Judah and Jerusalem (2:1), Zion (Jerusalem) is described as being established as the chief of all of other mountains.[65] It is the particular place to which the nations will "stream" in an upward direction.[66]

---

64. I am indebted to Craig Blaising for the building analogy.

65. Because of the similar language in Micah 4:1–3, there has been much discussion regarding the relationship of the passages. Normally, when the language is utilized among new creationists, there is a reference to both passages. For a brief introduction to the issue of the relationship between Isa 2:2–4 and Mic 4:1–3—including the role of Isa 2:1 and the origin of the language that appears in both texts—see Smith, *Isaiah 1–39*, 126–28.

66. The language describing the nations streaming up to Zion is interesting. As

According to the vision, the word of the Lord is going to proceed from a particular place and go out to other places all over the earth. The point is that the particular territory of Israel is envisioned as a portion of the whole earth.

The concept of the territory of Israel as a portion of the whole earth also can be seen in Isaiah 11, a text utilized by new creationists to argue for the peace that is to come upon the earth, especially in regards to the general effects that holistic salvation has upon the animal kingdom as a part of the renewed earth (11:6–8). In the context of the peace that is to come upon the earth, the particular place of God's holy mountain, Jerusalem, is mentioned in verse 9 immediately before the mention of the whole earth being full of the knowledge of the Lord. The particular territory of Jerusalem is distinguished from the whole earth in the vision of peace. Further, in verses 11–16, Isaiah speaks of a restored remnant which God will gather from all over the earth ("from the four corners of the earth," v. 12). There is even a mention of a highway on which the remnant can return to Jerusalem. Like Isaiah 2, Isaiah 11 includes a particular territory which is a portion of the whole.

The territory of Israel as a portion of the whole earth also is present in Isaiah 24–27, a text which new creationists utilize to inform their conception of the new earth.[67] In chapter 24, Isaiah envisions the earth being

Jonathan Magonet writes, "The root גהר is used metaphorically of people flowing towards a place (Jer 31:12; 51:44), but the overwhelming number of occurrences of the root are as a noun, meaning a river. Except in poetic texts (such as Psalm 114:3, 5) rivers do not flow upstream towards a mountain. So this paradoxical image reinforces the upward movement." Magonet, "Isaiah's Mountain," 175. J. Alec Motyer writes, "The presence and truth of the Lord (2–3a) exercises a supernatural magnetism, producing a reordered world (4a) and a new humanity (4b). . . . The incongruity of a *stream* flowing upwards to earth's highest point is intentional; a supernatural magnetism is at work." Motyer, *Prophecy of Isaiah*, 53–54. Cf. Wildberger, *Isaiah 1–12*, 90. Regarding Jerusalem at the time of Isaiah's writing, Smith writes, "The geographical setting of the historical city of Jerusalem is located on a lower mountain than the Mount of Olives to the east, which might imply something of an inferior status in the eyes of some ancient people. In the ancient Near Eastern world temples were usually built on the highest place available, so they would be closer to heaven. This new exaltation of God's dwelling place will symbolically demonstrate to the nations the superior glory and greatness of God." Smith, *Isaiah 1–39*, 129.

67. The use of Isa 24–27 among new creationists is not surprising given the connection of these chapters to the opening chapters of the book. Regarding the relationship between Isa 24–27 and Isa 2:2–4, Motyer writes, "In 2:2–4 a Zion hymn expressed a universal hope centred [sic] on the city as a magnet to the whole world. The companion truth, however, to the call to the nations ('Come, let us go up'; 2:3) is a call to the Lord's people, 'Come, let us walk' (2:5). Though they lived in Zion they had already lost the Zion

completely laid waste (Isa 24:1, 3). As a part of the judgment, God "will punish the host of heaven on high, And the kings of the earth on earth" (Isa 24:21). In verse 23, the vision includes the Lord reigning on Mount Zion and in Jerusalem. Language of territorial particularity continues in chapter 25 where it is said that "the hand of the Lord will rest on this mountain" (Isa 25:10). In chapter 26, Isaiah prophesies that there will be singing in the land of Judah and in chapter 27 that "Jacob will take root, Israel will blossom and sprout, And they will fill the whole world with fruit" (Isa 27:6). The presence of the territory of Israel as a portion of the whole earth is maintained throughout the four chapters, culminating in the final verses of the chapter 27: "In that day the Lord will start His threshing from the flowing stream of the Euphrates to the brook of Egypt, and you will be gathered up one by one, O sons of Israel. It will come about also in that day that a great trumpet will be blown, and those who were perishing in the land of Assyria and who were scattered in the land of Egypt will come and worship the Lord in the holy mountain at Jerusalem (Isa 27:12–13)."

Isaiah 35 expands upon the glorious future of Zion with descriptions of land and animal life, descriptions that new creationists utilize to inform their understanding of the new earth. The chapter distinguishes Zion from other territorial particularities such as the Arabah (Isa 35:1); Lebanon, Carmel, and Sharon (Isa 35:2); and, like in Isaiah 11, a highway, here called the Highway of Holiness (Isa 35:8–9). It is to the particular place, Zion, that the "ransomed of the Lord will return" (Isa 35:10). In this vision, the territory of Israel is a portion of the restored earth.

The last two chapters of Isaiah's prophecy are perhaps the most utilized OT texts by new creationists arguing for a restored or renewed earth. After noting the rebellion of his people in the early verses of Isaiah 65, God makes a promise to act in mercy by not utterly destroying all of the rebellious. Then he makes a promise concerning the way in which he will act:" 'I will bring forth offspring from Jacob, and an heir of My mountains from Judah; Even My chosen ones shall inherit it, and My servants will dwell there.

---

ideal and they too must come on pilgrimage back to the Lord. Chapters 24–27 express this double pilgrimage on a grand scale." Motyer, *Prophecy of Isaiah*, 194. Sweeney writes that "chs. 24–27 explain the manifestations of YHWH's world rule at Zion in relation to the judgment against the nations expressed in chs. 13–23 and the punishment and subsequent restoration of Israel and Judah expressed in chs. 1–12. Likewise, 2:2–4 conveys the central role that Zion will play in this scenario." Sweeney, *Isaiah 1–39*, 316. For a comprehensive treatment of Isa 24–27 as a distinct unit within the whole book of Isaiah, see Sweeney, *Isaiah 1–39*, 311–25.

'Sharon will be a pasture land for flocks, and the valley of Achor a resting place for My people who seek Me (Isa 65:9–10).' Following this declaration is the often quoted OT passage that corresponds to Revelation 21 in which God says that he will create new heavens and a new earth (Isa 65:17), that he will create Jerusalem for rejoicing (Isa 65:18), and that he will rejoice in Jerusalem (Isa 65:19). In the last verse of the chapter, a verse used by new creationists to argue for the end of animal predation in the new earth, God speaks of his holy mountain (Isa 65:25).

The call to "be joyful with Jerusalem and rejoice for her" continues in Isaiah 66:10. God says that he will extend peace to her like a river and the glory of the nations like an overflowing stream (Isa 66:12). He pronounces comfort for his people in Jerusalem (Isa 66:13). These statements describe a reversal of fortunes for the relationship between Jerusalem and the nations. The territorial particularities of Isaiah 66 increase as one progresses through the chapter. In verses 19–20, God proclaims the following:

> "I will set a sign among them and will send survivors from them to the nations: Tarshish, Put, Lud, Meshech, Tubal, and Javan, to the distant coastlands that have neither heard My fame nor seen My glory. And they will declare My glory among the nations. "Then they shall bring all your brethren from all the nations as a grain offering to the Lord, on horses, in chariots, in litters, on mules and on camels, to My holy mountain Jerusalem," says the Lord, "just as the sons of Israel bring their grain offering in a clean vessel to the house of the Lord (66:19–20).[68]

Israel and Jerusalem are described as distinct territories of the new earth mentioned in Isaiah 66:22. What seems to be a necessary feature of Isaiah's vision of new heavens and new earth (cf. Isa 65:17, 66:1, 22) is the territory of God's holy mountain/Zion/Jerusalem (cf. Isa 65:11, 18–25; 66:10, 13, 20) which is a portion of the new earth. The people from the nations are described as being brought to a particular place on the earth (Jerusalem) which is not the whole but a portion of it.

Like Isaiah, Jeremiah includes territorial particularity in his prophecy concerning the coming age in Jeremiah 30–31, texts also utilized by new creationists to argue for a restored earth. In Jeremiah 30:3, God declares that he will bring his people Israel and Judah "back to the land that I gave to their forefathers and they shall possess it." Clearly, the referent is the

---

68. The themes in Isa 66:18–21 should bring to mind the initial vision given to Isaiah in 2:2–4.

land of Israel which was promised to Abraham, Isaac, and Jacob. God also promises to destroy the nations to which his people have been scattered (Jer 30:11). In verses 18–24, he promises to restore the fortunes of the tents of Jacob and rebuild the city on its ruin, with the palace standing on its rightful place.

The territorial particularities inherent in God's promises about what is to occur in the latter days continue to be a theme in Jeremiah 31. Regarding the rebuilding of Israel, God states that his people "will plant vineyards on the hills of Samaria" (Jer 31:5). He also states that there will be a day in which watchmen "On the hills of Ephraim call out, 'Arise, and let us go up to Zion, To the Lord our God (Jer 31:6). God says that he is gathering them "from the north country" and "from the remotest parts of the earth" to return to Zion (Jer 31:8). They "will come and shout for joy on the height of Zion" (Jer 31:12), having returned from the land of the enemy (Jer 31:16). He promises that their children "will return to their own territory" (Jer 31:17). Then he makes the following proclamation: "Once again they will speak this word in the land of Judah and in its cities when I restore their fortunes, 'The Lord bless you, O abode of righteousness, O holy hill (Jer 31:23). In the promise of the new covenant (Jer 31:27–40), God likens the perpetuity of the particular nation of Israel to the fixed order of the whole creation which he created and sustains (Jer 31:35–37). The chapter ends with a promise that abounds with territorial particularities of Israel:

> "Behold, days are coming," declares the Lord, "when the city will be rebuilt for the Lord from the Tower of Hananel to the Corner Gate. "The measuring line will go out farther straight ahead to the hill Gareb; then it will turn to Goah. "And the whole valley of the dead bodies and of the ashes, and all the fields as far as the brook Kidron, to the corner of the Horse Gate toward the east, shall be holy to the Lord; it will not be plucked up or overthrown anymore forever" (Jer 31:38–40).

Again, what is clear in these chapters which new creationists utilize is that territorial Israel is emphasized as a portion of the whole earth.

The particular territory of Israel as a portion of the whole earth is present in Ezekiel 36–37, chapters which are utilized among new creationists. In Ezekiel 36, God speaks to the mountains, hills, ravines, valleys, wastes, and forsaken cities of Israel. He decries the nations who have taken possession of the land and reminds them that the land is his: "Surely in the fire of My jealousy I have spoken against the rest of the nations, and against all Edom, who appropriated My land for themselves as a possession with wholehearted joy and with scorn of soul, to drive it out for a prey" (Ezek 36:5). Then he makes prophecies concerning the particular land:

'Therefore prophesy concerning the land of Israel and say to the mountains and to the hills, to the ravines and to the valleys, "Thus says the Lord God, 'Behold, I have spoken in My jealousy and in My wrath because you have endured the insults of the nations.' "Therefore thus says the Lord God, 'I have sworn that surely the nations which are around you will themselves endure their insults. 'But you, O mountains of Israel, you will put forth your branches and bear your fruit for My people Israel; for they will soon come. 'For, behold, I am for you, and I will turn to you, and you will be cultivated and sown. 'I will multiply men on you, all the house of Israel, all of it; and the cities will be inhabited and the waste places will be rebuilt. 'I will multiply on you man and beasts; and they will increase and be fruitful; and I will cause you to be inhabited as you were formerly and will treat you better than at the first. Thus you will know that I am the Lord. 'Yes, I will cause men—My people Israel—to walk on you and possess you, so that you will become their inheritance and never again bereave them of children' (Ezek 36:6–12).

In these verses, God speaks directly to the particular territory of Israel, proclaiming a future blessing. After this word, God speaks to Ezekiel concerning his people's rebellion against him when they were in the land and the consequences of that rebellion—dispersion throughout the lands (Ezek 36:16–21). Following this pronouncement, God proclaims that he will gather them together again into their own land (Ezek 36:24). Receiving the Spirit, they will live in that particular land which he gave to their forefathers (Ezek 36:28).[69] God will inhabit the cities and rebuild the waste places (Ezek 36:33) and the nations will know that the Lord has accomplished it (Ezek 36:36).

Ezekiel's vision in chapter 37 is set in a valley full of dry bones. God gives Ezekiel direction to preach to the bones concerning their resurrection (Ezek 37:5–6), and, upon Ezekiel doing so, the bones come to life (Ezek 37:9). In the explanation of the vision God reveals that the referent of the bones in the vision is the whole house of Israel. God says that he will open

69. Living in the land will include the flourishing of crops and the multiplication of fruit trees so that famine will no longer occur and they will no longer be disgraced among the nations (Ezek 36:29–30).

their graves and cause them to come out of their graves. He promises to put his Spirit inside of them and bring them into the land of Israel (Ezek 37:11–14). After Ezekiel's vision, God gives him an object lesson to communicate that there will be a reunion of Judah and Israel (Ezek 37:19, 22) at which time God will regather them to their own land (Ezek 37:21, 22, 25). He also states that he will set his sanctuary in their midst forever (Ezek 37:26, 28).

According to Zechariah 2:11, "Many nations will join themselves to the Lord in that day and will become My people. Then I will dwell in your midst, and you will know that the Lord of hosts has sent Me to you." God's dominion is described as extending "from sea to sea" and "from the River to the ends of the earth" in Zechariah 9:10. Similarly, in Zechariah 14:9, it is proclaimed that "the Lord will be king over all the earth; in that day the Lord will be the only one, and His name the only one." Parallel to these passages are particular territorial references. For example, immediately following 2:11, Zechariah proclaims, "The Lord will possess Judah as His portion in the holy land, and will again choose Jerusalem" (Zech 2:12). Particular territorial references are prevalent throughout chapter 9, including the promise that God will encamp around his house and deliver his people. In the context of the promise in Zechariah 14 in which God's reign will extend to the entire earth, it is prophesied that God "will stand on the Mount of Olives, which is in front of Jerusalem on the east; and the Mount of Olives will be split in its middle from east to west by a very large valley, so that half of the mountain will move toward the north and the other half toward the south" (Zech 14:4). There will be topographical changes prior to his coming along with his holy ones (Zech 14:5). Living waters will flow out of Jerusalem (Zech 14:8). Immediately following the reference to God's dominion encompassing the whole earth (Zech 14:9), Zechariah gives particular prophesies with regard to the changes that are to take place in and around Israel (Zech 14:10). He also states that there will be inhabitants in a peaceful Jerusalem (Zech 14:11). In addition there are images akin to Isaiah 2 and Micah 4 regarding the movement of "families of the earth" up to Jerusalem to worship the Lord (Zech 14:16).

The language in the prophets in no way suggests that the particular territory of Israel or Jerusalem somehow envelops the territory of the rest of the world. More importantly, the idea that a particular territory of the earth somehow transforms into the entire earth makes no sense in a new creation conception that envisions the restoration of the present earth. As suggested in the following chapter, the alternative conception is that the key portion of the whole remains after the whole is renewed since the whole cannot be renewed without the renewal of its parts.

Inadequacy of Metaphorical Interpretations of the Land

The new creationists surveyed in the present work affirm a metaphorical fulfillment of the particular land promise, either in the way of universalization or Christification or some combination of the two. However, both views present problems when affirming a restored new earth, especially in light of the new creationists' utilization of OT texts. The problem with the universalizing view has to do with the relationship between materiality and particularity as articulated in chapter 2 of this work. The problem with arguing that the particular land becomes the whole earth in a new creation conception is that this is a material impossibility. How is one to think of the materiality of a particular land expanding to encompass (and replace?) the whole earth? What would happen to the materiality of the earth that is enveloped by the materiality of the particular land? For either to take place would be the result of a material anomaly. This line of thinking may seem odd to those who are not thinking through the lenses of a new creation conception. For new creationists, however, this line of thinking should be natural. The OT texts utilized highlight the particular land of Israel as a select feature of the earth. The whole earth is to be renewed in its materiality, and this includes the renewal of all its particularity. How is the particular matter of the territory of Israel discarded if it is part and parcel of the whole? Alternatively, how does the part of the whole become the whole itself?

In chapter 5 I examine a few of the NT texts used by new creationists to argue that the territory of Israel has been universalized to include the whole earth. It can be seen in the brief overview of OT passages above that language concerning the territory of Israel runs parallel to language referencing the whole earth. In fact, as we have seen, the universal [the restored earth] is present in many of the utilized OT texts alongside the particular territory. Would it not be more plausible to conclude that in both the OT and the NT the particular and the universal are complementary instead of mutually exclusive?

The belief that the particular land promise is in some way spiritually fulfilled is also inadequate for a new creation conception of the new earth.

A new creationist might claim that the land is fulfilled in Christ, for example, but how does one conceive of this fulfillment actually taking place in a new creation conception. Again, new creationists think in terms of materiality and particularity. How is a particular territorial promise fulfilled spiritually in a new creation conception that emphasizes a restored earth? The irony of the two-fold affirmation of a new creation in which the earth is renewed and in which Christ is the fulfillment of the particular land of Israel can be seen in Moore's position regarding Christ as the replacement of corporate Israel in the plan of God. Because in Moore's conception the promises to Israel are fulfilled in Christ alone (one might say that they are Christified), there is no longer a place for the particular territory of Israel. In new creation conceptions, how does one think of promises of earthly territory being fulfilled in a spiritual manner such as this?

Finally, many of the restoration texts include the geographical movement of nations—Israel and various Gentile nations—across the earth. The presence of geographical movement in texts that new creationists utilize to inform the reality of the new earth should not be overlooked. The affirmation of material and time-sequenced life on a restored earth would seem to include geographical movement upon that earth. The claim that there will be radical topographical changes between the present earth and the restored earth (e.g., Rev 21:1, 23; 22:5) must be taken into account. However, admitting radical topographical alterations does not necessitate the conclusion that particular geography is absent.[70] A new creation conception that appreciates the relationship between materiality and particularity demands geographical distinctions despite possible topographical alterations. Unless there is utter stasis among the inhabitants of the restored earth, there will be geographical movement. Why, then, would the restoration texts which speak clearly of geographical movement of Israel and the nations be interpreted as referring to something other than the actual geographical movement of peoples upon the earth, movement that is centered upon the particular territory of Israel?

70. The admission of geographical movement, at least in regard to the new Jerusalem, can be seen in Middleton. He writes, "The fact that the new Jerusalem does not encompass the entirety of the new creation, but instead represents the central locus of God's presence, might lead one to wonder if the cultural development of the earth is a continuing human task. Such development can happen as the redeemed do their part in filling the earth with the healing presence of God, thereby extending the parameters of the city and participating in the eschatological destiny of the world." Middleton, *A New Heaven and a New Earth*, 174–75.

Conclusion

There is general agreement among new creationists that OT restoration texts inform the earthly and material reality of the new earth. The issue that has been highlighted in the previous pages is the logical inconsistency in the way in which the new creationists treat these passages. This logical inconsistency is seen by noting the particular and the universal elements, respectively, in these passages. Against new creationists, many of the OT restoration texts envision the territorial particularity of Israel as a portion of the whole earth, a vision which necessarily excludes metaphorical interpretations of the particular territorial promise by means of spiritualization or universalization. In the next chapter, I will propose that a new creation conception of the final state coheres with upholding the territorial particularity of Israel as a portion of the renewed earth and harmonizes with NT texts commonly used among new creationists to deny the role of the territory of Israel in the new earth.

5

Territorial Particularity
in Consistent New Creationism

As shown in the previous chapter, a number of OT texts that are utilized by new creationists include language that emphasizes the particular territory of Israel as a portion of the whole earth. The new creationists surveyed in the present work seem to admit that territorial particularity is present in the various texts. However, as seen in chapter 3, none of them affirm a future relevance for that particular territory. Instead, they follow traditionally held views that the particular territory of Israel is superseded through spiritual fulfillment or through the universalization of the land such that it includes the whole earth.

In this chapter, I offer an alternative to the conclusion that the territorial particularity of Israel has been superseded. In an attempt to draw together the various elements of the present work, I suggest that affirming the territorial restoration of Israel 1) represents a consistent utilization of OT new creation texts, 2) is harmonious with NT texts commonly used to deny territorial restoration, and 3) leads to a consistent new creation eschatology that emphasizes the materiality of the final state. In doing so, I note a small group of theologians who have argued that upholding the territorial restoration of Israel actually bolsters a new creation conception.

Consistent Utilization of OT New Creation Texts

As argued in the previous chapter, there is a logical inconsistency in the way in which new creationists utilize certain OT prophecies to inform their conception of the new earth. A consistent approach would include the particular territory referenced in these texts that also envision the new earth. Because of the relationship between materiality and particularity (as argued in chapter 2) and the affirmation by new creationists that the present heavens and earth is going to be restored (hence, its current identity corresponds with its future identity), it seems that the utilization of OT texts to inform the nature of the new earth in its materiality would also lead to the affirmation of the territorial restoration of Israel as a part of the new earth. The inclusion of this restoration also would seem to suggest the wider inclusion of OT restoration texts in conceptions of the new creation.

The conclusion above seems to be bolstered by the concept of the partial and the whole in these texts. As argued in the previous chapter, a number of the texts utilized by new creationists include language concerning a new earth together with language concerning a particular portion of that earth—i.e., the land, the city, Jerusalem, or some other feature therof. As evidenced earlier, some new creationists argue that the NT universalizes the particular territory of Israel, that the particular territory of Israel in the OT is a metaphor for the entire earth. It is interesting to note, however, that none of them seem to appreciate the presence of both the universal and the particular in the OT prophecies which they utilize to inform their conception of the new earth. Could it be that the NT is simply emphasizing one of the two correlative ideas, the whole as opposed to the particular, instead of substituting one for the other, implying that the particular is universalized to become the whole? The fact that the NT is not as focused as the OT is on the territory of Israel could be because the OT conception of that territory was so ingrained in the original hearers that it did not need to be reiterated and the emphases of the NT were to inform the OT teaching of place, not replace it.

Harmony with NT Texts

Affirming the territorial particularity of Israel in texts that inform the conception of the new earth is harmonious with the concept that God is going to restore all things (cf. Matt 17:11; Mark 9:12; Col 1:20), a concept that new creationists readily affirm. New creationists typically emphasize the inherent goodness of the created order, humanity's sin subsequent to the completion of that created order, and God's plan to reverse the effects of the sin and restore the original goodness of all creation. God's power and might are signified in his desire and plan to redeem that which is in bondage, which includes not only his human creation, but all of creation (cf. Rom 8). As argued in chapter 2, a new creation conception that affirms a restored present heavens and earth involves a correspondence of identity between the materiality of the present earth and the materiality of the new earth. The correspondence of identity in the material particularity of the whole seems to imply a correspondence of identity of portions of the whole.

Not only is the affirmation of territorial particularity harmonious with the general concept of God restoring all things, it also is harmonious with certain NT texts sometimes used to discard the particular land promises of the OT. Contrariwise, many new creationists prefer to view the NT interpretation of the relationship between the part and the whole as one of mutual exclusivity. In other words, new creationists tend to discard the particular territory because certain NT texts seem to focus on the whole earth.[1] The point is not to argue that these texts explicitly teach that the particular land promises of the OT should be upheld, but simply to show that these texts can be understood in a way that harmonizes with the affirmation of the particular territorial promise to Israel in the OT.[2]

---

1. In an essay on Paul's use of the phrase "new creation," Moo states, probably correctly, "It is quite unlikely, given the usual meaning of 'creation' in Paul, that he would use 'new creation' to allude to [the] Isaianic expectation without some reference to the cosmos." Moo, "Creation and New Creation," 45–46. Regarding the Isaianic echo in Rom 7, Moo writes that Paul's "conviction about the physical restoration of the entire world is to some extent derived from the prophetic hope for the restoration of Israel to her land—a restoration that in these chapters, and in a manner typical of Isaiah's prophecy, ultimately encompasses the whole world (see esp. 24:21–23; 27:6, 13)." Moo, "Nature in the New Creation," 463. Moo's conclusion is that the purpose of Paul's emphasis on the whole is to disregard the part. However, it does not follow that a reference to the cosmos as a whole means that the particular territory has been obliterated. The point to be made is that Paul's reference to the cosmos more likely includes its territorial particularities such as Israel.

2. Psalm 37:11, 22 is referenced by new creationists along with the NT texts discussed here to teach that the particular territory of Israel has been universalized. See, for example, Moore, "Personal and Cosmic Eschatology," 907, who, like Hoekema (cf. Hoekema, *Bible and the Future*, 278–81), argues that Jesus utilizes the Psalm to universalize the inheritance language of Israel in regard to the particular land to believers in regard to the whole earth.

Matthew 5:5

Jesus' words in the Beatitudes are used by new creationists to argue that the territorial promise of the OT has been universalized to include the whole earth: "Blessed are the meek, for they shall inherit the earth" (Matt 5:5, ESV).[3] Evans rightly states, "The promise that the meek will 'inherit the earth' . . . recalls God's promise to Abraham: 'I am the Lord who brought you out of Ur of the Chaldeans, to give you this land" (Gen 15:7 RSV; cf. 28:4)."[4] New creationists argue that Jesus is expanding the promise of the particular territory promised to Abraham through offering the whole earth instead. While this interpretation may at first be appealing, one must ask if universalization is the only valid interpretation. In other words is there a way to affirm that Jesus' pronouncement of blessing on the meek does not discard the territorial restoration of Israel promised in the OT? While we cannot be dogmatic regarding Jesus' intent in the blessing for the meek, it seems unlikely that in this context he is intending to obliterate a long held Jewish belief of territorial inheritance or suggesting that the territorial promise of Israel per se should now be expanded to the whole earth. Granted, those who utilize this passage may respond by saying that this passage stands with other passages which speak to the idea of universalization. Still, the likelihood that Jesus is attempting such a drastic change in worldview in such few words should be questioned.[5]

Against the new creation view of understanding Jesus' words as universalizing the territorial promise, a number of scholars argue that the language concerning the meek inheriting the land is not to be taken as literally referring to geography in any sense. For example, W. D. Davies seems to

---

3. It is widely acknowledged that there is a relationship between Matt 5:5 and Psalm 37. Hagner notes the following: "The third beatitude is practically a quotation of the LXX of Ps 36[37]:11:οἱ δὲ πραεῖς κληρονομήσουσιν τὴν γῆν, 'the meek will inherit the earth.'" Hagner, *Matthew 1–13*, 92.

4. Evans, *Matthew*, 106. Evidence of the relationship between Jesus' statement and God's promise to Abraham is the verbal repetition in the Greek.

5. In light of the repetition of God's promise to Abraham (e.g., in Ex 23:30; Deut 4:1; Isa 60:21; and Isa 61:7), Evans concludes the following: "Jesus' third beatitude . . . speaks to Israel's hope for national renewal, which includes, in some instances, regaining the land itself. It must be remembered that many in Israel in Jesus' day were poor and had been disinherited, possibly because the law of the jubilee (cf. Leviticus 25), whereby debts are forgiven and land seized in foreclosure is returned, had not been observed. Jesus' beatitude and its allusion to the promised re-inheriting of the land would strike a hopeful chord in the hearts of his hearers." Ibid., 106.

exclude the common view of new creationists as a possible interpretation. He states, "The reference [in Matt 5:5] is not to a merely geographic earth, but to the 'redeemed' earth of the Age to Come, 'which eye hath not seen nor ear heard.'"[6] Then, he states that the interpreter has two possible choices regarding the meaning of the language: "either . . . hold that Matt. 5:5 refers to inheriting, not the earth, but the land of Israel in a transformed world, in the Messianic Age or the Age to Come, or to recognize that for Matthew 'inheriting the land' is synonymous with entering the Kingdom and that this Kingdom transcends all geographic dimensions and is spiritualized."[7] Davies concludes "that in Mt 5.5 'to inherit the land' has been spiritualized, and 5.5b is no more concrete than any of the other promises made in the beatitudes. It is just another way of saying, 'The one who humbles himself will be exalted (in the kingdom of God).'"[8] France takes a similar approach:

> In echoing [Psalm 37:7–9] so closely, Jesus clearly intended to promise a reversal of fortunes such as the psalm envisages, but whereas the "inheriting of the land" in the psalm seems to be understood in terms of earthly reversal, the overall tone of these beatitudes does not encourage us to interpret his words here quite so literally . . . . There is a general tendency in the NT to treat OT promises about "the land" as finding fulfillment in nonterritorial ways, and such an orientation seems required here too. The focus is on the principle of reversal of fortunes rather than on a specific "inheritance."[9]

Even if the whole earth as territory is in view in Matthew 5:5, as new creationists contend, there is an alternative view of the passage which seems to be more appropriate for its context than one which universalizes the promised territory into the whole earth. The preaching of both John the Baptist and Jesus was one of repentance from sin in light of the kingdom of heaven which was to come to the earth (e.g., Matt 3:2; 4:23). While going throughout all of Galilee, Jesus taught in the synagogues, proclaiming the gospel of the kingdom and healing diseases. When the crowd around him grows, he goes up on the mountain and begins to preach there. In the context of the kingdom which is coming upon the earth, Jesus speaks about the meek inheriting the earth. The logic is 1) The promised kingdom is coming

6. Davies, *Gospel and the Land*, 362.
7. Ibid.
8. Davies and Allison, *Gospel According to Saint Matthew*, 450–51.
9. France, *Gospel of Matthew*, 166–67.

upon the earth; 2) Repent in light of its coming; and 3) Those who repent and live according to that repentance inherit the very earth upon which the kingdom will come.[10] While the emphasis in this interpretation is upon the coming of an earthly kingdom, the interpretation does not inherently exclude the promise of a particular territory of the earth being given to a particular people.[11] In fact, it seems to make sense in light of the fact that Jesus at that time is preaching only to Israel.

John 4:19–24

Jesus' words to the woman as recorded in John 4 are also sometimes used as evidence that the particular territory has been universalized to include the whole earth. In the passage, Jesus speaks of a radical change in the relationship between place and worship. In the first century the particular places of worship were well-known and followed from the history of God's interaction with his people in the OT (e.g., Gen 12:6, 7; Deut 11: 29, 30; 12:5; 2 Sam 7:5–13; 2 Chron 6:6). Jesus speaks of an hour which is to come when the woman will worship "neither in this mountain nor in Jerusalem" (John 4:20). An hour is coming, he says, in which "true worshipers will worship the Father in spirit and truth." (John 4:23). As seen in chapter 3, a common interpretation of this passage among new creationists is that Jesus is discarding any future relevance for the particular territory which was promised to Israel as an everlasting inheritance. However, this interpretation is certainly not the only one that makes sense.

Aside from the fact that, like the other two passages covered in this section, it is unlikely that a whole worldview is being challenged in such a

10. Hagner's comments should not necessarily be denied. He writes, "The 'earth' (τὴν γῆν) originally referred to the land of Israel, i.e., what was promised to the Jews beginning with the Abrahamic covenant (cf. Gen. 13:15). But in the present context of messianic fulfillment it connotes the regenerated earth (19:28; cf. Rom 4:13, where κόσμοσ, 'world,' replaces γῆ), promised by the eschatological passages in the prophets (e.g., Isa 65–66)." Hagner, *Matthew 1–13*, 92–93. For a discussion of the various uses of the biblical terminology of land and earth, see Uemura, *Land or Earth?*.

11. Nolland argues that the particular territory of Israel is actually in view in the passage. He writes, "In Ps. 36(37):11 the γῆ ('land') to be inherited is clearly the land of Israel, in the context of God's covenant promise to his people. But since γῆ can also mean the 'earth', what about the meaning in Matthew? The interest in 4:25 in the scope of historic Israel . . . and the evocation of exile and return in the opening beatitudes weigh in favour of Matthew's also intending γῆ to refer to Israel as the land of covenant promise." Nolland, *Gospel of Matthew*, 202.

brief interaction, there seems to be questions regarding the legitimacy of interpreting Jesus' words as a denunciation of the territorial particularity of Israel. According to Köstenberger, Jesus' words to the woman became reality in the first century: "Jesus' prophecy was literally fulfilled through the events of A.D. 66–70 when the Romans, under Titus, razed Jerusalem, including the temple (cf. Luke 21:20, 24). Spiritually speaking, the crucified and resurrected Christ would serve as a substitute for the Jerusalem temple as the new center of worship for God's people (John 2:19–22)."[12] In light of the historical events that were imminent, according to Köstenberger, it makes sense that Jesus would tell the woman that worship on the mountain and in Jerusalem would come to an end. However, it does not necessitate the conclusion which Köstenberger himself seems to adopt that Jesus is denying the importance of territorial particularity in the consummation, specifically that particularity of which the OT prophecies spoke frequently and specifically.

Further, Jesus' words could be seen as minimizing the importance of location for true worship with his emphasis on the importance of worshipping in spirit and in truth.[13] Commenting on Jesus' response, McHugh writes, "The gospel . . . is not concerned to determine the correct locality for earthly liturgy, but to transcend that question by declaring that the very principle of worship is about to be altered, irrevocably."[14] Regarding the

---

12. Köstenberger, *John*, 155.

13. Ridderbos correctly notes that Jesus' language regarding worshipping in Spirit and in truth is not intended to separate worship from the sphere of materiality: "The mark of [the] future is worship 'in Spirit and truth,' as contrasted with worship that is bound to a specific place. This is not to be understood as saying that true worship is realized totally in the sphere of the supersensuous and elevated above the visible temporal world or any cultic form. 'Spirit'—here linked with 'truth' in a hendiadys as with 'grace and truth' in 1:17—refers to the time of salvation that has come with Christ and to the concomitant new way in which God wants to relate to human beings. Whereas 'grace and truth' above all describe the compassion and love God displayed in the sending of his Son (cf. 3:16), 'Spirit and truth' refer to the fellowship thus established in its life-creating and life-giving power, as leading to the fullness of God's gifts (cf. 1:16) that is no longer mediated by all sorts of provisional and symbolic forms, but by the Spirit of God himself, which is why it is repeatedly called worship of the 'Father.'" Ridderbos, *Gospel According to John*, 163–64.

14. McHugh, *John 1–4*, 285. McHugh adds an interesting note regarding Jesus' wording: "In v. 20 the woman had used the verb προσκυνεῖν absolutely, and in the past tense, of her own community; here in v. 21 Jesus speaks of the future, uses the dative (the common LXX form for offering liturgical praise to Yahweh), and introduces the term τῷ πατρί." Ibid.

emphasis on worshipping in Spirit and in truth, Köstenberger writes that "true worship is not a matter of geographical location (worship in a church building), physical posture (kneeling or standing), or following a particular liturgy or external rituals (cf. Matt. 6:5–13); it is a matter of the heart and of the Spirit."[15] The point seems to be that Jesus is countering the woman's concern regarding geographical territory, not refocusing her attention on a greater territory, specifically that of the whole earth. Regarding the language of the true worshippers, Carson writes,

> The expression *the true worshippers* does not make a distinction between worshippers *after* the ministry of Jesus (the *true* worshippers) and those *before* the ministry of Jesus (presumably the *false* worshippers). Both true and false worshipper [*sic*] could be found under the terms of the old covenant, and both can be found appealing to the new covenant as well. Rather, the point is that with the coming of the 'hour' the distinction between true worshippers and all others turns on factors that make the ancient dispute between the conflicting claims of the Jerusalem temple and Mount Gerizim obsolete. Under the eschatological conditions of the dawning hour, the true worshippers cannot be identified by their attachment to a particular shrine, but by their worship of the Father *in spirit and truth*. . . . To worship the Father 'in spirit and truth' clearly means much more than worship without necessary ties to particular holy places (though it cannot mean any less).[16]

So, against the universalization interpretation of the passage, a common position is that Jesus' words are not focused upon geography—whether portions of the earth or the whole earth—but on the heart of the worshipper. Ultimately, it seems unlikely that Jesus' point is that the OT promises regarding particular geographical territories are being discarded and therefore have no significance for the future.

Romans 4:13

Another text often used by new creationists to argue that the OT territorial promise has been universalized to include the whole earth is Romans 4:13. In the process of arguing that Abraham was justified by faith and not by works, Paul makes what seems to be a passing comment regarding the

15. Köstenberger, *John*, 157.
16. Carson, *Gospel According to John*, 224–26. Cf. Beasley-Murray, *John*, 61–62.

inheritance God promised to Abraham: "For the promise to Abraham or
to his descendants that he would be heir of the world was not through the
Law, but through the righteousness of faith" (Rom 4:13). The legitimacy of
interpreting this verse in a universalizing manner is supported by Paul's use
of inclusive language in his discussion of circumcision:

> How then was it [faith as righteousness] credited? While he was
> circumcised, or uncircumcised? Not while circumcised, but while
> uncircumcised; and he received the sign of circumcision, a seal of
> righteousness of the faith which he had while uncircumcised, so
> that he might be the father of all who believe without being cir-
> cumcised, that righteousness might be credited to them, and the
> father of circumcision to those who also follow in the steps of the
> faith of our father Abraham which he had while uncircumcised
> (Rom 4:10–12).

However, to argue that Paul is utilizing the term "κόσμου" to communicate that the territorial promise of the OT has been expanded to
the territory of the whole earth is tenuous at best. The conclusion seems
to overemphasize the role of geographical territory in Paul's statement.
Though material prosperity cannot necessarily be excluded, Paul's argument is more complex, including both both the spiritual and the material.[17]
While one cannot rule out that Paul had in mind landedness as a part of
the overall blessing, it is unlikely that he was arguing that the nature of the
OT territorial promise had been universalized. Instead, Paul seems to be
summarizing the complex fulfillment of the promise to Abraham and is
doing so in a general way and with an emphasis on people (descendants)
rather than the earth.[18] So, Middendorf concludes that "rather than being

17. Regarding the nature of the promise to the heir, Morris writes, "It could be understood as an enthusiastic description of great material prosperity, but we expect something in the way of spiritual blessing here. Perhaps material blessing is used as a symbol
of spiritual blessing. It is possible to see the prosperity in terms of the family of faith that
Abraham would beget, a worldwide family." Morris, *Romans*, 206. It is not necessary
to conclude, like Davies, that Paul's "interpretation of the promise is a-territorial," and
fulfilled christologically. Davies, *Gospel and the Land*, 179.

18. Cf. Cranfield, *Epistle to the Romans*, 239. While Moo admits that Paul is summarizing the fulfillment of the promise, he still concludes that this verse teaches that
the particular land promise has been expanded to include the entire world. He writes,
"The clause 'that they should be heirs of the world' explains what the promise is. This
language does not exactly match any promise to Abraham found in the OT but succinctly
summarizes the three key provisions of the promise as it unfolds in Genesis: that Abraham would have an immense number of descendants, embracing 'many nations' (Gen.
12:2; 13:16; 15:5; 17:4–6, 16–20; 22:17), that he would possess 'the land' (Gen. 13:15–17;

an illegitimate expansion, Paul's phrasing encompasses the implications of the overall promise."[19]

Even if Paul's point is that Abraham's descendants would inherit the territory of the whole earth, it would not necessarily follow that the promise of the particular territory and the particular people or nation of Israel should be excluded from it. The promise that every believer would take part in the renewal of the earth in the final state is in no way antithetical to the promise that all ethnic Jewish believers would inherit a particular portion of that renewed earth. Like Matthew 5:5 and John 4:19–24, Romans 4:13 does not offer definitive justification to the claim that OT territorial promises have been universalized or expanded in such a way as to lose their particular place in the consummation. Yet these texts are often cited as the primary evidence of the process of territorial universalization in the NT. Instead of denying the fulfillment of the particular territorial promise, the texts at minimum allow it.

Fulfillment in Christ?

The question of fulfillment does not have to do with the legitimacy of christological fulfillment of the particular land promise per se, but the meaning behind that language. As seen in the previous two chapters, it is common to understand the territorial promise to Israel as spiritually fulfilled in Christ's person and work. In this understanding the fulfillment of the promise has taken place already in history. However, there is another notion of christological fulfillment that could potentially be utilized in a new creation conception that affirms territorial particularity in the final state. In this sense, the meaning is that the particular territorial promises to Israel are fulfilled through Christ's victory over sin and death, that is, through his

---

15:12–21; 17:8), and that he would be the medium of blessing to 'all the peoples of the earth' (Gen. 12:3; 18:18; 22:18). . . . Against this background—to which we can add Jesus' beatitude, 'Blessed are the gentle, for they shall inherit the earth'—Paul probably refers generally to all that God promised his people." Moo, *Epistle to the Romans*, 274. See also Thomas Schreiner's extensive treatment on the meaning of the promise of inheritance. While Schreiner may in fact agree that the land promise has been universalized in the NT, he does not state that this text teaches such a point, but instead focuses, like Moo, on the three features of the promise to Abraham, and the universal character of the promise of blessing that is set forth throughout the OT. Schreiner, *Romans*, 226–29.

19. Middendorf, *Romans 1–8*, 353.

sacrificial atonement for the sins of the world.[20] The point is that the only way in which the particular territorial restoration takes place is through the person and work of Christ. Furthermore, the fact that this restoration is extended to the entire earth does not exclude the restoration of the particular territory of Israel.

Consistent Emphasis on the Materiality of the Final State

Finally, the affirmation of a future role for the territorial particularity of Israel seems to bolster the new creation conception of the final state. As noted above, it would open up the possibility of a variety of other OT prophetic texts to inform one's conception of the final state. It would also support the conclusion that the final state is an existence within materiality, rather than absent from it.

Two dispensationalists who recently have argued for a new creation understanding are Craig Blaising and Michael Vlach.[21] Not wanting to limit the promises regarding territorial particularity to the millennial kingdom, these theologians argue that the millennial kingdom is a transition to the eternal kingdom, but that the transition is not from a material and time-sequenced existence on earth to an immaterial, eternal existence in heaven. Instead, the transition is one to a material and time-sequenced everlasting existence on a restored earth with the New Jerusalem being the focal point. The restoration, according to these theologians, has territorial implications. OT prophecies regarding the particular territory of Israel are fulfilled for national Israel in the final state as a part of the restoration of the earth.

Vlach argues, though, that national particularities do not begin and end with Israel: "Nations appear to have a place in God's future plans. Although nations are a postfall development and they often act contrary to God's purposes in this present age, there is no indication that the concept of nations is inherently unspiritual or wrong."[22] Vlach argues that the diversity of nations is God's intention and that God has used specific nations

---

20. Cf. fn 103 in chapter 1 in the present work.

21. See Blaising, "Premillennialsim,"; Blaising, "New Creation Eschatology,"; and Vlach, *Has the Church Replaced Israel?*. See also Vlach's recent work *He Will Reign Forever* which offers a comprehensive biblical theology of the kingdom of God. I regret that the schedule of this book did not allow me to give Vlach's new work its proper due here.

22. Vlach, *Has the Church Replaced Israel?*, 169. For Vlach's full argument for the ongoing importance of nations, see chapter 14 entitled "God's Future Plan for the Nations."

to fulfill his purpose.[23] Further, he writes, "It appears that there is more to God's plans for nations than select members of each nation being saved. The nations of the world as a whole also appear headed for some form of restoration."[24] Vlach sees the vision of this restoration described at various points throughout the book of Revelation.[25] There is to be a corporate restoration of nations, all of which consist of individuals who have been redeemed by the blood of Christ.[26] In other words, there will be no individuals that experience the restoration whose sins have not been atoned for by Christ and through individual acts of faith and repentance. However, each individual there will be a part of a distinct corporate nationality.[27] The point to be made regarding the importance of territorial particularity to the materiality of the final state is that if there is such a role for nations as Vlach describes, there is by implication a role for the particular nation of Israel, a role which would seem to include promises regarding a particular land.

Another theologian who argues for a new creation conception and seems to affirm territorial particularity in the final state is Vern Poythress. Poythress, an amillennialist himself, critiques traditional amillennial thought regarding the fulfillment of OT prophecy: "Amillennialists sometimes spoke *only* of prophecy being fulfilled in the church, paying little attention to the consummate fulfillment of those prophecies in the new earth. In many circles people looked forward primarily to death and the intermediate state rather than to the Second Coming, the resurrection of the body, and the new heavens and the new earth, which are the primary focus of New Testament hope."[28] Poythress emphasizes, like Hoekema, the

23. Ibid., 170.

24. Ibid., 171–72.

25. Ibid., 172–73.

26. As Vlach puts it, "The concept of nations in eternity does not contradict passages that speak of unity among God's people (see Rev 5:9–10). Nations can coexist in harmony with the equality of salvation and spiritual blessings of which all believers partake. In regard to salvation, there is one people of God, but this concept does not rule out all ethnic, geographical, or gender distinctions." Ibid., 176.

27. Vlach notes that both Anthony Hoekema and Randy Alcorn affirm that Scripture teaches that there will be a variety of ethnic contributions in the final state. Vlach, *Has the Church Replaced Israel*, 173–75. (cf. Alcorn, *Heaven*, 290, 380, 382; and Hoekema, *Bible and the Future*, 286).

28. Poythress, "Currents Within Amillennialism," 21–25. He pleas with his amillennial brethren, "Amillennialists today must try to be increasingly faithful to the biblical accent, and speak not only of a first stage of fulfillment in the life of Christ, the New Testament age and the church, but also, of a second, consummate stage in the new heavens

new heavens and new earth. He notes the influence of Platonism and the focus on the intermediate state that envisions "a kind of ethereal existence of vaporous souls playing harps on clouds."[29] Opposed to this ethereal existence, he says, is one which remembers the materiality of the new earth: "The problem with the old world is not materiality but sin. The solution is redemption and transfiguration, not vaporization."[30]

In his affirmation that the new heavens and new earth is the present heavens and earth restored, Poythress sounds much like the new creationists surveyed in the present work. However, he diverges from the new creation proponents in that he seems to affirm territorial particularity in the final state:

> Hope for the new earth thus gives us a picture that is startlingly similar to premillennialism. I believe that Jesus will return bodily to the world, that all people will be judged and that the earth itself will be renewed. Jesus will reign over the nations and usher in an era of great peace and prosperity. Faithful Jews will possess the land of Palestine, as well as the entirety of the renewed earth. When I hear premillennialists describe what happens in the millennial kingdom, I respond, "I believe that too." If I may play with words, I would say that I am an optimistic premillennialist. I believe the things that premillennialists typically say about the millennium. But I am "optimistic" in that I believe that what they call the millennium is even better than they imagine. It is so exceedingly good that no evil and no death remain. And it goes on forever. Thus, it is already the eternal state and not "the millennium" as we have traditionally defined it.[31]

Unlike the new creationists surveyed here, Poythress is open to affirming the promise to ethnic Jews of a particular land.[32] He does not feel it necessary to argue that territorial particularity is fulfilled in some metaphorical way such as the land being "Christified" or universalized to include the whole earth. Further, he implies that there is nothing inherent

---

and the new earth." Ibid., 21–22. Poythress notes Hoekema's *Bible and the Future* as having "set the pace in this area." Ibid., 22.

29. Ibid., 23.

30. Ibid.

31. Ibid.

32. Poythress expresses hope that "Sympathetic listening between dispensationalists and nondispensationalists may have also opened up room for exploration concerning the future of the Jewish people." Ibid.

within amillennialism that should be a barrier to the literal fulfillment of the particular land promise:

> I think that earthy amillennialists should find no problem in af-
> firming that all faithful Jews will join with Abraham in inheriting
> the land of promise and fully enjoying the blessing of God in the
> new world. Amillennialism should not be understood as disinher-
> iting Jews, but rather as affirming the incorporation of Gentiles
> into the family of promise through their union with Christ. Hence,
> Gentiles also will share with Jews as coheirs in Christ (Eph 3:6;
> Rom 8:17). The question is not whether Jews will come into pos-
> session of the wealth of privileges of Old Testament promises (they
> will), but whether a new middle wall of partition will be erected by
> granting them some unique priestly or religious status from which
> Gentiles are excluded (Eph 2:14).[33]

Poythress's openness to the affirmation of territorial particularity is especially intriguing in light of the fact that traditionally the dominant belief within amillennialism has been that the church replaces or fulfills national Israel and, as a result, the promises for Israel, including that of territorial restoration, have been fulfilled in some spiritual sense.

Conclusion

In this chapter, I have suggested that affirming the territorial restoration of Israel 1) represents a consistent utilization of OT new creation texts, 2) is har-monious with NT texts commonly used to deny territorial restoration, and 3) leads to a consistent new creation eschatology that emphasizes the ma-teriality of the final state. New creationists have predominantly understood the fulfillment of OT promises regarding the particular territory promised to Israel to be metaphorical. However, there are a small number of scholars who affirm a new creation conception that includes the territorial restoration of Israel. This evidence suggests that a metaphorical understanding of the fulfillment of the OT territorial promise to Israel is not a necessary feature of new creationism. In fact, if those such as Blaising, Vlach, and Poythress are correct, the inclusion of the territorial particularity of Israel enhances a new creation conception in at least the three ways noted above.

---

33. Ibid., 24. Poythress argued similarly six years prior to "Currents Within Amillen-nialism" in the second edition of *Understanding Dispensationalists*. Poythress, *Under-standing Dispensationalists*, 132–37. The first edition was published in 1987.

6

Conclusion

In the previous chapters, I have argued that a there is a logical inconsistency in the arguments of recent new creationists regarding territorial particularity. At the heart of the inconsistency is the new creationists' use of OT restoration texts to inform their understanding of a renewed earth. Instead of affirming the essential element of territorial particularity in these texts and allowing that to inform their conception of the final state, they argue that the particular territory of Israel is metaphorical for what is believed to be a greater fulfillment. The result is a new creation conception that lacks consistency regarding descriptions of materiality in the texts.

The argument of the present work holds only for those proponents of new creationism who 1) argue that the present heavens and earth will be renewed, and 2) utilize OT restoration texts to inform their conception of the final state of the redeemed upon a new earth. Those who argue that the current heavens and earth will be annihilated and replaced with an utterly new creation do not see continuity between the present state and the final state, especially in the sense of a correspondence of identity as argued in chapter 2. Therefore, even if they utilize OT restoration texts in some way to inform their understanding of the final state, they may not be restrained by the particularities referenced in the texts since those particularities in their materiality will be annihilated and replaced by an utterly new earth. The importance of the present work lies in the fact that within the growing interest in new creationism the dominant position is that the present creation is to be restored.

This book argues that the new creationists surveyed here, along with others who argue for a restored creation that excludes the territorial particularity of Israel, should reconsider their conclusion that the territorial promise to Israel has been superseded. Acknowledging territorial particularity in the final state coheres with a proper reading of the OT restoration texts and is in line with a consistent new creationism that appreciates the materiality of earthly promises for the new creation. My hope is that the present work may lead to further discussions of the importance of language regarding territorial restoration in discussions of eschatology, specifically those involving the nature of the final state in a new creation conception. Perhaps the shared affirmation among new creationists that territorial particularity must be considered when utilizing OT restoration texts to inform the final state will lead to further discussions on the question of the role of the territory of Israel as a consistent feature of biblical new creationism.

Areas of Further Research

There are a number of areas for further research which logically issue from the current work. The first was alluded to in chapter 4. There needs to be a comprehensive examination and critique of the broad hermeneutic of new creationists who argue for an earthly material reality on the one hand, and a metaphorical fulfillment of the promise of particular land materiality, on the other.[1]

Another area in which further work is needed is the question of the role of territorial particularity in the final state. Those who argue for new creationism should explain the exegetical and hermeneutical reasons for including or excluding territorial particularity in their respective conceptions. The modest conclusion of chapter 5 is that the affirmation of the territorial restoration of Israel in a new creation conception is harmonious with OT and NT texts that describe God's plan to restore all things and that it is logically consistent with a view that affirms materiality in the final state. The next step is to offer descriptions of a final state which includes territorial particularity. This step would include examining additional OT prophetical texts in which territorial particularity plays a role, such as those which include detailed descriptions, boundaries, and measurements of a variety of objects and places in a future age (e.g., Ezek 40–49). An appreciation of the contribution of OT prophetic texts to an understanding of

---

1. Again, for a brief explanation of the issue, see Blaising, "Israel and Hermeneutics."

the final state could have implications on how the book of Revelation as a whole is interpreted, specifically the description of the New Jerusalem in Revelation 21–22. In addition, it could have implications on how one understands Jesus' statements concerning the coming kingdom or age to come, Jesus' words to his disciples in Matthew 19:28, the understanding of the two disciples on the road to Emmaus of Jesus' mission (Luke 24:21), and the nature of the disciples' question in Acts 1 (especially as it relates to the context of Acts and its relation to Joel 2). The more advanced need is a comprehensive argument for a new creation conception that not only allows for but shows the necessity for particular land fulfillment in God's plan of redemption.

Another area of further research that issues from the current work has to do with features other than territorial particularity in texts that are utilized to inform the nature of the final state. One example of such a feature is the question of the role of particular nations in the final state.[2] In supersessionist hermeneutics, the particular elements that are superseded have to do with the nation of Israel. However, if particularities regarding the nation of Israel are to inform a consistent new creation eschatology, it seems that particularities regarding other nations also may inform new creation conceptions.[3]

Another area of research has to do with the OT prophetic passages utilized in the arguments for a new creation conception of the final state. More work needs to be done to investigate the question of whether the particular language seen in many prophetic passages can be discarded without the texts' meaning either being diminished or altered. If the particular language in the OT prophetic texts utilized by new creation proponents is shown to be inherent to the framework of the texts, it would seem to be further evidence that there is a logical inconsistency in utilizing those texts to inform one's conception of a renewed new earth in its materiality and yet not allowing the particularities in the text to inform that materiality.

2. E.g., as noted in the previous chapter, Michael Vlach argues that particular nations will have a role in the final state. See Vlach, *Has the Church Replaced Israel?*, especially ch. 14, "God's Future Plan for the Nations."

3. I appreciate the promising affirmations regarding national diversity by Middleton. He writes, "The reference to kings and nations in the new creation is a telling signal that cultural, even national, diversity is not abrogated by redemption. Salvation does not erase cultural differences, rather, the human race, still distinguished by nationality, now walks by the glory or light of the holy city, which is itself illuminated by the Lamb (Rev. 21:24)." Middleton, *A New Heaven and a New Earth*, 212.

Not so much an area of research as a call to a group of scholars is the question of the involvement of dispensational theologians in discussions about the final state. From its beginnings, the tradition of dispensational premillennialism has held to a future for national Israel, so it is not surprising that earthly elements have been a part of dispensational eschatologies. The affirmation of an everlasting earthly and time-sequenced existence for at least some portion of the redeemed is present throughout the history of the dispensational tradition. However, influenced by spiritual vision conceptions of the final state, certain forms of dispensationalism have affirmed that following a literal thousand-year kingdom, in which earthly prophecies are fulfilled, there will be a *less*-material, everlasting existence. Classical dispensationalism included both elements of new creation eschatology and elements of spiritual vision eschatology.[4] Revised dispensationalists, jettisoning the eternal duality of classical dispensationalism, were in one of two camps. One of these camps emphasized what could be understood as a spiritual vision conception while the other emphasized aspects that are more consistent with a new creation conception. While a small group of progressive dispensationalists have attempted to advance the dialogue regarding the nature of the final state, the advancement seems inadequate.[5]

4. There seems to be justification for using the categories of classical, revised, and progressive for describing the historical development of dispensationalism. Even though the term "dispensationalism" was not used to refer to a movement within evangelicalism until the controversy primarily within Presbyterianism between 1936–1944 (see Mangum, *The Dispensational-Covenantal Rift*), it seems justified to include the theology of J. N. Darby as the starting point for early forms of dispensationalism. Classical dispensationalism, then, includes the time period from the Niagara Bible Conferences (late 1800s) until the decade or so leading up to the revision of the *Scofield Reference Bible* notes (1967). Revised dispensationalism primarily begins in the writings of Charles Ryrie and John Walvoord from 1959–66. Subsequently there was a second turning point in the 1980s at which time various dispensational theologians began to discuss development within the tradition, questioning some elements of previous dispensational writings. There are those, like Charles Ryrie, who do not affirm a change significant enough for the term 'revised.' Instead, Ryrie prefers to understand the form of dispensationalism that he espouses as closely connected to previous forms so that he specifies the period from Darby (1800–1882) to the 1980s as 'Systematized Dispensationalism' and the period following this as 'Recent Neodispensationalism,' one in which he sees major shifts in interpretation. See Blaising and Bock, *Progressive Dispensationalism*, 23–56 and Ryrie, *Dispensationalism*.

5. Examples of works from a progressive dispensationalist position that have presented new creation conceptions of the final state include Blaising, "Premillennialism,"; Blaising, "New Creation Eschatology,"; and Vlach, *Has the Church Replaced Israel?* (see especially ch. 14, "God's Future Plan for the Nations"). Most progressive dispensationalists,

In addition to some areas of further research which issue logically from the present work, there are some prospective research areas that are tangential to the current argument. As seen in chapter 1, interest in new creation conceptions of the final state is on the rise so that the conversation regarding the nature of the final state is ongoing.[6] As a result there is an ongoing need for research that surveys and analyzes recent works on new creationism. More work needs to be done regarding the manner in which land is being considered as a biblical theological theme. The synthesis offered in chapter 3 helps to show the context for treatments of land among new creationists. However, a comprehensive survey and critique of treatments of land as a broad theological theme is needed.

Another area of research that is tangentially related to the current book is the concept of space/place in theology. Craig Bartholomew's work *Where Mortals Dwell: A Christian View of Place for Today* is perhaps the broadest treatment of the issue of place in the Bible.[7] Not only does Bartholomew show the prevalence of place in the Bible, he also discusses the concept of place in Western philosophy and in the Christian tradition. The church, at least in America, has seemed to discard place as irrelevant for doctrine and theology. Jake Meador describes the situation as follows: "Like much of Western philosophy generally, many recent forms of American evangelicalism marginalize or ignore the particular settings within which divine and human dramas unfold. We assume that place is trivial, merely incidental to the Bible's core message of salvation. And then, predictably enough, we read Scripture in such a way that our assumptions are confirmed."[8] An appreciation of the role of place in the Bible could change the way we read and understand it. Helpful for this appreciation are several recent contributions in biblical theology to the theme of restoration and geography in ancient

---

however, seem ambivalent or apathetic when it comes to the nature of the eternal state. The question of continuity/discontinuity between the various stages of the kingdom is important to the dispensational discussion of biblical descriptions which refer to the church age, the millennial kingdom, and the everlasting kingdom, respectively. Cf. Busenitz, "Kingdom of God and the Eternal State," 255–74.

6. Middleton's *A New Heaven and a New Earth* will be foundational for future discussions on new creationism. I believe that a pressing need is a thorough analysis and critique of Middleton's comprehensive defense of new creation eschatology.

7. Bartholomew, *Where Mortals Dwell*. One reviewer has said that Bartholomew's work "ought to become the introductory book for evangelicals interested in issues of place-making." Meador, "Location, Location, Location," 67.

8. Meador, "Location, Location, Location," 67.

text and worldview.[9] New creationists who affirm a restored new heavens and new earth should be interested in the theology of space/place because of their interest in materiality and continuity between the present heavens and earth and the new heavens and new earth. Further, the affirmation of continuity between the present heavens and earth and the new heavens and earth has implications on how the particular language of territorial place in the Scripture should be understood both in the future and in the present day. It is one thing to appreciate the prevalence of place in Scripture and even proclaim that it has implications for the way we live and for understanding God's redemptive plan, it is quite another to articulate what those implications are and how one should understand the role of particular places in God's redemptive plan.

The current work also has implications regarding how one thinks about the current state of the nation of Israel. If territorial particularities have relevance for conceptualizing the final state in a new creationist conception, does the current possession or treatment of particular territories also have meaning? If creation care should be a concern for believers because the present earth is to be renewed and restored, should believers also be concerned about events that affect particular territories in the current day? Further, is there theological meaning to the large number of Jews who have returned to Palestine over the past one hundred years?

A Final Plea

In essence, this book is a call for those who are attempting to articulate the nature of what God has promised for the future to continue the difficult work of biblical theology. In Romans 5:1-2, Paul writes, "Therefore, having being justified by faith, we have peace with God through our Lord Jesus Christ." The perfect peace that exists between the believer and God is a picture of the perfect peace that will come upon the whole earth. While the Christian has entered this peace through faith, he waits by faith for the completion not only of his individual redemption, but for the redemption of all creation (Rom 8). The rising interest in this all-encompassing

---

9. E.g., Scott, ed., *Restoration*; Scott, *Geography in Early Judaism and Christianity*; Scott, "Jesus' Vision for the Restoration of Israel," 129–43. Also helpful, specifically in regards to a proper understanding regarding biblical terminology of land and earth is Uemura, *Land or Earth?*.

redemption and its implications is encouraging for future theological discussions of anthropology and eschatology. As Klaus Nürnberger writes,

> Because human need occurs in all dimensions of reality, an escha-
> tology for today must be comprehensive or holistic. The personal
> core of one's being (the soul) must be seen in the context of its
> physical existence, the individual in the context of the community,
> the community in the context of society, society in the context of
> the natural world, and earthly nature within the vast dimensions
> of the universe. The hope for the reunion of a disembodied soul
> with a personal Saviour in heavenly bliss is as inadequate as the
> hope for a transition from the class struggle to the classless society.
> According to biblical faith, God's ultimate intention is the com-
> prehensive well-being of creation as a whole. It encompasses the
> personal, communal, social-structural and ecological dimensions
> of life.[10]

The encouragement that comes as a result of the hope for the future
also has ecclesiological implications. Not only does the church look forward with faith to the future promises articulated throughout the pages of
God's Word, but she evidences that hope by living it out. Middleton states
well the current situation and task of the church:

> In the present, as the church lives between the times, those being
> renewed in the *imago Dei* are called to instantiate an embodied
> culture or social reality alternative to the violent and deathly for-
> mations and practices that dominate the world. By this conformity
> to Christ—the paradigm image of God—the church manifests
> God's rule and participates in God's mission to flood the world
> with the divine presence. In its concrete communal life the church
> as the body of Christ is called to witness to the promised future
> of a new heaven and a new earth in which righteousness dwells.[11]

It is my hope that this book plays a small role in working toward a better understanding of the nature of this promised future and, in turn, a better understanding of the church's witness in the present age in light of that
future age as she awaits for the reality of Christ's revelation to the Apostle
John: "Then I saw a new heaven and a new earth; for the first heaven and
the first earth passed away . . . He will wipe away every tear from their eyes;

10. Nürnberger, "Towards a New Heaven and a New Earth," 148.
11. Middleton, *A New Heaven and a New Earth*, 214.

and there will no longer be any death; there will no longer be any mourning, or crying, or pain; the first things have passed away" (Rev 21:1,4).

Bibliography

Alcorn, Randy. *Heaven*. Carol Stream, IL: Tyndale House, 2004.

Alexander, T. Desmond. "Beyond Borders: The Wider Dimensions of Land." In *The Land of Promise: Biblical, Theological and Contemporary Perspectives*, ed. Philip Johnston and Peter Walker, 35-50. Leicester; Downers Grove, IL: Apollos; InterVarsity, 2000.

—————. *From Eden to the New Jerusalem: An Introduction to Biblical Theology*. Grand Rapids: Kregel, 2008.

—————. *From Paradise to the Promised Land: An Introduction to the Pentateuch*. 3rd ed. Grand Rapids: Baker Academic, 2012.

Anderson, Bernhard W. "Biblical Theology and Sociological Interpretation." *ThTo* 42 (1985) 292-306.

—————. *From Creation to New Creation*. Overtures to Biblical Theology. Minneapolis: Fortress, 1994.

—————. *Understanding the Old Testament*. 5th ed. Upper Saddle River, NJ: Prentice Hall, 2006.

Arand, Charles P., and Erik Herrman. "Attending to the Beauty of the Creation and the New Creation." *CJ* 38 (2012) 313-31.

Bartholomew, Craig G. *Where Mortals Dwell: A Christian View of Place for Today*. Grand Rapids: Baker Academic, 2011.

Bauckham, Richard J. *The Bible and Ecology: Rediscovering the Community of Creation*. Sarum Theological Lectures. Waco, TX: Baylor University Press, 2010.

—————. *Bible and Mission: Christian Witness in a Postmodern World*. Grand Rapids: Baker Academic, 2003.

—————. *God Will Be All in All: The Eschatology of Jürgen Moltmann*. Edinburgh: T and T Clark, 1999.

—————. *Jude, 2 Peter*. WBC, vol. 50. Nashville: Thomas Nelson, 1996.

—————. *Living With Other Creatures: Green Exegesis and Theology*. Waco, TX: Baylor University Press, 2011.

Bauckham, Richard, and Trevor A. Hart. *Hope Against Hope: Christian Eschatology at the Turn of the Millennium*. Grand Rapids: Eerdmans, 1999.

Bavinck, Herman. *Reformed Dogmatics*. 4 vols. Grand Rapids: Baker, 2003-8.

Beagley, A. J. *The 'Sitz im Leben' of the Apocalypse with Particular Reference to the Role of the Church's Enemies*. BZNW 50. Berlin/New York: de Gruyter, 1987.

Beale, Gregory. K. "Eden, the Temple, and the Church's Mission in the New Creation." *JETS* 48 (2005) 5-31.

―――. "The Eschatological Conception of New Testament Theology." In *Eschatology in Bible and Theology*, ed. Kent E. Brower and Mark W. Elliot, 11–52. Downers Grove, IL: InterVarsity, 1997.

―――. *A New Testament Biblical Theology: The Unfolding of the Old Testament in the New*. Grand Rapids: Baker Academic, 2011.

―――. "The New Testament and New Creation." In *Biblical Theology: Retrospect and Prospect*, ed. Scott J. Hafemann, 53–65. Downers Grove, IL: InterVarsity, 2002.

―――. *The Temple and the Church's Mission: A Biblical Theology of the Dwelling Place of God*. New Studies in Biblical Theology 17. Downers Grove, IL: Apollos; InterVarsity, 2004.

Beale, G. K., and Mitchell Kim. *God Dwells Among Us: Expanding Eden to the Ends of the Earth*. Downers Grove, IL: InterVarsity, 2014.

Beasley-Murray, George R. *John*. WBC. Vol. 36. Nashville: Nelson Reference & Electronic, 1999.

Berkhof, Hendrikus. *Christ: The Meaning of History*. Translated by Lambertus Buurman. Grand Rapids: Baker, 1966.

Berkouwer, G. C. *The Return of Christ*. Translated by James Van Oosterom. Studies in Dogmatics. Grand Rapids: Eerdmans, 1972.

Blaising, Craig A. "The Day of the Lord Will Come: An Exposition of 2 Peter 3:1–18." *BibSac* 169 (2012) 387–401.

―――. "Israel and Hermeneutics." In *The People, the Land, and the Future of Israel: Israel and the Jewish People in the Plan of God*, ed. Darrell L. Bock and Mitch Glaser, 151–67. Grand Rapids: Kregel, 2014.

―――. "New Creation Eschatology and Its Ethical Implications." In *Ethics and Eschatology: Papers Presented at the Annual Theological Conference of Emanuel University*, ed. Corneliu C. Simut, 7–24. Oradea, Romania: Emanuel University Press, 2010.

―――. "Premillennialism." In *Three Views on the Millennium and Beyond*, ed. Darrell L. Bock, 157–227. Grand Rapids: Zondervan, 1999.

Blaising, Craig A., and Darrell L. Bock. *Progressive Dispensationalism*. Grand Rapids: Baker, 1993.

Blaising, Craig, et al. "A Review of *Kingdom Through Covenant: A Biblical Understanding of the Covenants* by Peter Gentry and Stephen Wellum." San Diego, November 19–21, 2014.

Blanchard, William Maurice. "Changing Hermeneutical Perspectives on 'The Land' in Biblical Theology." Ph.D. diss., Southern Baptist Theological Seminary, 1986.

Bock, Darrell. "Kingdom through Covenant: A Review by Darrell Bock." http://thegospelcoalition.org/article/kingdom-through-covenant-a-review-by-darrell-bock/.

Borg, Marcus J., and N. T. Wright. *The Meaning of Jesus: Two Visions*. San Francisco: HarperSanFrancisco, 1999.

Bouma-Prediger, Steven. *For the Beauty of the Earth: A Christian Vision for Creation Care*. Engaging Culture. Grand Rapids: Baker Academic, 2001.

Brown, R. E. *The Gospel According to John*. AB. Vol. 29. Garden City, NY: DoubleDay, 1966.

Brueggemann, Walter. *The Land: Place as Gift, Promise, and Challenge in Biblical Faith*. Overtures to Biblical Theology 1. Philadelphia: Fortress, 1977.

————. *The Land: Place as Gift, Promise, and Challenge in Biblical Faith.* 2nd ed. Overtures to Biblical Theology 1. Minneapolis: Fortress, 2002.

————. *Old Testament Theology: An Introduction.* Library of Biblical Theology. Nashville: Abingdon, 2008.

Burge, Gary M. *The Anointed Community: The Holy Spirit in the Johannine Tradition.* Grand Rapids: Eerdmans, 1987.

————. *Interpreting the Fourth Gospel.* Guides to New Testament Exegesis 3. Grand Rapids: Baker, 1992.

————. *Jesus and the Land: The New Testament Challenge to "Holy Land" Theology.* Grand Rapids: Baker Academic, 2010.

————. *The Letters of John.* NIVAC. Grand Rapids: Zondervan, 1996.

————. "Rejoinder to Boyd Luter—*Jesus and The Land: The New Testament Challenge to Holy Land Theology.*" *CTR* 9 (2012) 77.

————. *Who are God's People in the Middle East?* Grand Rapids: Zondervan, 1993.

————. *Whose Land? Whose Promise? What Christians are Not Being Told about Israel and the Palestinians.* Cleveland: Pilgrim, 2003.

Busenitz, Nathan. "The Kingdom of God and the Eternal State." *MSJ* 23 (2012) 255–74.

Calvin, Jean. *The Epistle of Paul the Apostle to the Hebrews and the First and Second Epistles of St. Peter.* Calvin's New Testament Commentaries. Vol. 12. Grand Rapids: Eerdmans, 1963.

Carson, D. A. *The Gospel According to John.* PNTC. Apollos; Eerdmans: Leicester; Grand Rapids, 1991.

Chapman, Colin. *Whose Promised Land?* Tring: Lion, 1983.

Charles, R. H. *Eschatology: The Doctrine of a Future Life in Israel, Judaism and Christianity.* New York: Schocken, 1963.

Childs, Brevard S. *Biblical Theology of the Old and New Testaments: Theological Reflection on the Christian Bible.* Minneapolis: Fortress, 1992.

Church, Philip, et al, eds. *The Gospel and the Land of Promise: Christian Approaches to the Land of the Bible.* Eugene, OR: Pickwick, 2011.

Clapp, Rodney. "Animals in the Kingdom." *ChrCent* 129, no. 13 (2012) 45.

Colwell, John. *Called to One Hope: Perspectives on the Life to Come.* Carlisle, PA: Paternoster, 2000.

Cranfield, C. E. B. *A Critical and Exegetical Commentary on the Epistle to the Romans.* Vol. 1. ICC. Edinburgh: T & T Clark, 1975.

Daley, Brian E. *The Hope of the Early Church: A Handbook of Patristic Eschatology.* Cambridge: Cambridge University Press, 1991.

Danker, Frederick W. "2 Peter 3:10 and Psalm of Solomon 17:10." *ZNW* 53 (1962) 82–86.

Davids, Peter H. *The Letters of 2 Peter and Jude.* PNTC. Apollos; Eerdmans: Nottingham; Grand Rapids, 2006.

Davies, W. D. *The Gospel and the Land: Early Christianity and Jewish Territorial Doctrine.* Berkeley, CA: University of California Press, 1974.

————. *Paul and Rabbinic Judaism: Some Rabbinic Elements in Pauline Theology.* New York: Harper Torchbooks, 1948.

————. *The Territorial Dimension of Judaism.* Berkeley, CA: University of California Press, 1982.

Davies, W. D., and Dale C. Allison. *A Critical and Exegetical Commentary on The Gospel According to Saint Matthew.* Vol. 1. ICC. London: T & T Clark, 1988.

Deyoung, James Calvin. *Jerusalem in the New Testament: The Significance of the City in the History of Redemption and in Eschatology.* Amsterdam: J.H. Kok/N.V. Kampen, 1960.

Diprose, R. E. *Israel in the Development of Christian Thought.* Rome: Istituto Biblico Evangelico Italiano, 2000.

Dodd, C. H. *New Testament Studies.* Manchester: Manchester University Press, 1953.

Dumbrell, William J. *The Search for Order: Biblical Eschatology in Focus.* Eugene, OR: Wipf and Stock, 1994.

Dyrness, William A. *Let the Earth Rejoice: A Biblical Theology of Holistic Mission.* Westchester, IL: Crossway, 1983.

Evans, Craig A. *Matthew.* NCBC. Cambridge: Cambridge University Press, 2012.

Field, David N. "Confessing Christ in the Context of Ecological Degradation." *JTSA*, no 98 (1997) 32–44.

France, R. T. *The Gospel of Matthew.* NICNT. Grand Rapids: Eerdmans, 2007.

Frankel, David. *The Land of Canaan and the Destiny of Israel: Theologies of Territory in the Hebrew Bible.* Siphrut: Literature and Theology of the Hebrew Scriptures. Winona Lake, IN: Eisenbrauns, 2011.

Fretheim, Terrence E. *God and World in the Old Testament: A Relational Theology of Creation.* Nashville: Abingdon, 2005.

Gentry, Peter J., and Stephen J. Wellum. *Kingdom through Covenant: A Biblical-Theological Understanding of the Covenants.* Wheaton, IL: Crossway, 2012.

Goheen, Michael W., and Craig G. Bartholomew. *The Drama of Scripture.* Grand Rapids: Baker Academic, 2004.

Gowan, Donald E. *Eschatology in the Old Testament.* 2nd ed. Edinburgh: T and T Clark, 2000.

Granberg-Michaelson, Wesley. "Covenant and Creation." In *Liberating Life: Contemporary Approaches to Ecological Theology*, ed. Charles Birch, William Eakin, and Jay B. McDaniel, 27–36. Maryknoll, NY: Orbis, 1990.

Guy, H. A. *The New Testament Doctrine of the 'Last Things': A Study of Eschatology.* London: Oxford University Press, 1948.

Habel, Norman C. *The Land is Mine: Six Biblical Land Ideologies.* Overtures to Biblical Theology 16. Minneapolis: Fortress, 1995.

Hagner, Donald. *Matthew 1–13.* WBC. Vol. 33A. Nashville: Nelson, 1993.

Hahne, Harry Alan. *The Corruption and Redemption of Creation: Nature in Romans 8:19–22 and Jewish Apocalyptic Literature.* LNTS 336. London: T & T Clark, 2006.

Hamner, Phil, and Andy Johnson. "Holy Mission: The 'Entire Sanctification' of the Triune God's Creation." *Didache* 5 (2005) 1–8.

Hare, D. R. A. "Davies, W(illiam) D(avid)." In *Dictionary of Major Biblical Interpreters.* Edited by Donald K. McKim. Downers Grove, IL: IVP Academic, 2007.

Harris, Murray J. *The Second Epistle to the Corinthians: A Commentary on the Greek Text.* NIGTC. Grand Rapids: Eerdmans, 2005.

Hegeman, David Bruce. *Plowing in Hope: Toward a Biblical Theology of Culture.* Moscow, ID: Canon, 1999.

Heide, Gale Z. "What is New About the New Heaven and the New Earth? A Theology of Creation From Revelation 21 and 2 Peter 3." *JETS* 40 (1997) 37–56.

Hoekema, Anthony A. *The Bible and the Future.* Grand Rapids: Eerdmans, 1979.

Jacobsen, Eric O. *Sidewalks in the Kingdom: New Urbanism and the Christian Faith.* The Christian Practice of Everyday Life. Grand Rapids: Brazos, 2003.

————. *The Space Between: A Christian Engagement with the Built Environment.* Cultural Exegesis. Grand Rapids: Baker, 2012.

————. "We Can't Go Back to the Garden: Critiquing Evangelicals' Over-Ruralized Eschatology." Christianity Today. http://www.Christianitytoday.com/thisisourcity /7thcity/ruralizedeschatology.html.

James, Steven Lee. "Has Yahweh Come to Zion? A Critique of N. T. Wright's Interpretation of the Parable of the Talents." Th.M. thesis, Southwestern Baptist Theological Seminary, 2009.

Jammer, Max. "Matter: 1. Philosophy" and "Matter: 2. Natural Sciences." In *TRE.* Edited by Hans Dieter Betz, Don S. Browning, Bernd Janowski, and Eberhard Jüngel. Leiden: Boston, 2010.

Johnston, Philip, and Peter Walker, eds. *The Land of Promise: Biblical, Theological, and Contemporary Perspectives.* Leicester; Downers Grove, IL: Apollos; InterVarsity, 2000.

Kaiser, Walter. "Israel and Its Land in Biblical Perspective." In *The Old Testament in the Life of God's People: Essays in Honor of Elmer A. Martens,* ed. John Isaak, 245-56. Winona Lake, IN: Eisenbrauns, 2009.

Keesmaat, Sylvia C. *Paul and His Story: (Re)interpreting the Exodus Tradition.* JSNTSup 181. Sheffield: Sheffield Academic, 1999.

Kim, Joon-Sik. " 'Your Kingdom Come on Earth': The Promise of the Land and the Kingdom of Heaven in the Gospel of Matthew." Ph.D. diss., Princeton Theological Seminary, 2002.

Knox, Wilfred L. *St. Paul and the Church of the Gentiles.* Cambridge: Cambridge University Press, 1939.

Köstenberger, Andreas J. *John.* BECNT. Grand Rapids: Baker Academic, 2004.

Kuyper, Abraham. *De Gemeene Gratie.* Leiden: Donner, 1902.

Lampe, Peter. "Paul's Concept of a Spiritual Body." In *Resurrection: Theological and Scientific Assessments,* ed. Ted Peters, Robert John Russell, and Michael Welker, 103–114. Grand Rapids: Eerdmans, 2002.

Lawrence, David. *Heaven: It's Not the End of the World.* London: Scripture Union, 1995.

Leder, Arie C. *Waiting for the Land: The Story of the Pentateuch.* Phillipsburg, NJ: P&R, 2010.

Lilburne, Geoffrey R. *A Sense of Place: A Christian Theology of the Land.* Nashville: Abingdon, 1989.

Luter, Boyd. "Review of Gary M. Burge, *Jesus and the Land: The New Testament Challenge to 'Holy Land' Theology.*" *JETS* 54 (2011) 217-20.

Magonet, Jonathan. "Isaiah's Mountain or The Shape of Things to Come." *Prooftexts* 11 (1991) 175–81.

Mangum, Todd R. *The Dispensational-Covenantal Rift: The Fissuring of American Evangelical Theology from 1936 to 1944.* Studies in Evangelical History and Thought. Waynesboro, GA: Paternoster, 2007.

Marshall, Paul, and Lela Gilbert. *Heaven is Not My Home: Living in the Now of God's Creation.* Nashville: Word, 1998.

Martens, Elmer A. *God's Design: A Focus on Old Testament Theology.* 3rd ed. N. Richland Hills, TX: BIBAL, 1998.

Martin, Oren Rhea. "Bound for the Kingdom: The Land Promise in God's Redemptive Plan." Ph.D. diss., Southern Baptist Theological Seminary, 2013.

———. *Bound for the Promised Land: The Land Promise in God's Redemptive Plan*. NSBT 34. Leicester; Downers Grove, IL: Apollos; InterVarsity, 2015.

McCartney, Dan G. "*ECCE HOMO*: The Coming of the Kingdom as the Restoration of Human Vicegerency." *WTJ* 56 (1994) 1–21.

McDannell, Colleen, and Bernhard Lang. *Heaven: A History*. Princeton, NJ: Yale University Press, 1988.

McGinn, Bernard. *The Flowering of Mysticism: Men and Women in the New Mysticism (1200–1350)*. Vol. 3, *The Presence of God: A History of Western Christian Mysticism*. New York: Crossroad, 1998.

———. *The Foundations of Mysticism*. Vol. 1, *The Presence of God: A History of Western Christian Mysticism*. New York: Crossroad, 1991.

———. *The Growth of Mysticism*. Vol. 2, *The Presence of God: A History of Western Christian Mysticism*. New York: Crossroad, 1994.

———. *The Harvest of Mysticism in Medieval Germany (1300–1500)*. Vol. 4, *The Presence of God: A History of Western Christian Mysticism*. New York: Crossroad, 2005.

———. *The Varieties of Vernacular Mysticism (1350–1550)*. Vol. 5, *The Presence of God: A History of Western Christian Mysticism*. New York: Crossroad, 2012.

McGrath, Alister E. *A Brief History of Heaven*. Oxford: Blackwell, 2003.

McHugh, John F. *A Critical and Exegetical Commentary on John 1–4*. ICC. London: Bloomsbury T & T Clark, 2014.

Meacham, Jon. "Heaven Can't Wait: Why Rethinking the Hereafter Could Make the World a Better Place." *Time*, 16 April 2012, 30–36.

Meador, Jake. "Location, Location, Location." *Christianity Today* 55, no. 11 (2011) 67–69.

Middendorf, Michael P. *Romans 1–8*. ConC. Saint Louis: Concordia, 2013.

Middleton, J. Richard. *The Liberating Image: The Imago Dei in Genesis 1*. Grand Rapids: Brazos, 2005.

———. "A New Heaven and a New Earth: The Case for a Holistic Reading of the Biblical Story of Redemption." *JCTR* 11 (2006) 73–97.

———. *A New Heaven and a New Earth: Reclaiming Biblical Eschatology*. Grand Rapids: Baker Academic, 2014.

Middleton, J. Richard, and Michael J. Gorman. "Salvation." In *NIDB*. Edited by Katharine Doob Sakenfeld. Nashville: Abingdon, 2009.

Moltmann, Jürgen. *The Coming of God: Christian Eschatology*. Minneapolis: Fortress, 1996.

———. *Theology of Hope: On the Ground and the Implications of a Christian Theology*. New York: Harper and Row, 1967.

Moo, Douglas J. "Creation and New Creation." *BBR* 20 (2010) 39–60.

———. *The Epistle to the Romans*. NICNT. Grand Rapids: Eerdmans, 1996.

———. "Kingdom through Covenant: A Review by Douglas Moo." http://thegospelcoalition.org/article/kingdom-through-covenant-a-reveiw-by-douglas-moo/.

———. "Nature in the New Creation: New Testament Eschatology and the Environment." *JETS* 49 (2006) 449–88.

Moore, Russell D. *The Kingdom of Christ: The New Evangelical Perspective*. Wheaton, IL: Crossway, 2004.

———. "Personal and Cosmic Eschatology." In *A Theology of the Church*, ed. Daniel L. Akin, 858–926. Nashville: B&H Academic, 2007.

Bibliography

————. "A Purpose Driven Cosmos." Global Gospel Project. *Christianity Today*, February 2012, 31-33.

Morris, Leon. *The Epistle to the Romans*. Apollos; Eerdmans: Leicester; Grand Rapids, 1988.

Motyer, J. Alec. *The Prophecy of Isaiah: An Introduction & Commentary*. Downers Grove, IL: IVP Academic, 1993.

Munck, Johannes. *Paul and the Salvation of Mankind*. London: SCM, 1959.

Neyrey, Jerome H. *2 Peter, Jude*. AB. Vol. 37C. New York: Doubleday, 1993.

Nolland, John. *The Gospel of Matthew: A Commentary on the Greek Text*. NIGTC. Grand Rapids; Bletchley: Eerdmans, Paternoster, 2005.

Nürnberger, Klaus. "Towards a New Heaven and a New Earth." In *Doing Theology in Context: South African Perspectives*, ed. John W. de Gruchy and Charles Villa-Vicencio, 139-49. Theology and Praxis: Volume One. Maryknoll, NY: Orbis, 1994.

Overstreet, R. Larry. "A Study of 2 Peter 3:10-13." *BibSac* 137 (1980) 354-71.

Pannenberg, Wolfhart. *Systematic Theology*. 3 vols. Grand Rapids: Eerdmans, 1991.

Perrin, Nicholas. *Jesus and the Temple*. Grand Rapids: Baker Academic, 2010.

Pilcher, Charles Venn. *The Hereafter in Jewish and Christian Thought*. New York: Macmillan, 1940.

Plantinga, Jr., Cornelius. *Engaging God's World: A Christian Vision of Faith, Learning, and Living*. Grand Rapids: Eerdmans, 2002.

Polkinghorne, John. *The God of Hope and the End of the World*. New Haven, CT: Yale University Press, 2002.

Polkinghorne, J. C., and Michael Welker. *The End of the World and the Ends of God: Science and Theology on Eschatology*. Theology for the Twenty-First Century. Harrisburg, PA: Trinity, 2000.

Poythress, Vern S. "Currents Within Amillennialism." *Presbyterion* 26 (2000) 21-25.

————. *Understanding Dispensationalists*. Grand Rapids: Academie, 1987.

————. *Understanding Dispensationalists*. 2nd ed. Phillipsburg, NJ: Presbyterian and Reformed, 1994.

Rad, Gerhard von. "The Promised Land and Yahweh's Land in the Hexateuch." In *The Problem of the Hexateuch and Other essays*, 79-93. London: SCM, 1966.

Reddish, Mitchell G. "Heaven." In *ABD*, ed. David Noel Freedman, 3:90-91. New York: Doubleday, 1992.

Ridderbos, Herman N. *The Gospel According to John: A Theological Commentary*. Translated by John Vriend. Grand Rapids: Eerdmans, 1997.

Rietkerk, Wim. *Millennium Fever and the Future of This Earth: Between False Expectations and Biblical Hope*. Rochester, MN: Ransom Fellowship Publications, 2008.

Robertson, O. Palmer. *The Israel of God: Yesterday, Today, and Tomorrow*. Phillipsburg, NJ: P&R, 2000.

————. "The Land of the Bible in the Age of the New Covenant." In *Understanding the Land of the Bible*, 109-32. Phillipsburg, NJ: P&R, 1996.

Robinson, Charles K. "Materiality and Eschatology." *JRT* 19 (1963) 109-18.

Russell, David. *The "New Heavens and New Earth": Hope for Creation in Jewish Apocalyptic and the New Testament*. Studies in Biblical Apocalyptic Literature 1. Philadelphia: Visionary, 1996.

Russell, Jeffrey Burton. *A History of Heaven: The Singing Silence*. Princeton, NJ: Princeton University Press, 1997.

Ryrie, Charles C. *Dispensationalism*. Rev. and Exp. ed. Chicago: Moody, 2007.

Santmire, H. Paul. *The Travail of Nature: The Ambiguous Ecological Promise of Christian Theology*. Philadelphia: Fortress, 1985.

Schreiner, Thomas R. *1, 2 Peter, Jude*. NAC, vol. 37. Nashville: Broadman & Holman, 2003.

———. *Romans*. BECNT. Grand Rapids: Baker, 1998.

Scott, James M. *Geography in Early Judaism and Christianity*. Cambridge: Cambridge University Press, 2002.

———. "'Jesus' Vision for the Restoration of Israel as the Basis for a Biblical Theology of the New Testament." In *Biblical Theology: Retrospect and Prospect*, ed. Scott J. Hafemann, 129–43. Downers Grove, IL: InterVarsity, 2002.

Scott, James M., ed. *Restoration: Old Testament, Jewish, and Christian Perspectives*. JSJSup 72. Leiden: Brill, 2001.

Simpson, J. A., and E. S. C. Weiner. *OED*. 2nd ed. 20 vols. Oxford: Clarendon, 1989.

Smith, Gary V. *Isaiah 1–39*. NAC. Vol. 15A. Nashville: B&H, 2007.

Snyder, Howard S. *Models of the Kingdom*. Nashville: Abingdon, 1991.

———. "Salvation Means Creation Healed: Creation, Cross, Kingdom, and Mission." *AJ* 62 (2007) 9–47.

Snyder, Howard A., and Joel Scandrett. *Salvation Means Creation Healed: The Ecology of Sin and Grace: Overcoming the Divorce Between Earth and Heaven*. Eugene, OR: Cascade, 2011.

Soulen, R. Kendall. *The God of Israel and Christian Theology*. Minneapolis: Fortress, 1996.

Stanford, Peter. *Heaven: A Traveller's Guide to the Undiscovered Country*. London: HarperCollins, 2003.

Starr, J. M. *Sharers in Divine Nature: 2 Peter 1:4 in Its Hellenistic Context*. ConBNT 33. Stockholm: Almqvist & Wiksell, 2000.

Stewart, Robert B., ed. *The Resurrection of Jesus: John Dominic Crossan and N. T. Wright in Dialogue*. Minneapolis: Fortress, 2005.

Surburg, Mark P. "Good Stuff! The Material Creation and the Christian Faith." *CJ* 36 (2010) 245–62.

Sweeney, Marvin A. *Isaiah 1–39 with An Introduction to Prophetic Literature*. FOTL. Vol. 16. Grand Rapids: Eerdmans, 1996.

Thiede, Carsten Peter. "A Pagan Reader of 2 Peter: Cosmic Conflagration in 2 Peter 3 and the Octavius of Minucius Felix." *JSNT* 26 (1986) 79–96.

Thiselton, Anthony C. *The First Epistle to the Corinthians*. NIGTC. Grand Rapids: Eerdmans, 2000.

Thurneysen, Eduard. *Eternal Hope*. Translated by Harold Knight. London: Lutterworth, 1954.

Tresham, Aaron. "A Test Case for Conjectural Emendation: 2 Peter 3:10d." *MSJ* 21, no. 1 (2010) 55–79.

Troeger, Thomas H. "A Spirituality of Materiality." *Living Pulpit* 15, no. 2 (2006) 12.

Truesdale, Al. "Last Things First: The Impact of Eschatology on Ecology." *PSCF* 46 (1994) 116–22.

Uemura, Shizuka. *Land or Earth? A Terminological Study of Hebrew 'eres' and Aramaic 'ara' in the Graeco-Roman Period*. Library of Second Temple Studies 84. London: Bloomsbury T&T Clark, 2012.

Viviano, Benedict T. *The Kingdom of God in History*. Good News Studies, vol. 27. Wilmington, DE: Michael Glazier, 1988.

Vlach, Michael J. *Has the Church Replaced Israel? A Theological Evaluation*. Nashville: B&H, 2010.

———. "Have They Found a Better Way? An Analysis of Gentry and Wellum's *Kingdom Through Covenant.*" *MSJ* 24 (2013) 10-12.

———. *He Will Reign Forever: A Biblical Theology of the Kingdom of God.* Silverton, OR: Lampion, 2017.

Walker, P. W. L. "Gospel Sites and 'Holy Places': The Contrasting Attitudes of Eusebius and Cyril." *TynB* 41 (1990) 89-108.

———. *Holy City, Holy Places? Christian Attitudes to Jerusalem and Holy Land in the Fourth Century.* Oxford: Oxford University Press, 1990.

———. "Jerusalem and the Holy Land in the Fourth Century." In *The Christian Heritage in the Holy Land: Past, Present and Future*, ed. A. O'Mahoney et al, 22-34. London: Scorpion Cavendish, 1995.

———. "Jerusalem in the Early Christian Centuries." In *Jerusalem Past and Present in the Purposes of God*, ed. P. W. L. Walker, 2nd ed., 79-97. Carlisle; Grand Rapids: Paternoster; Baker, 1994.

———. *Jesus and the Holy City: New Testament Perspectives on Jerusalem.* Grand Rapids: Eerdmans, 1996.

Walker, P. W. L. ed. *Jerusalem Past and Present in the Purposes of God.* 2nd ed. Carlisle; Grand Rapids: Paternoster; Baker, 1994.

Walsh, Brian J., and Richard J. Middleton. *The Transforming Vision: Shaping a Christian World View.* Downers Grove, IL: InterVarsity, 1984.

Waltke, Bruce K. *An Old Testament Theology: An Exegetical, Canonical, and Thematic Approach.* Grand Rapids: Zondervan, 2007.

Ware, Bruce. "Extent of the Atonement: Outline of the Issue, Positions, Key Texts, and Key Theological Arguments." Eternal Perspective Ministries. www.epm.org/static/uploads/downloads/Extent_of_the_Atonment_by_Bruce_Ware.pdf.

Wenham, David. "Being 'Found' on the Last Day: New Light on 2 Peter 3:10 and 2 Corinthians 5:3." *NTS* 33 (1987) 477-79.

Wesley, John. *Explanatory Notes Upon the New Testament.* London: Epworth, 1958.

Wildberger, Hans. *Isaiah 1-12: A Commentary.* Translated by Thomas H. Trapp. CC. Minneapolis: Fortress, 1991.

———. Sermon 60, "General Deliverance." In *The Bicentennial Edition of the Works of John Wesley*, ed. Frank Baker, Richard Heitzenrater, et al, 2:449. Nashville: Abingdon, 1984.

Williams, Michael D. *Far as the Curse is Found.* Phillipsburg, NJ: P&R, 2005.

———. "On Eschatological Discontinuity: The Confession of an Eschatological Reactionary." *Presbyterion* 25 (1999) 13-20.

———. "Rapture or Resurrection." *Presbyterion* 24 (1998) 9-37.

———. "Regeneration in Cosmic Context." *EJ* 7 (1989) 68-80.

Wittmer, Michael E. *Heaven is a Place on Earth: Why Everything You Do Matters to God.* 2nd ed. Grand Rapids: Zondervan, 2004.

Wolters, Albert M. *Creation Regained: Biblical Basics for a Reformational Worldview.* Grand Rapids: Eerdmans, 2005.

———. "Worldview and Textual Criticism in 2 Peter 3:10." *WTJ* 49 (1987) 405-13.

Wright, Christopher J. H. "A Christian Approach to Old Testament Prophecy Concerning Israel." In *Jerusalem Past and Present in the Purposes of God*, ed. P. W. L. Walker, 2nd ed., 1-19. Carlisle; Grand Rapids: Paternoster; Baker, 1994.

———. *An Eye for an Eye: The Place of Old Testament Ethics Today.* Downers Grove, IL: InterVarsity, 1983.

—. *God's People in God's Land: Family, Land, and Property in the Old Testament.* Grand Rapids; Exeter: Eerdmans; Paternoster, 1990.

—. *Living as the People of God: The Relevance of Old Testament Ethics.* Leicester: Inter-Varsity, 1983.

Wright, N. T. "4QMMT and Paul: Justification, 'Works,' and Eschatology." In *History and Exegesis: New Testament Essays in Honor of Dr. E. Earle Ellis on His 80th Birthday*, ed. SangWon (Aaron) Son, 104-32. New York: T and T Clark, 2006.

—. *The Challenge of Jesus: Rediscovering Who Jesus Was and Is.* Downers Grove, IL: InterVarsity, 1999.

—. *The Climax of the Covenant: Christ and the Law in Pauline Theology.* Minneapolis: Fortress, 1992.

—. *Jesus and the Victory of God.* Vol. 2 of Christian Origins and the Question of God. Minneapolis: Fortress, 1997.

—. *Justification: God's Plan and Paul's Vision.* Downers Grove, IL: IVP Academic, 2009.

—. *The Millennium Myth.* Louisville, KY: Westminster John Knox, 1999.

—. *New Heavens, New Earth: The Biblical Picture of Christian Hope.* Grove Biblical Series B11. Cambridge: Grove, 1999.

—. "New Perspectives on Paul." In *Justification in Perspective: Historical Developments and Contemporary Challenges*, ed. Bruce L. McCormack, 243-64. Grand Rapids: Baker Academic, 2006.

—. *The New Testament and the People of God.* Vol. 1 of Christian Origins and the Question of God. Minneapolis: Fortress, 1992.

—. *Paul and the Faithfulness of God.* 3 vols. Vol. 4 of Christian Origins and the Question of God. Minneapolis: Fortress, 2013.

—. *Paul: Fresh Perspectives.* Minneapolis: Fortress, 2005.

—. *Pauline Perspectives: Essays on Paul, 1978-2013.* Minneapolis: Fortress, 2013.

—. "Redemption from the New Perspective." In *Redemption*, ed. S. T. Davis, D. Kendall, and G. O'Collins, 69-100. Oxford: Oxford University Press, 2004.

—. *The Resurrection of the Son of God.* Vol. 3 of Christian Origins and the Question of God. Minneapolis: Fortress, 2003.

—. *Surprised by Hope: Rethinking Heaven, the Resurrection, and the Mission of the Church.* New York: HarperOne, 2008.

—. *What Saint Paul Really Said.* Grand Rapids: Eerdmans, 1997.

Author Index

Scripture Index

Jeremiah